This book was conceived,
edited and designed
by **nextquisite** Ltd

First published in Great Britain in 2023
by NQ Publishers, an imprint of Nextquisite Ltd.
Copyright © 2023 Nextquisite Ltd

www.nqpublishers.com, www.nextquisite.com

Project Director Anne McRae
Art Director Marco Nardi
Illustrations John Devolle
Texts Marcus Johnson
Editing Pauline Townsend
Layouts Richard Smyth

ISBN 978-1-912944-55-2

Printed in China

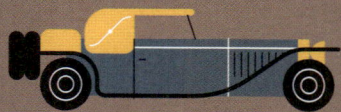

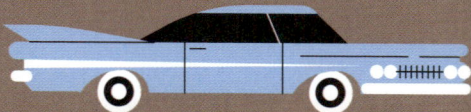

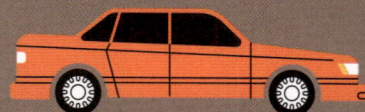

JOHN DEVOLLE & MARCUS JOHNSON

#TECHNOLOGY

NQ PUBLISHERS
For enquiring minds

Contents

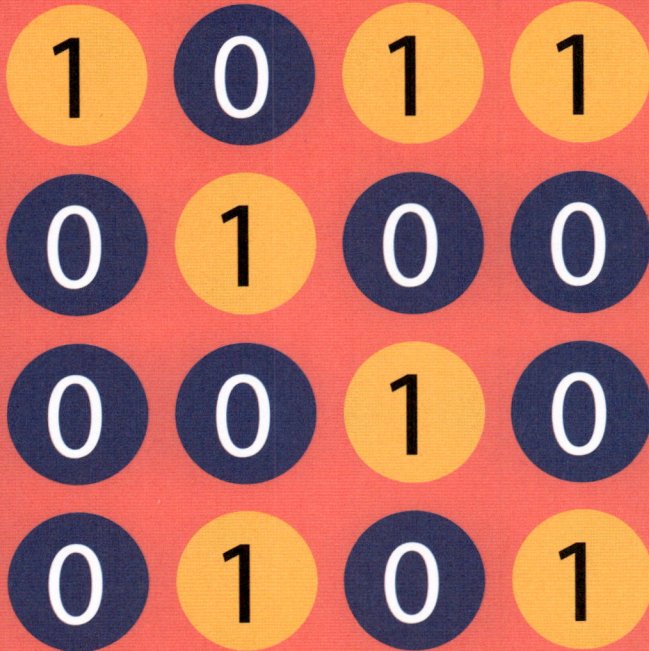

42
INDUSTRIAL & DOMESTIC

54
MATERIALS & CONSTRUCTION

66
BIO & MEDICAL

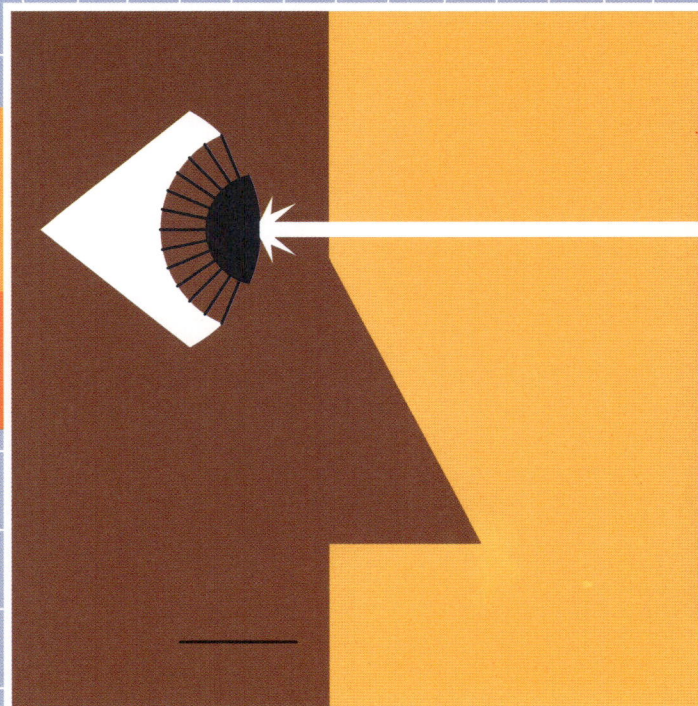

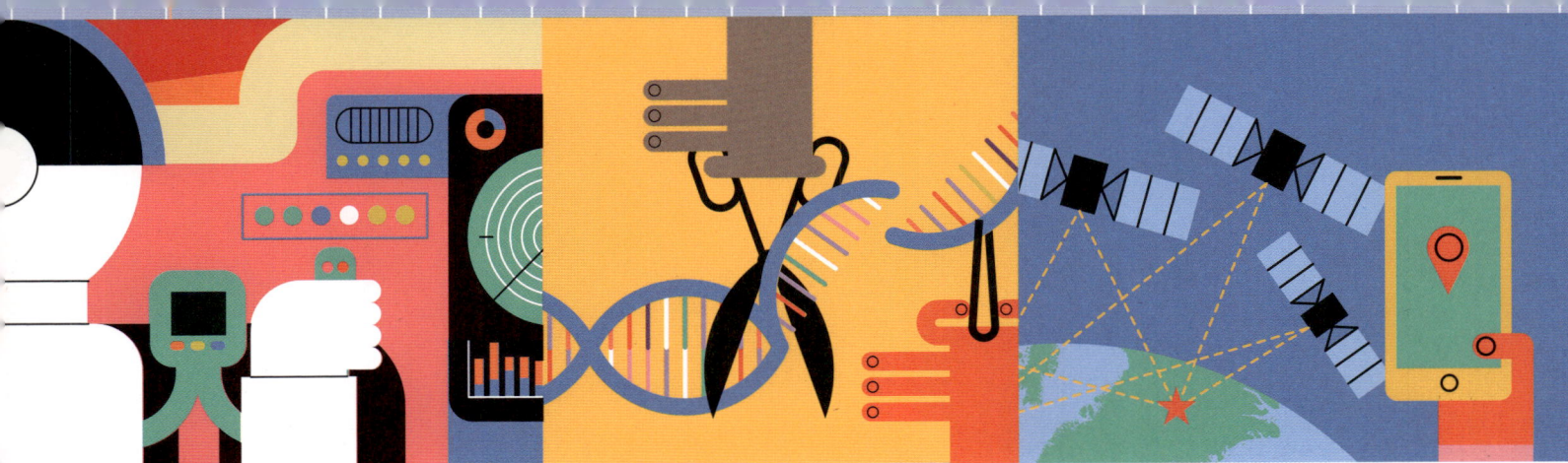

INTRODUCTION

Technology is about applying scientific knowledge to the practical side of life, to resolve problems and to make things work in the most efficient way. In our ultramodern lives, technology is all around us. When you wake up in the morning, what is the first thing you do? Do you check your smartphone or tablet? Perhaps you just slip out of bed and go to the bathroom? In either case you are making use of technology: your smartphone contains some of the most recent and advanced technology on the planet, whereas the indoor plumbing and running water in your bathroom places you in the wealthiest part of the world where technology makes clean water available to all. Everything else in your home is also the result of technology, from the heating and lighting to the flooring and stairs, and even the structure of the building itself. If we didn't have skilled architects and builders carefully designing and planning houses and blocks of flats, they might just collapse!

What did you have for breakfast? Some cereal perhaps, or toast and jam? These products are made by the food industry which uses technology to produce, harvest and process them. When ready to be sold, they are sent to supermarkets using transport technology. Meanwhile, medical technology helps keep you well. Technology is a part of daily life, making things simpler, healthier and more comfortable.

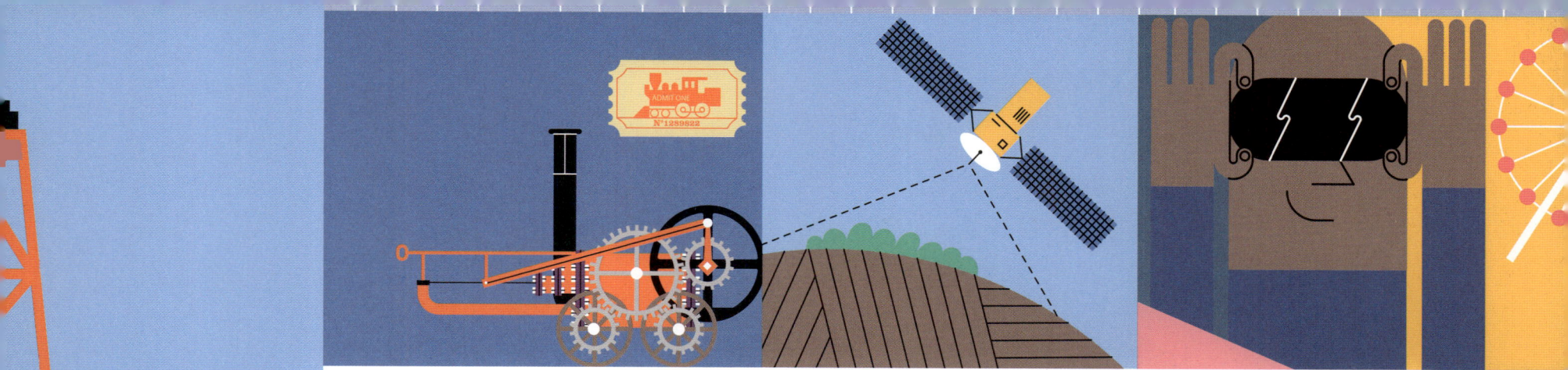

But technology also has an exciting, futuristic side too. Like the science behind it, technology expresses a uniquely human desire to discover and invent new things, and to use creativity, knowledge and skills to go where we have never been before.

Engineers, computer scientists, roboticists and space technologists are currently working on the following: an Interstellar Space Probe that will make a decades-long trip into deep space, beaming back information as it goes; gene-editing techniques that will wipe out malaria (which currently kills more than 500,000 people a year) by introducing malaria-resistant mosquitoes; the 3D printing of bones and organs to replace ones that are failing in elderly or sick people; developing hydrogen-powered planes that can fly 250 people halfway round the world in a single zero-carbon flight; creating artificial eyes to restore sight in the blind; manufacturing tiny "living robots" that can swim through the seas gobbling up every last piece of microplastic. We could go on, the list of the technological research in progress is as long as it is inspiring.

In this book you will find an overview of some of what's going forward, alongside a glance at technology in the past.

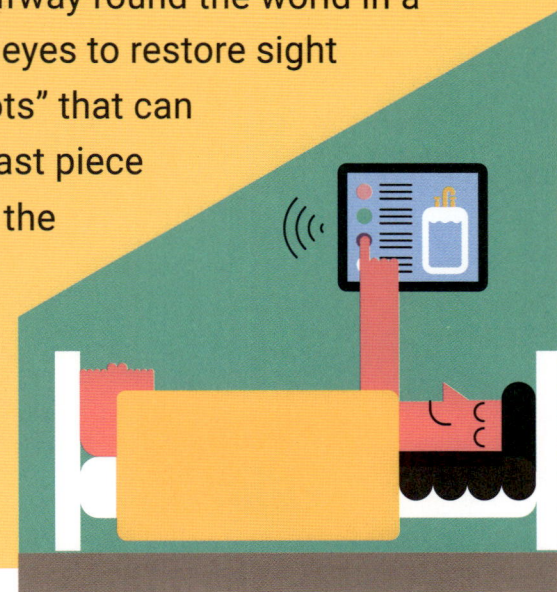

TIMELINE

There's nothing new about technology. The earliest examples predate modern humans by millions of years. What has changed is the amount of technology and the speed of change. Here you can see an overview of the first 3.3 millions years.

Irrigation

Farmers needed constant access to water, so they dug canals, built terraces and invented tools to control water and get it onto their fields.

The iron age

Prehistoric people discovered metals like gold and silver thousands of years ago. They learned to smelt metals such as copper and bronze to make tools and jewellery. Human society developed more quickly after iron was invented. Iron ploughs and other farm tools made farming easier and more food could be grown.

★ The earliest irrigation systems were built in Mesopotamia and Egypt about 8,000 years ago.

★ The first coins were made of a gold and silver alloy.

Invention of tools

★ Stone tools are the first examples of human technology.

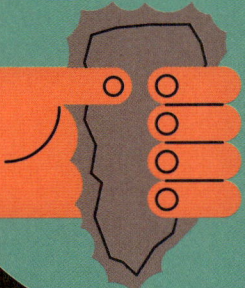

Using a shaduf to lift water out of the Nile in Egypt. **Irrigation**

Iron tools

★ Iron had to be fired at very high temperatures then beaten into shape. Iron tools were tough and long-lasting.

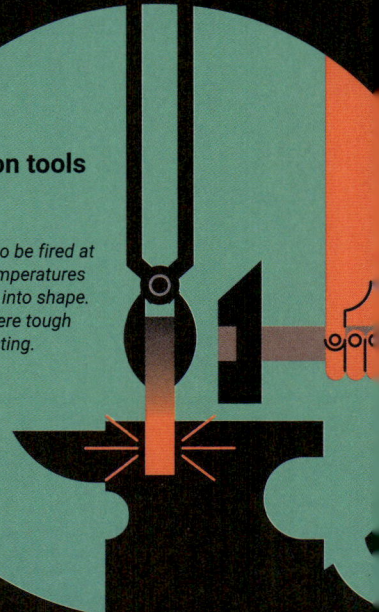

3.3 million years ago

World's earliest technology

The earliest examples of technology date from 3.3 million years ago. Some of our very early ancestors made sharp flakes of stone and used them as tools for cutting, chopping and scraping.

★ The element symbol for iron is Fe. It comes from the Latin word for iron – "ferrum."

| 12,000 years ago | 11,000 years ago | 10,000 years ago | 9,000 years ago | 8,000 years ago | 7,000 years ago | 6,000 years ago |

★ The birth of farming, also known as the Neolithic Revolution, changed the way people lived. It led directly to the first Industrial Revolution and our modern societies.

Sailing

When people learned to harness the energy of the wind using sails to power their boats they could travel further and trade more widely. Fishing also became easier, increasing food supply.

The birth of farming

About 12,000 years ago people began settling in permanent villages. They became farmers, raising livestock and growing crops instead of hunting wild animals and gathering plants.

Taming the flames

The control of fire gave our ancestors warmth, light and protection from predators. It also improved their diet. They could absorb more nutrients from cooked food, which made them bigger, stronger and more intelligent.

2-1 million years ago

▶ Their new way of life led to many inventions. They needed tools like the plough to farm and building materials such as bricks for permanent homes. They invented pottery to store food. Farming was a great step forward.

▶ Sailing technology was invented in Mesopotamia and Egypt about 6,000 years ago.

Sailing boats

Control of fire

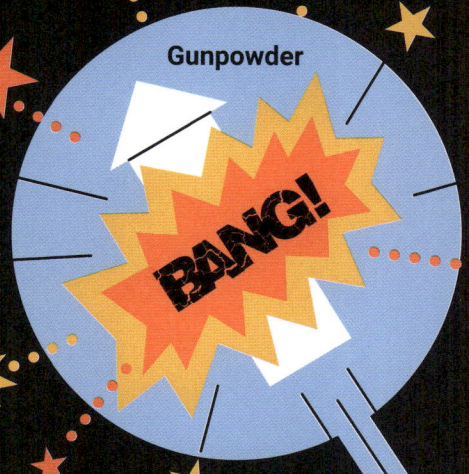

Gunpowder

Gunpowder

The recipe for the explosive mix of the three chemicals in gunpowder – **saltpetre**, charcoal and sulphur – was discovered by Chinese monks. They were searching for an elixir to extend human life but instead they stumbled upon an explosive that would increase the use of weapons and warfare across the globe.

★ *Chinese civilisation is credited with four big inventions: the compass, gunpowder, paper and printing.*

★ *Before antibiotics were discovered, people often died of minor infections.*

Medical breakthroughs

It is hard to imagine a time when we didn't know what germs were and how they spread sickness and disease. French chemist Louis Pasteur proved his "germ theory" in 1861 (see page 70). **Anaesthesia** was first used in 1846, removing pain during surgery. Surgeons used carbolic acid as an antiseptic to stop their patients getting infections.

Antibiotics

The first antibiotic, called penicillin, was discovered by accident when Dr Alexander Fleming went on holiday leaving a petri dish with bacteria growing in his lab. On his return, he noticed a mould had formed that stopped the bacteria from growing – penicillin!

▶ Fibre optic scopes can look inside dark and difficult places like under the sea or inside the human body.

Fibre optics

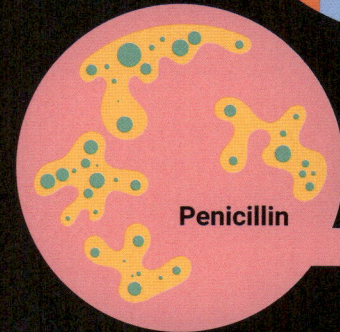

An optical fibre is a strand of pure glass about as thick as a human hair. When bundled together in a cable, the strands can send masses of information very quickly. They have revolutionised communications.

★ *The steam engine was the power behind the first Industrial Revolution.*

Steam engines

These engines used steam from boiling water as a source of power. The first useful steam engines became widespread at the end of 17th century. They were used in many different ways, in factories, mines, trains and steamboats.

Penicillin

5,000 years ago   **4,000** years ago   **3,000** years ago   **2,000** years ago   **1,000** years ago   **NOW**

Paper

Paper was invented in China about 2,000 years ago. It was made of mulberry bark, hemp and rags mixed with water. The mix was pressed and left to dry in the sun.

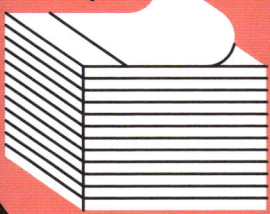

Paper

▶ Gutenberg's press could print large numbers of books cheaply. More people could afford to buy them, spreading knowledge.

The compass

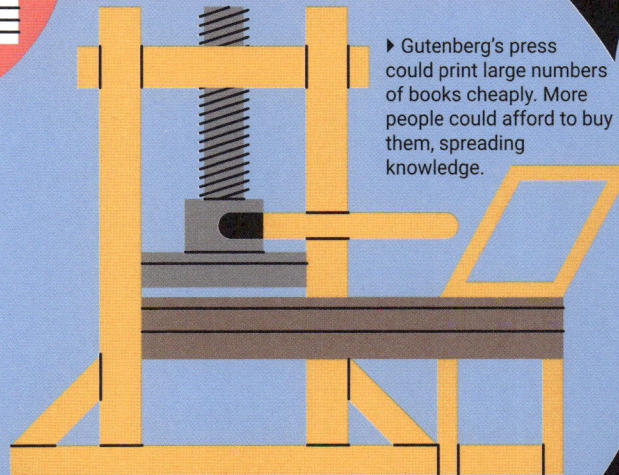

Printing

The Chinese began printing on paper in the 7th century. In Europe, the first printing press was invented in Germany in the 15th century by Johannes Gutenberg.

The compass

Magnetic compasses were first invented in China over 2,000 years ago. Chinese travellers began using them for navigation in the 11th century. Their use soon spread across the world.

Electricity

Electricity

Benjamin Franklin is credited with the discovery of electricity, although many scientists studied the subject before him. Thomas Edison invented the light bulb and in 1882 he flipped the switch on the first power company, providing electricity for people in Manhattan, New York.

Nuclear fission

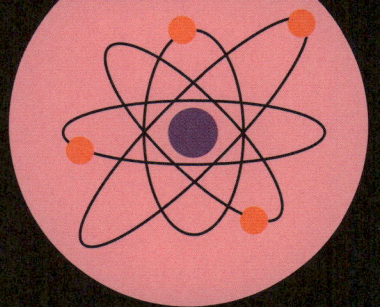

Nuclear power

Nuclear power is made by splitting atoms to release the energy in their cores. The process is called nuclear fission. The first nuclear power plant opened in Russia in 1954.

The world's energy needs are expanding rapidly, just as we realise that we need new, cleaner energy technologies to protect our planet from the effects of global warming. Rising prices, international conflict and emerging economies are some of the other forces driving the search for new sources of energy.

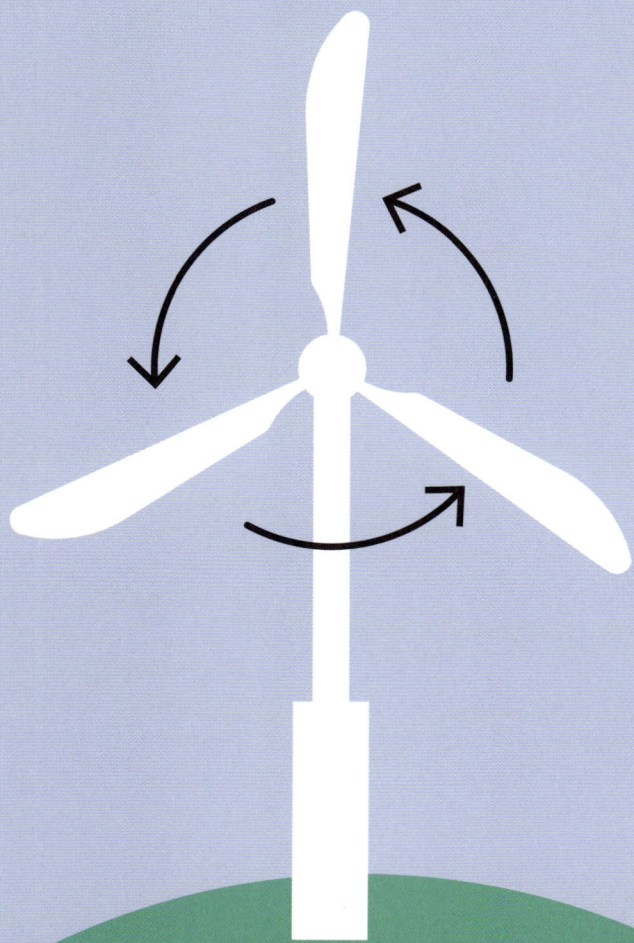

ENERGY
& POWER

POWER STATIONS

Electricity is one of the most common forms of energy. We use it for everything, from lighting, heating and cooling for our homes, offices and shops to powering factories, computers and transport systems. Most of the electricity we use is generated in large industrial plants known as power stations.

▶ The dense white clouds above power stations are not smoke but steam. Harnessing this energy using **CHP technology** can greatly increase a plant's efficiency.

How a coal-fired power station works

Coal-fired stations make electricity by burning coal in a furnace or boiler to produce steam. The steam, under immense pressure, flows into turbines that spin a generator to create electricity. The electricity is sent via a transformer to the supply grid for use in homes, offices and factories. The steam is condensed back into water and then either returned to rivers and lakes, or cooled and returned to the boiler.

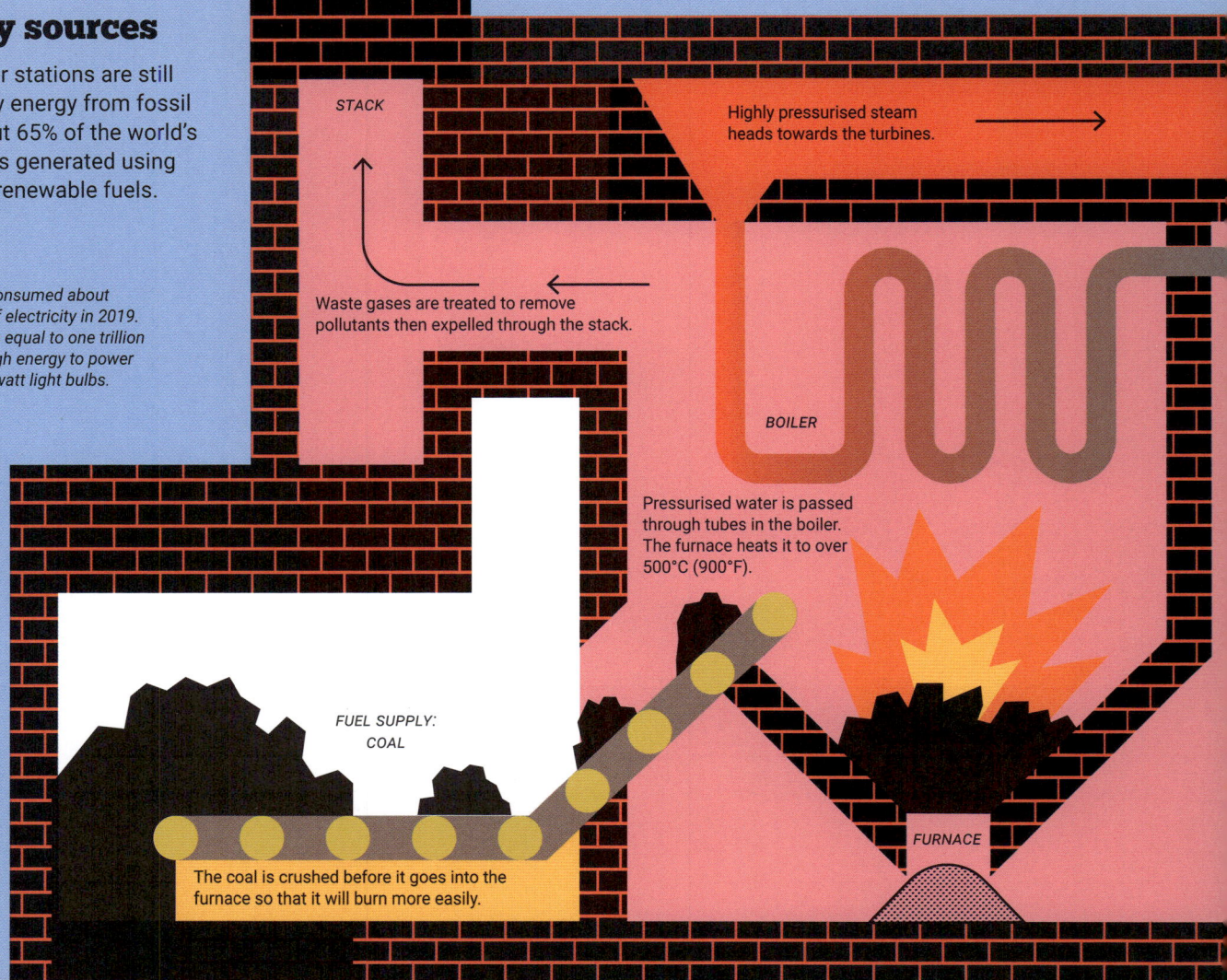

Electricity generation by energy source

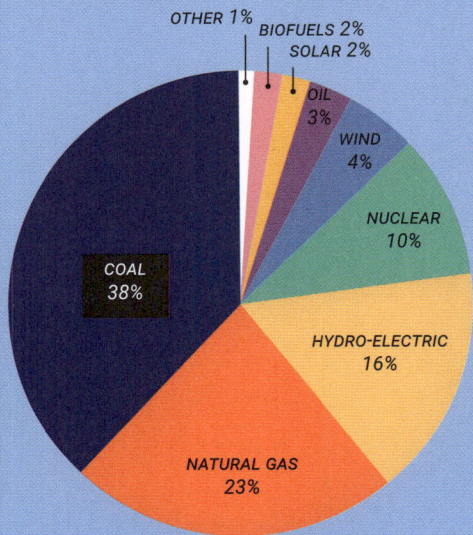

Energy sources

OTHER 1%
BIOFUELS 2%
SOLAR 2%
OIL 3%
WIND 4%
NUCLEAR 10%
COAL 38%
HYDRO-ELECTRIC 16%
NATURAL GAS 23%

Most power stations are still powered by energy from fossil fuels. About 65% of the world's electricity is generated using these non-renewable fuels.

★ The world consumed about 23 terawatts of electricity in 2019. One terawatt is equal to one trillion watts, or enough energy to power 10 billion 100-watt light bulbs.

STACK

Highly pressurised steam heads towards the turbines.

Waste gases are treated to remove pollutants then expelled through the stack.

BOILER

Pressurised water is passed through tubes in the boiler. The furnace heats it to over 500°C (900°F).

Fossil fuels

Fossil fuels were formed millions of years ago when plants and tiny animals were buried beneath layers of rock and sediment. There are three main types of fossil fuels.

Coal
A kind of sedimentary rock made mostly of carbon.

Oil
A liquid made up primarily of carbon and hydrogen.

Natural gas
An odourless gas composed mainly of methane.

FUEL SUPPLY: COAL

The coal is crushed before it goes into the furnace so that it will burn more easily.

FURNACE

Environmental impact

Coal-fired power stations are a major cause of pollution and global warming. They emit large amounts of greenhouse gases such as carbon dioxide, as well as other substances like sulphur dioxide that damage animal and plant health. In recent years Europe has closed more than half its coal-fired stations. In the United States over 65% of plants have closed, or will close in the next ten years.

★ About a third of the world's carbon emissions come from burning coal. It is the single largest contributor to climate change.

Greenhouse effect
When the Sun shines on our planet some of its heat is absorbed and some is reflected. When clouds of gases build up in the Earth's atmosphere, heat cannot be reflected and our planet becomes hotter.

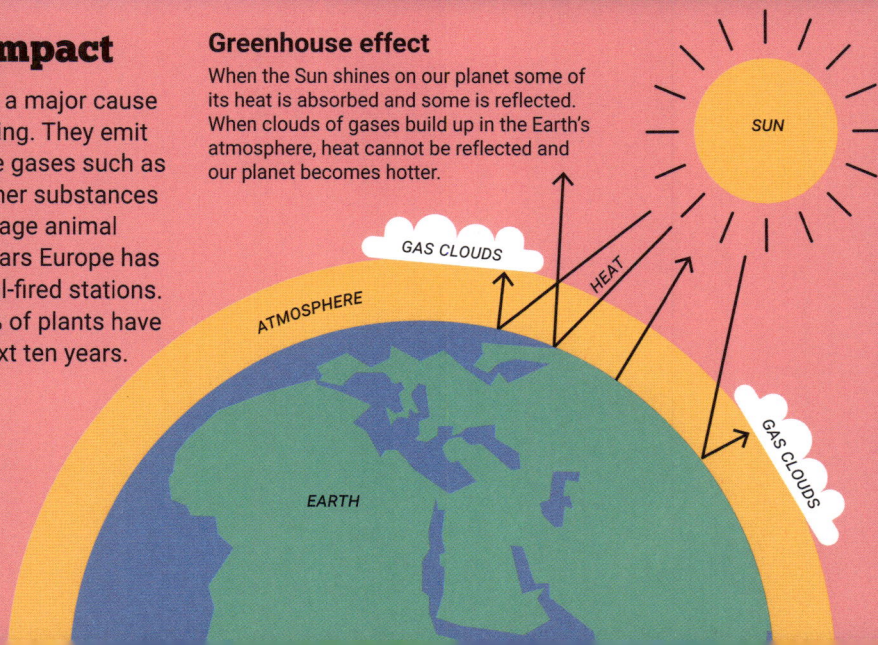

SUN
GAS CLOUDS
HEAT
ATMOSPHERE
GAS CLOUDS
EARTH

Why do we still use fossil fuels?

Now that we know that burning fossil fuels is damaging our planet, why we are still using them? There are three main reasons. Firstly, they are very efficient. Compared to greener alternatives, small amounts of fossil fuels are good at making large amounts of energy. Secondly, they are ready-made, just sitting there waiting to be collected. Thirdly, we are used to using them. Everything, from our cars to our offices and homes, is set up to run on energy produced by fossil fuels. We must switch to alternative forms of energy, but it won't be simple.

★ In many countries, especially those with fast-growing economies and high demand for energy, coal is the cheapest fuel available.

The discovery of electricity

▶ To prove that lightening was electricity, Franklin tied a metal key to a kite and flew it during a thunderstorm. The metal conducted the electricity in the storm clouds and gave him a nasty shock, but it proved he was right!

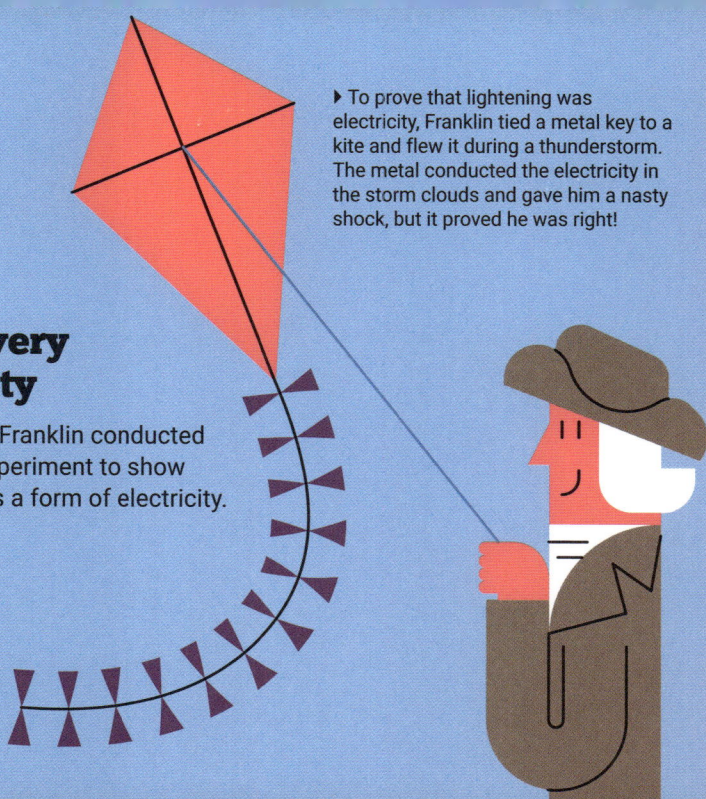

In 1752, Benjamin Franklin conducted his famous kite experiment to show that lightening was a form of electricity.

▶ Electricity exists in nature so it didn't need to be invented. Instead, it needed to be discovered, and understood.

Natural gas stations

Power stations fuelled by natural gas work in much the same way as coal-fired plants, only they burn natural gas instead of coal. They are slightly less bad for the environment than coal, although they do release greenhouse gases, especially carbon dioxide.

Coal versus natural gas

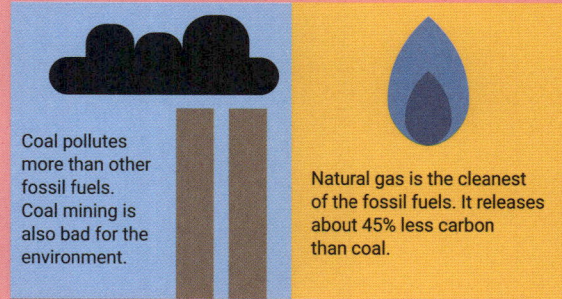

Coal pollutes more than other fossil fuels. Coal mining is also bad for the environment.

Natural gas is the cleanest of the fossil fuels. It releases about 45% less carbon than coal.

What is natural gas?

Natural gas is colourless, odourless and highly flammable. There are large reserves around the world and it is easily transported in pipelines.

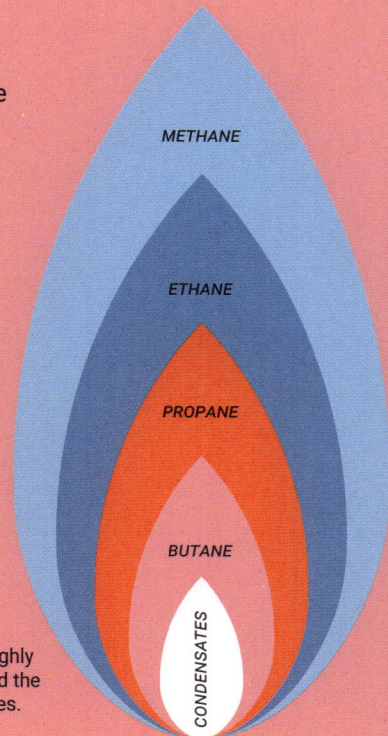

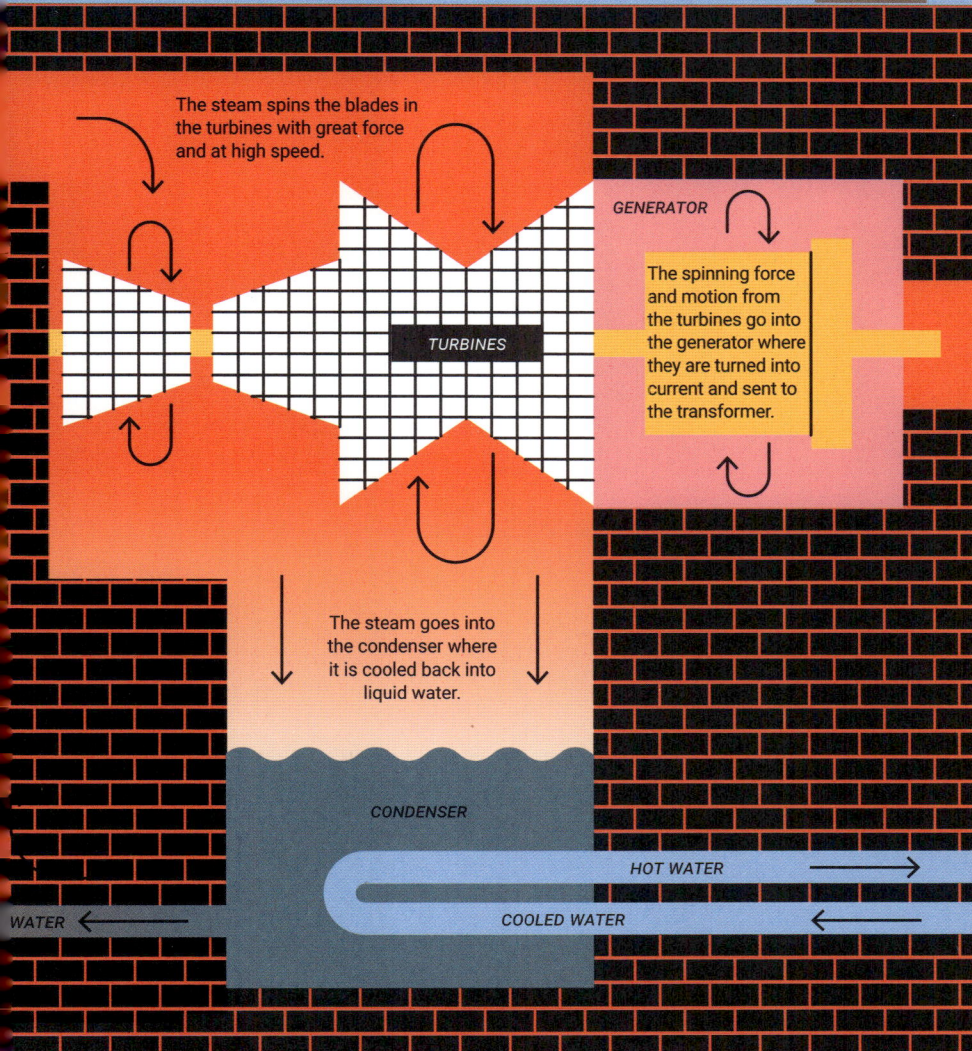

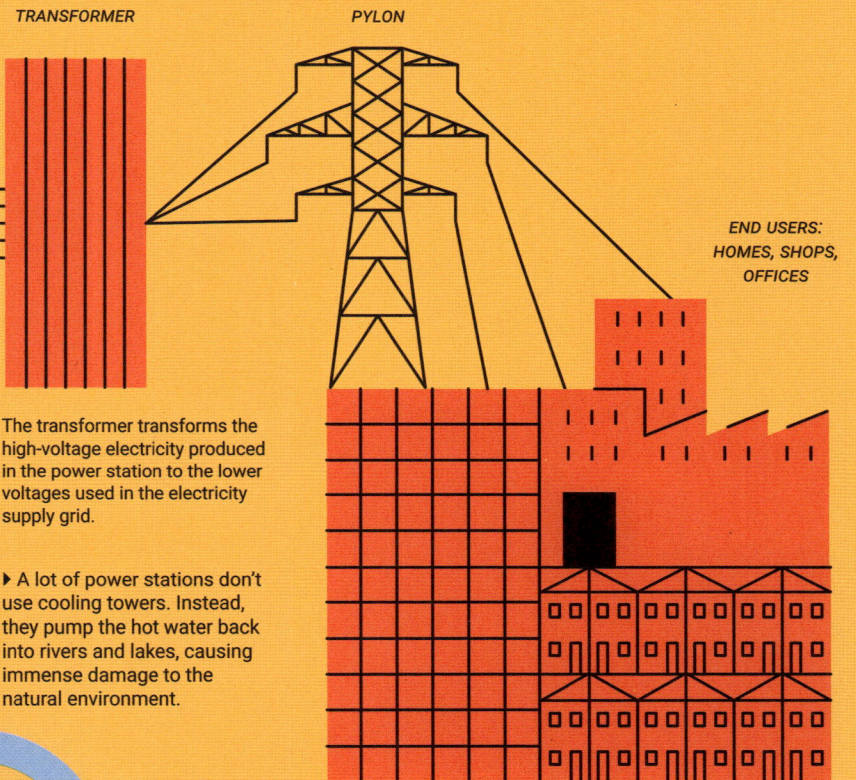

METHANE
ETHANE
PROPANE
BUTANE
CONDENSATES

The steam spins the blades in the turbines with great force and at high speed.

GENERATOR

The spinning force and motion from the turbines go into the generator where they are turned into current and sent to the transformer.

TURBINES

The steam goes into the condenser where it is cooled back into liquid water.

CONDENSER

HOT WATER

COOLED WATER

◀ WATER

TRANSFORMER **PYLON**

END USERS: HOMES, SHOPS, OFFICES

The transformer transforms the high-voltage electricity produced in the power station to the lower voltages used in the electricity supply grid.

▶ A lot of power stations don't use cooling towers. Instead, they pump the hot water back into rivers and lakes, causing immense damage to the natural environment.

STEAM CLOUDS **STEAM CLOUDS**

COOLING TOWERS

Hot water from the condenser is sent to the cooling towers, then back to the condenser where it

begins its journey all over again. Some steam is also emitted from the cooling towers.

Efficiency

Traditional coal-fired power stations are quite wasteful. The average fossil-fuelled power station is about 35% efficient. This means that around two-thirds of the energy produced is given off as clouds of heat and steam! Power plants that are equipped with Combined Heat and Power technology (known as **CHP technology**) are much more efficient. They capture the steam and hot water that is usually wasted and re-use it.

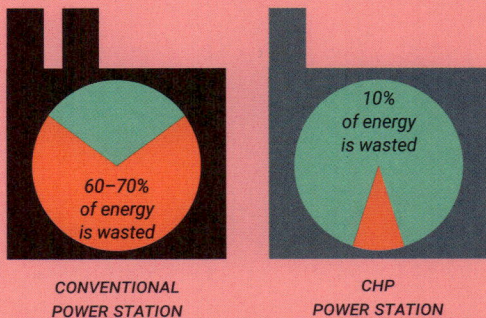

60–70% of energy is wasted

CONVENTIONAL POWER STATION

10% of energy is wasted

CHP POWER STATION

★ Until we are able to replace fossil-fuelled power stations with greener alternatives, CHP technology is less damaging for the environment.

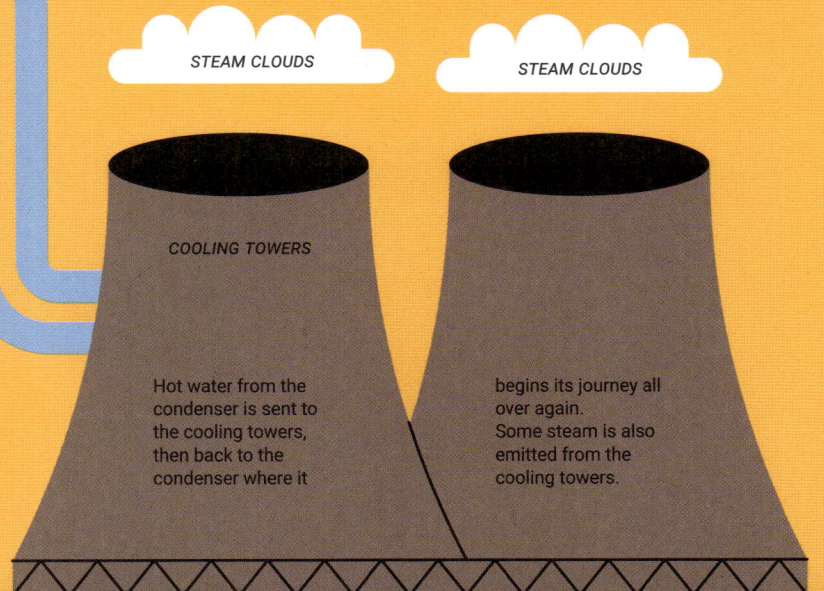

ALTERNATIVE ENERGY

Fossil fuels are not the only way to generate electricity. There are lots of cleaner ways, including wind, hydro-electric, solar and geothermal processes. We already have the technology to generate power in these ways and they are being used more and more.

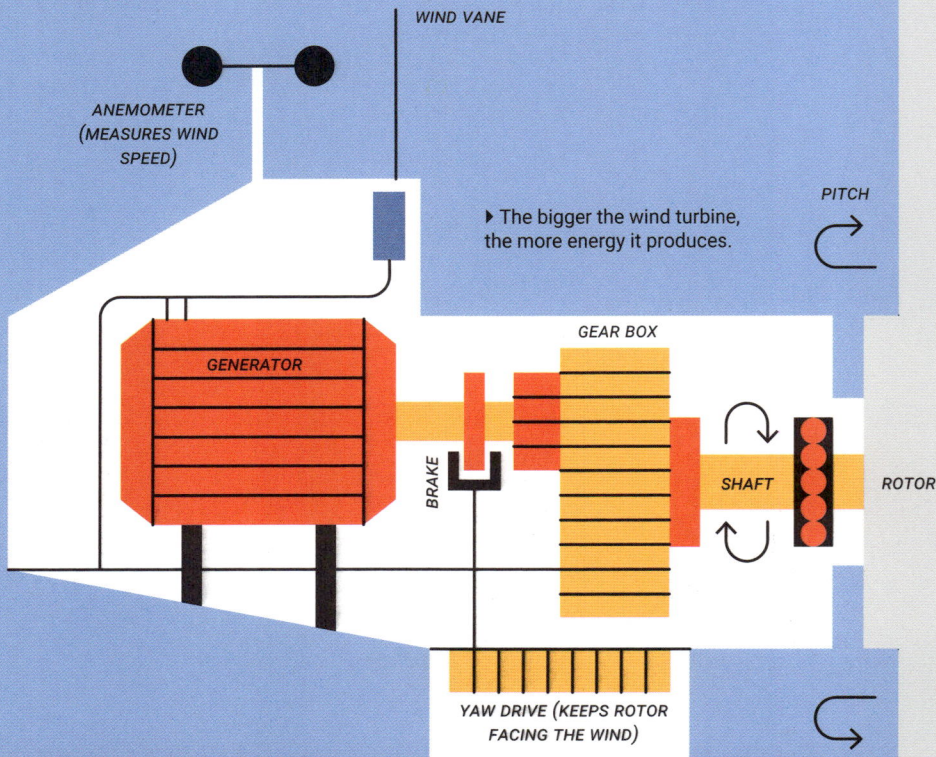

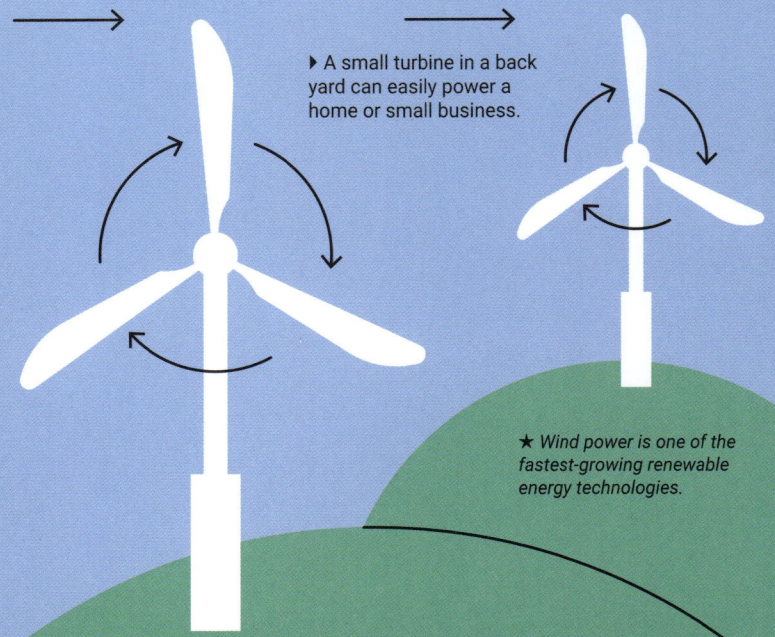

▶ A small turbine in a back yard can easily power a home or small business.

★ Wind power is one of the fastest-growing renewable energy technologies.

WIND VANE

ANEMOMETER (MEASURES WIND SPEED)

BLADES

PITCH

▶ The bigger the wind turbine, the more energy it produces.

GENERATOR

GEAR BOX

BRAKE

SHAFT

ROTOR

YAW DRIVE (KEEPS ROTOR FACING THE WIND)

Wind farms

A wind farm is a group of wind turbines in the same area that generate electricity. Wind farms can be made up of just a few turbines or they can be huge, with hundreds of turbines harnessing the power of the wind together. Wind farms can be onshore (on land) or offshore (at sea).

How wind turbines work

The wind turns the blades which are connected to a rotor that makes a shaft spin. The shaft is linked to a gear box which increases the speed at which the blades rotate. The shaft leads to the generator which converts the mechanical energy into electricity.

Renewable versus non-renewable

There are two types of energy: renewable and non-renewable. Renewable energy sources do not run out, and include solar, wind and hydropower. Non-renewable energy sources, such as oil and coal, are finite and will eventually be all used up.

SOLAR POWER

▶ Renewable energy sources are much better for the environment than non-renewable ones.

WIND POWER

Rapid growth of renewables

Experts predict that by 2035 more than half the electricity produced worldwide will come from renewable energy sources.

★ Renewable energy is growing fast. For the first time, in 2021 wind and solar generated more than 10% of global electricity.

Hydro-electric power

Hydro-electric, or hydropower, uses falling or fast-running water to power machinery that produces electricity. It is by far the most common way renewable energy is generated globally.

★ Hydropower currently supplies around 18% of the world's electricity, the third-largest source after coal and natural gas.

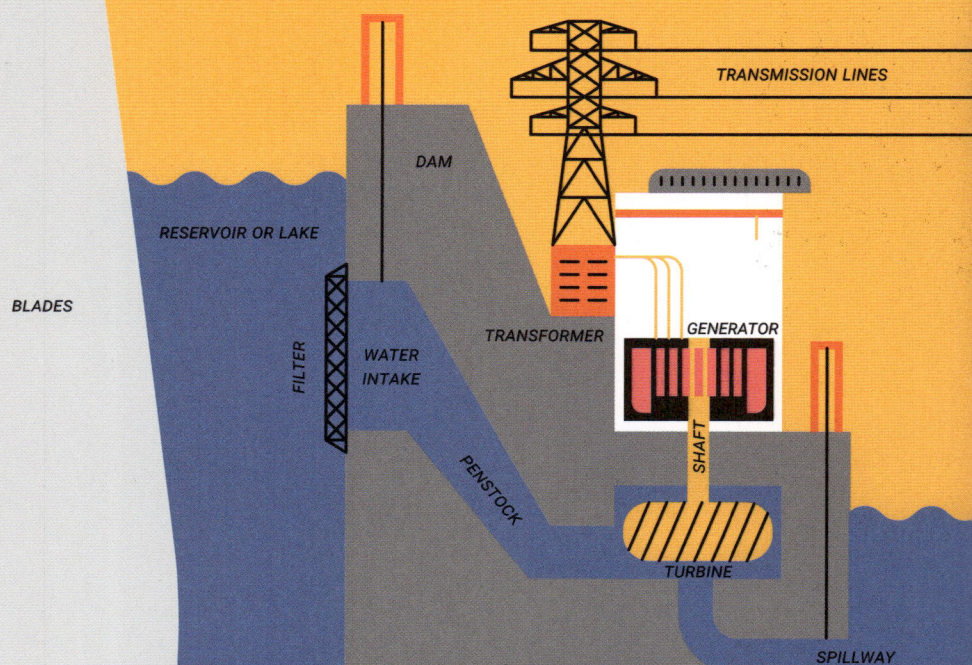

TRANSMISSION LINES

DAM

RESERVOIR OR LAKE

BLADES

FILTER

WATER INTAKE

TRANSFORMER

GENERATOR

SHAFT

PENSTOCK

TURBINE

SPILLWAY

How it works

A dam is built across a river so that water builds up behind it. The intake is opened and water flows down a pipe called the penstock, gaining speed (kinetic energy) as it goes. When it reaches the turbine it makes the blades spin. The turbine shaft is attached to a generator which transforms the spinning force into electricity. The water flows out of a spillway and the river continues its journey.

Nuclear power stations

Nuclear power plants use **nuclear fission** to produce energy to turn water into steam. The super-heated steam drives a turbine connected to a generator which produces electricity.

▸ The nuclear reactor is encased in a concrete dome to prevent radiation leakage.

Nuclear fission

Nuclear fission occurs when the nucleus of an atom splits into two or more smaller parts. The reaction releases an enormous amount of energy, as well as nuclear waste. In the future, scientists hope to use **nuclear fusion** to generate energy because it doesn't produce dangerous radioactive waste.

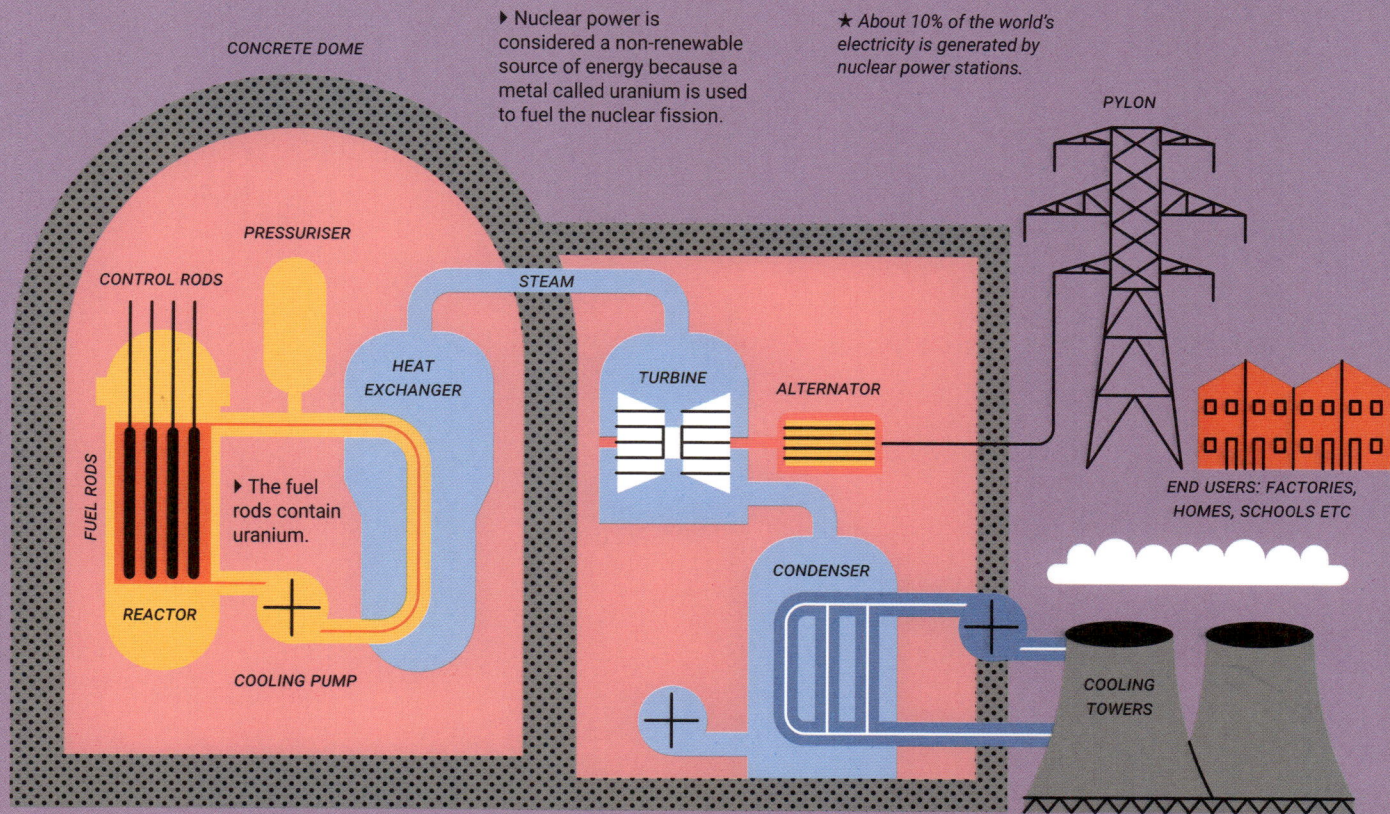

CONCRETE DOME

▸ Nuclear power is considered a non-renewable source of energy because a metal called uranium is used to fuel the nuclear fission.

★ About 10% of the world's electricity is generated by nuclear power stations.

PRESSURISER

CONTROL RODS

STEAM

HEAT EXCHANGER

TURBINE

ALTERNATOR

PYLON

FUEL RODS

▸ The fuel rods contain uranium.

REACTOR

COOLING PUMP

CONDENSER

END USERS: FACTORIES, HOMES, SCHOOLS ETC

COOLING TOWERS

Waste disposal

Nuclear power stations generate radioactive waste that is highly toxic. Radioactive waste has to be stored for thousands of years before it becomes non-toxic. A lot of nuclear waste is processed into solid glass which is easier to manage and store than liquid waste. It is usually buried deep underground.

★ People worry that stored nuclear waste may be released unintentionally by earthquakes or other natural disasters, or by terrorists or during a war.

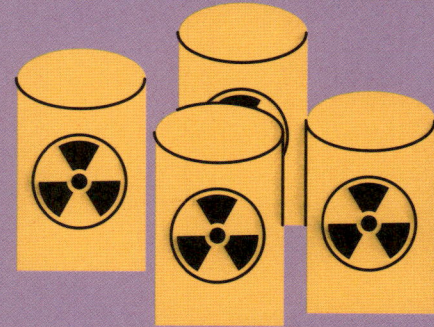

Geothermal power

A geothermal power plant pumps very hot water or steam from wells located deep in the Earth's crust. The hot water gushes up, driving turbines connected to generators that transform the energy into electricity. The water is cooled then pumped back into the ground.

▸ Geothermal power is a very clean, renewable source of energy.

★ There is enough **geothermal energy** in the Earth's crust to meet all our energy needs for millions of years.

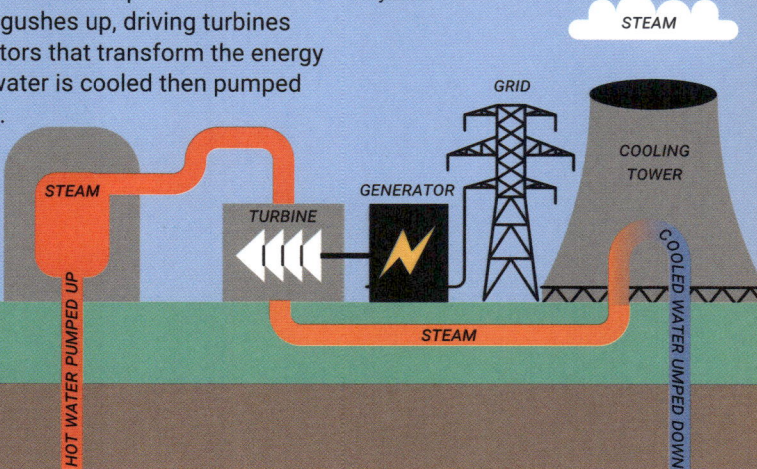

STEAM

GRID

COOLING TOWER

STEAM

TURBINE

GENERATOR

STEAM

HOT WATER PUMPED UP

COOLED WATER UMPED DOWN

Biofuels

Biofuels are made from renewable resources such as plants, algae or animal waste. There are many different types of biofuel and not everyone agrees that they are all good for the environment.

Some sources of biofuel

RUBBISH

WOOD

CROPS

LANDFILL GAS

ALCOHOL FUELS

▸ Biofuels and tidal power are not widely used. More research is needed to make them viable on a large scale.

Solar power

Solar power works by converting light and heat from the Sun into energy. Solar panels on solar farms or rooftops absorb sunlight and use it to create electrical charges. The electricity can be used or stored by homes, or sent off to the national grid.

★ Solar energy is the third biggest renewable power source in the world today.

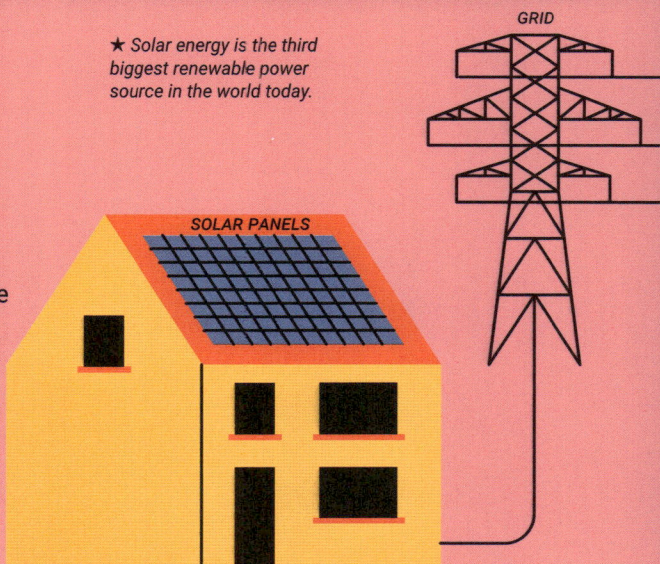

GRID

SOLAR PANELS

▸ There are two ways of generating solar energy. One uses panels to convert light into electricity, while the other uses thermal technology to capture the Sun's heat.

Tidal power

Tidal energy is produced by harnessing the surging sea waters during the rise and fall of tides. There are a few different technologies being developed.

▸ Tidal power works a bit like an undersea wind turbine.

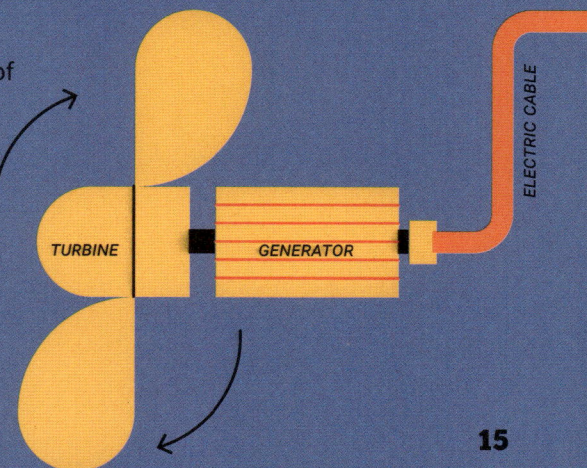

INCOMING TIDE TURNS GIANT UNDERWATER TURBINES

TURBINE

GENERATOR

ELECTRIC CABLE

▸ Tidal power is a clean and renewable energy source. However, it is quite expensive to set up and can also damage delicate coastal ecosystems.

15

WATER SUPPLY

As world population surges towards nine billion, we need to find new and better ways to use and conserve the water on our planet. A wide range of high-tech solutions are used to tackle water scarcity and to extend access to unpolluted, germ-free water to as many people as possible.

Water treatment

In many countries almost everyone has clean running water in their homes. This diagram shows how water is treated before it flows from household taps.

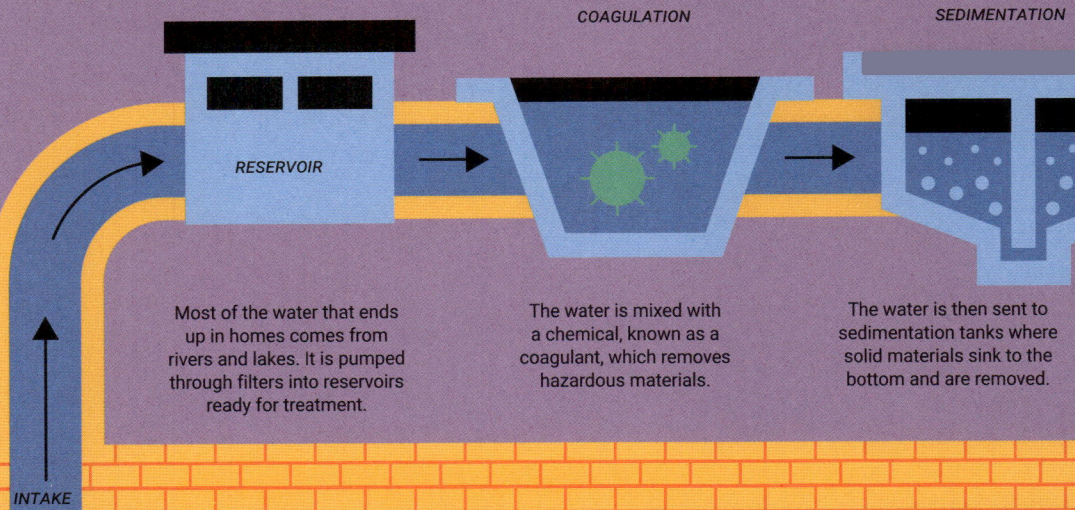

RESERVOIR

COAGULATION

SEDIMENTATION

INTAKE

Most of the water that ends up in homes comes from rivers and lakes. It is pumped through filters into reservoirs ready for treatment.

The water is mixed with a chemical, known as a coagulant, which removes hazardous materials.

The water is then sent to sedimentation tanks where solid materials sink to the bottom and are removed.

Issues

Climate change

Global warming leads to extreme weather, causing flooding and droughts. Clean water is less readily available or is contaminated.

▶ Rising temperatures make deserts larger and increase the need for irrigation to grow food crops.

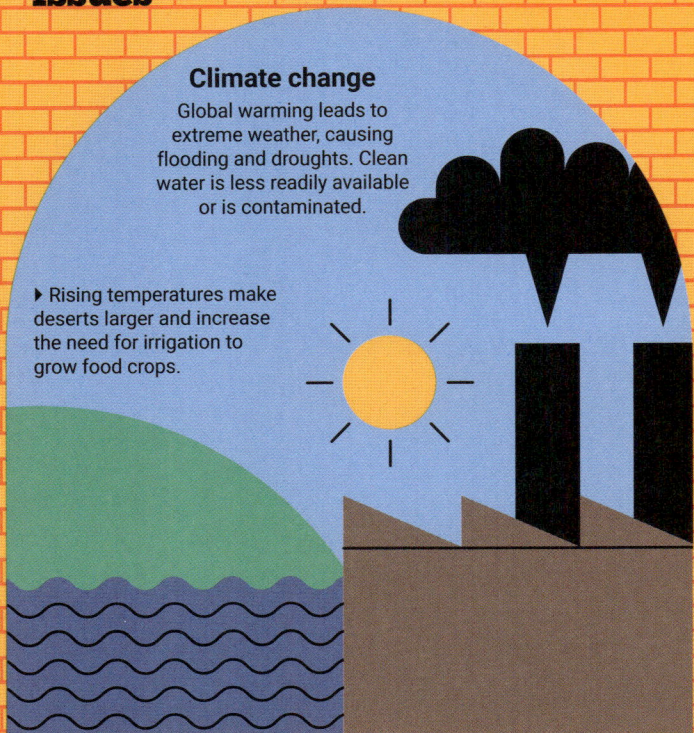

Treating waste water

Water that has been used in homes, factories or farms should be treated before being used again or returned to the natural environment. Treating waste water can be difficult and expensive.

★ The World Health Organisation (WHO) estimates that over 800,000 people die every year from drinking contaminated water.

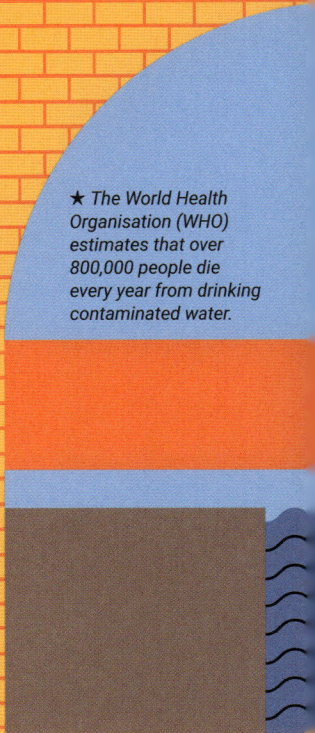

▶ At present only about half of the water used in homes and industry is treated.

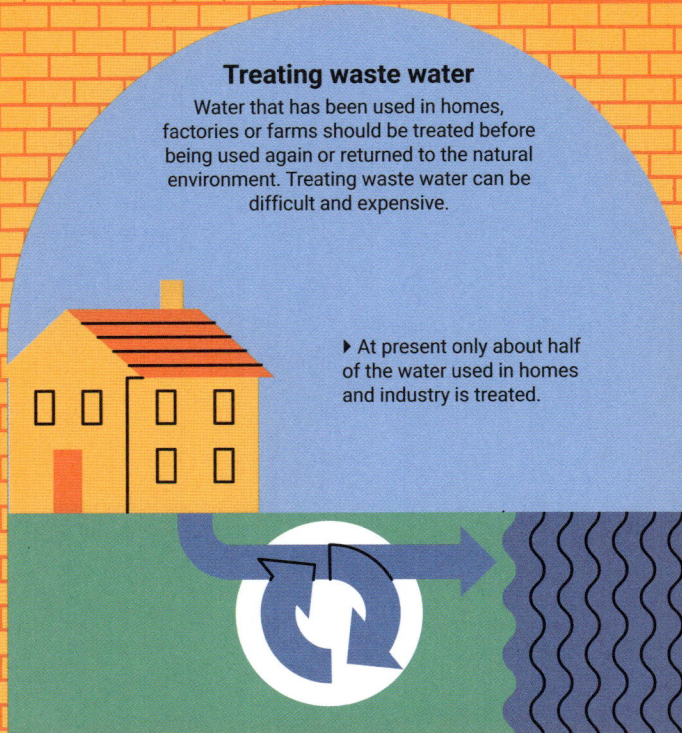

Some solutions

Water in the desert

More than two billion people live in very dry regions. Scientists have found a way to extract moisture from the desert air.

A metal frame captures humidity at night. During the day, heat from the Sun turns it into water.

HEAT FROM THE SUN

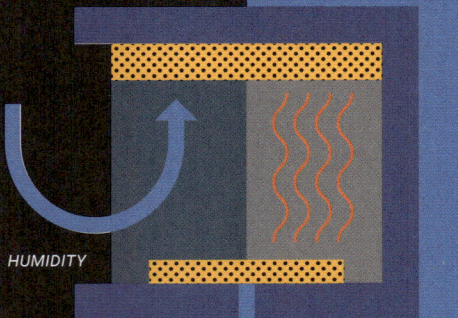

HUMIDITY

WATER IS COLLECTED FOR USE

Removing the salt

People living next to the ocean often have no fresh water to drink. Salt can be removed from seawater to make it drinkable. This is called desalination. New "reverse osmosis" technology has made it easier and cheaper to do this.

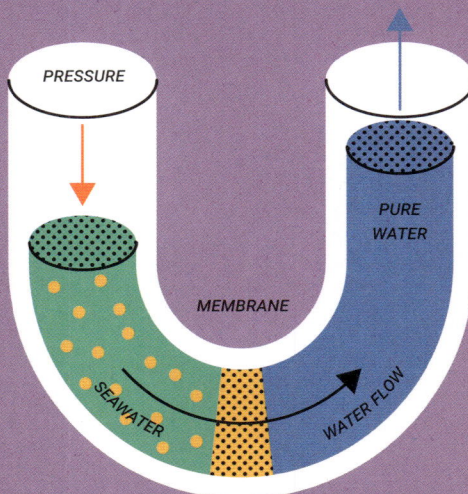

PRESSURE

PURE WATER

MEMBRANE

SEAWATER

WATER FLOW

LifeStraw

Some people live close to water but it is too polluted to drink. Researchers invented a filter in the shape of a fat straw. They called it a LifeStraw.

▶ Each LifeStraw can purify up to 4,000 litres (870 gallons) of water, enough to last one person for three years.

LIFESTRAW

POLLUTED WATER

After filtration, the water is disinfected using chlorine which kills any remaining germs.

FILTRATION

DISINFECTION

STORAGE AND DISTRIBUTION

READY TO USE IN HOUSEHOLD TAPS

At the next stage, the water is filtered through layers of different materials, such as sand and gravel, which removes more germs and dirt.

The clean water is stored ready for use.

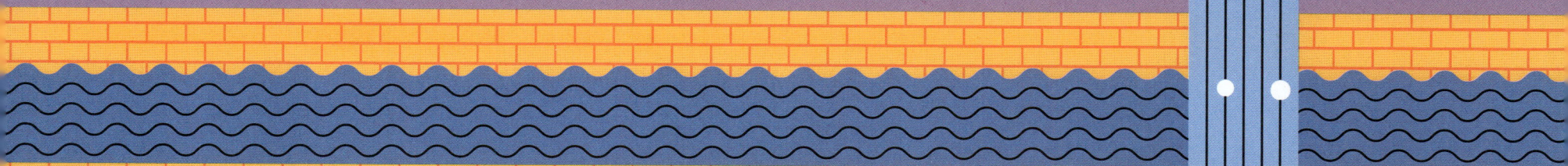

Save water!

There are lots of ways to save water. For example, you can take shorter showers, turn the tap off while you brush your teeth, and only run appliances like washing machines and dishwashers with full loads. Look online for more ideas about how to save water.

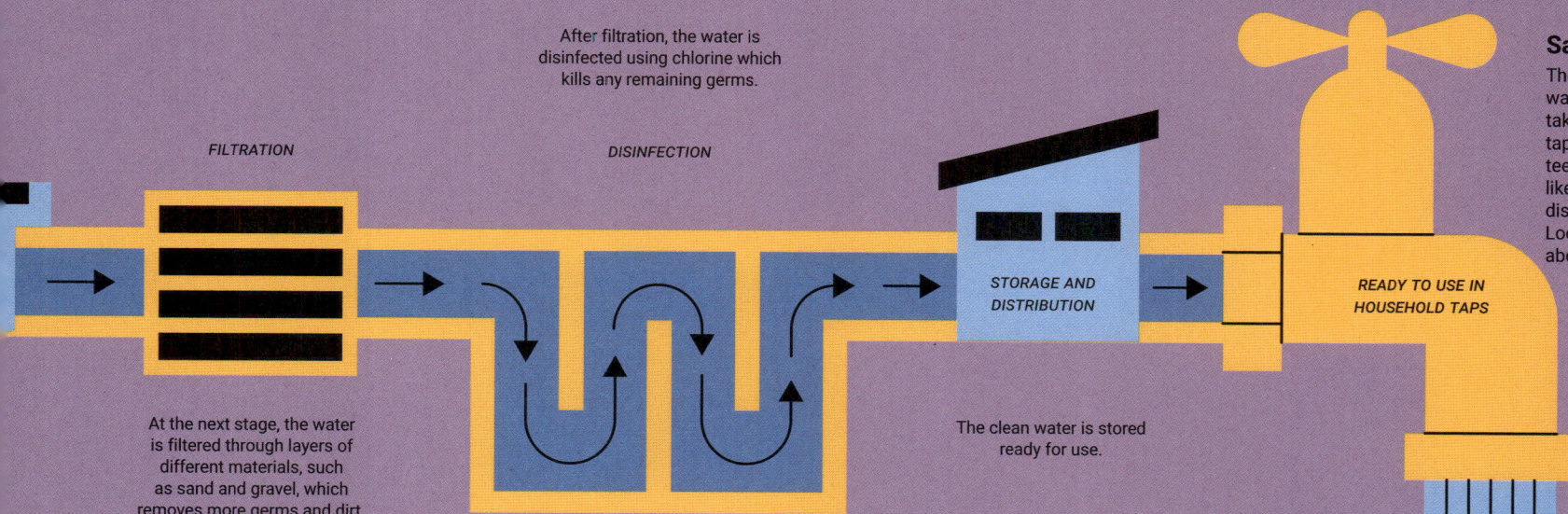

Polluted water

Contaminated water spreads diseases such as cholera and dysentery. Chemicals from industry, fossil fuels and sewage are the main causes of water pollution.

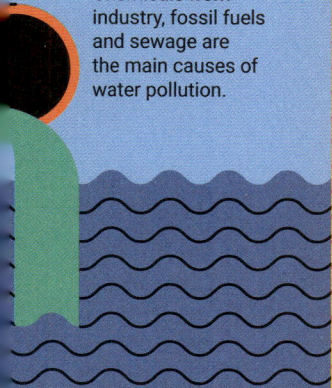

Access to safe water

Globally, over two billion people do not have safe drinking water at home. Half the people in the world do not have toilets in their homes.

▶ In some countries women walk miles every day to collect water for drinking, cooking and washing.

Water Fresh water is a precious resource. We can't live without it. We need it to drink and for sanitation in our homes, but also for food production and industry.

Solar-powered filtration

Germs and pollution can be filtered out of dirty water using energy generated by solar panels.

▶ Small solar-powered filtration plants can be moved around easily to wherever they are needed.

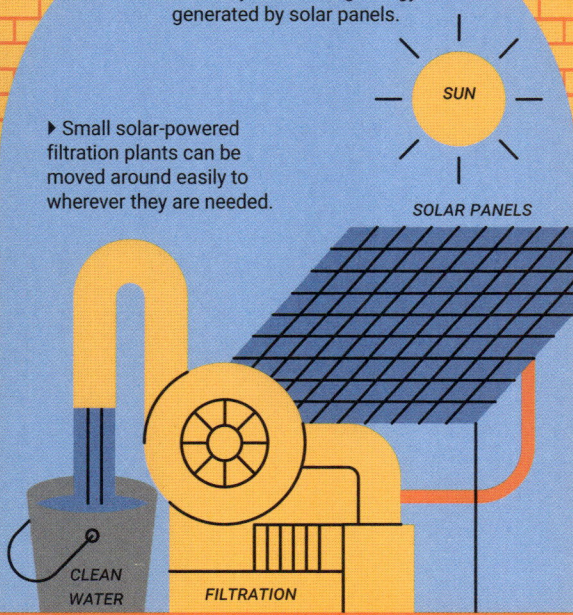

SUN

SOLAR PANELS

CLEAN WATER

FILTRATION

Conservation

Technology can be used in many ways to conserve water, for example by reducing evaporation and stopping seepage from pipelines and canals.

SMART

00001.00

METRE

Smart metres use wireless technology to tell people how much water they are using.

Installing efficient household appliances like dishwashers and toilets reduces water consumption.

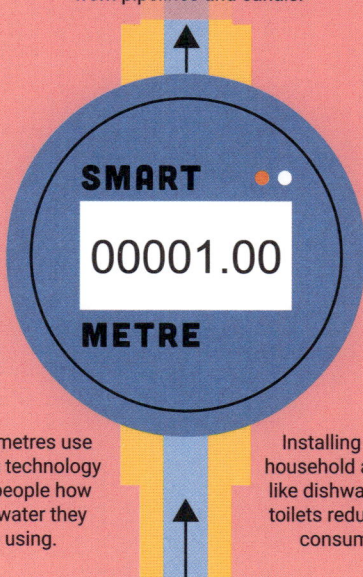

Cloud seeding

Involves spreading substances in the air, usually to try and make it rain. Not everyone agrees that it works.

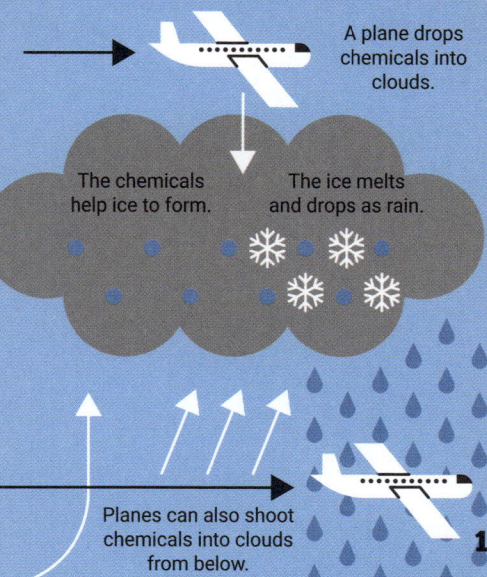

A plane drops chemicals into clouds.

The chemicals help ice to form.

The ice melts and drops as rain.

Planes can also shoot chemicals into clouds from below.

17

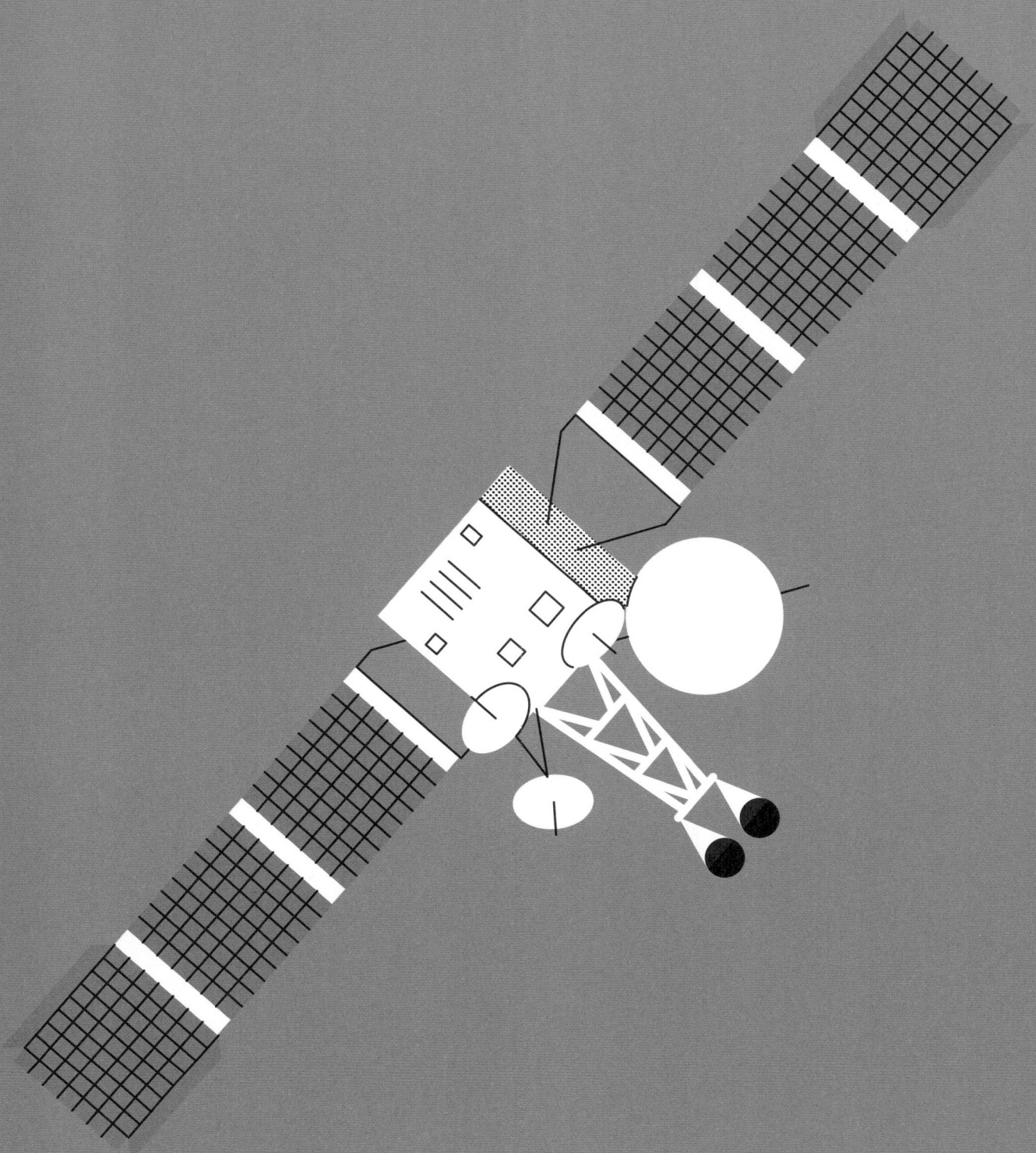

INFORMATION & COMMUNICATION

Information and Communication Technologies (ICT) encompass all the tools and resources we use to create, transmit, store, share and exchange information, from telephones and computers to satellites and media.

THE TELEPHONE

Telephones allow people to speak when they far apart. They do this by converting the sound waves in the human voice into signals and transferring them to other phones which turn them back into speech. Traditional phones, or **landlines**, use electrical signals to so this, while mobile phones use radio waves.

AHOY!

★ Bell first became interested in the science of sound because his mother was deaf. His wife, whom he met while teaching at a school for the hearing-impaired, was also deaf.

BELL'S CENTENNIAL MODEL (1876)

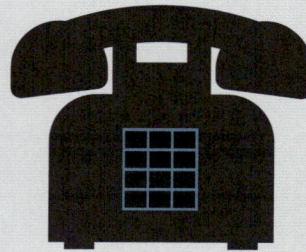

★ Bell's telephone patent was challenged by over 600 lawsuits.

Alexander Graham Bell

Scottish-born scientist and engineer Alexander Graham Bell invented the telephone in 1876. He spoke the first historic — and humdrum — words on a telephone on 10 March of the same year, saying to his assistant "Mr Watson, come here, I want to see you."

★ Bell wanted "Ahoy-hoy!" to be the standard telephone greeting. Luckily, "hello" was chosen instead.

1876
Telephone invented.

1879
First telephone numbers issued.

1891
Automatic switchboard invented.

1915
First coast-to-coast call from San Francisco to New York.

CANDLESTICK PHONE (1890s)

★ Telephone comes from the Greek words tele, meaning "distant," and phone, meaning "voice."

1927
First transatlantic telephone call between New York and London. The official call was made on 7 January, but a test call was made a day earlier. During that call one caller said to the other: "Distance doesn't mean anything anymore. We are on the verge of a very high-speed world..." How right they were!

CRADLE DESK SET (1926)

Telegraph
The electric telegraph was a forerunner of the telephone. Invented in the mid 19th century, it was the first machine that could transmit messages instantly over long distances.

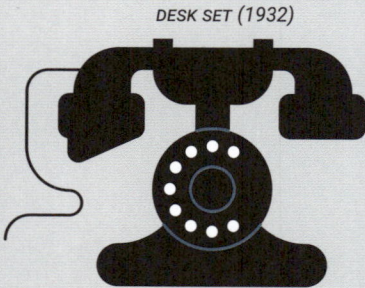

DESK SET (1932)

DESK SET (1964)

1960s & 70s
Touch-tone dial pads begin to replace rotary from 1963. Cordless phones invented in 1966. Caller ID invented in 1976.

1980s
The first hand-held mobile phone by Motorola appeared in 1983. Answering machines were invented in the 1930s but only became popular in the 1980s.

CORDLESS PHONE

TELEPHONE BOX

How it works

SPEAKER

Landlines
An old-fashioned handset like this one had an inbuilt speaker and a microphone. It was connected by a cord to a device that could dial numbers, and to a duplex coil (to stop you from hearing your own voice), a ringer, and a hook switch (which connected and disconnected you from the network).

MICROPHONE

CORDS

ANTONIO MEUCCI

ELISHA GREY

In the air
The "talking telegraph" idea was in the air in the 1870s and at least two other people invented a similar device at around the same time as Bell. Antonio Meucci, an Italian immigrant in New York, filed a patent in 1871, but failed to complete the paperwork. Elisha Grey, an American engineer, filed for his invention just hours after Bell in 1876.

Booths and books
Before mobile phones, our towns and cites were full of telephone boxes where people could go with coins or cards to make calls. At home, people kept two giant books with lists of telephone numbers, one for private phones and one for businesses.

TELEPHONE BOOKS

Landlines vs mobile phones

In most places mobile phone use has displaced landlines. Mobile phones are cheaper and more convenient than landlines.

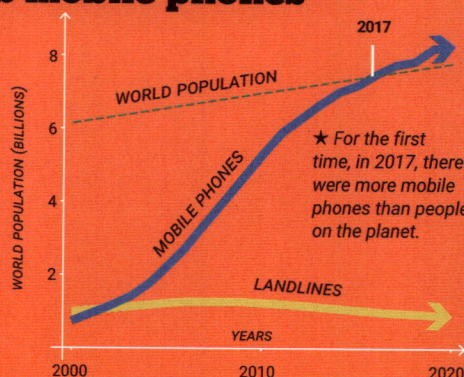

2017

WORLD POPULATION

MOBILE PHONES

LANDLINES

★ For the first time, in 2017, there were more mobile phones than people on the planet.

WORLD POPULATION (BILLIONS)

8
6
4
2

YEARS

2000   2010   2020

Mobile coverage

When you make a call on your mobile it connects via radio link to the nearest mobile tower. The tower forwards your link to a mobile exchange and from there to the end user, wherever in the world they may be.

ANTENNAE

SIGNALS

TOWER

TALL BUILDING ROOF

▶ Mobile towers, or masts, are often perched on top of tall buildings so they can provide a strong signal over a wider area.

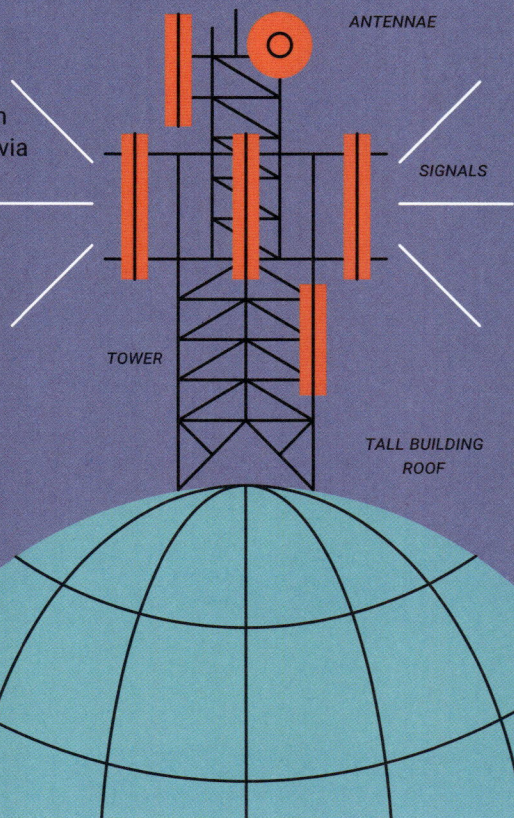

Smartphones

Smartphones are like handheld computers with voice-calling capacity. They communicate via a mobile network (mainly GSM), Bluetooth, Wi-Fi and GPS. They have inbuilt cameras, microphones, loudspeakers and sensors and can be customised by installing apps.

★ Smartphones can be used as wearables, for example as a Fitbit. But they can also hold the app which communicates with wearables, such as headphones.

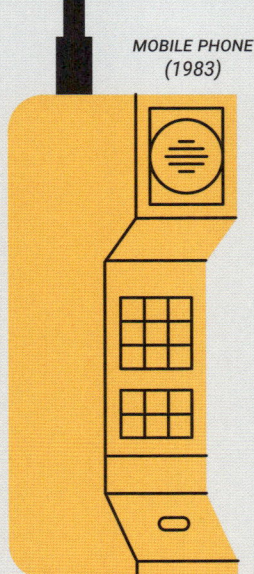

▶ The IBM Simon, released in 1994, was the first smartphone. It was a phone with touchscreen and with email, fax and calendar functions.

★ The iPhone wasn't the first smartphone but it was a game changer. Apple left all the other phone companies scrambling to catch up.

MOBILE PHONE (1983)

1990s
First touchscreen phone: IBM Simon (1994). First internet voice calls. First flip phone (Motorola 1996).

2000s
Golden age of the BlackBerry. First colour screens appear, along with built-in cameras. First iPhone. Users can access and download multimedia content.

2010s
The smartphone era: Used for everything, from banking to finding a hotel or a date. 4G brings 10x faster speed. Flexible phones appear.

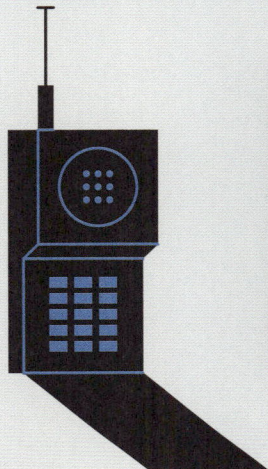

FLIP PHONE (1996)

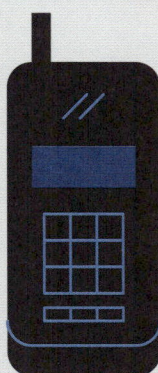

2020s
Better cameras, higher quality displays. 5G will make mobiles faster and more reliable. It will also vastly improve mobile connection to the IoT (Internet of Things).

The Future
Mobile phones will be paper thin and will recharge wirelessly.

MOBILE PHONE

Satellite phones

Unlike mobile phones, satphones send and receive messages via satellites that orbit the Earth. They are expensive and are mainly used for voice and text messages. They are very useful in remote regions where there is no mobile phone coverage.

Mobile phones can be...

DIRTY
Mobile phones have more germs than a toilet flush.

DISTRACTING
More than 60% of Americans admit to texting while driving.

SPORTING
Mobile phone throwing is an official sport in Finland.

DANGEROUS!
Many more people die each year taking selfies than are killed in shark attacks.

WATERPROOF
In Japan, 90% of mobile phones are waterproof because children use them even in the shower.

ADDICTIVE
The average mobile phone owner checks their phone about 150 times a day.

ECONOMICAL
It costs less than £1.00 a year to keep your phone charged.

INCREDIBLY POWERFUL
Your mobile phone has more computing power than the computers used for the Apollo 11 moon landing in 1969.

A SOURCE OF NEW WORDS
"Phubbing" (phone snubbing) is a new word that means ignoring your friends in favour of your phone.

PATENTED
The technology behind smartphones relies on 250 different patents.

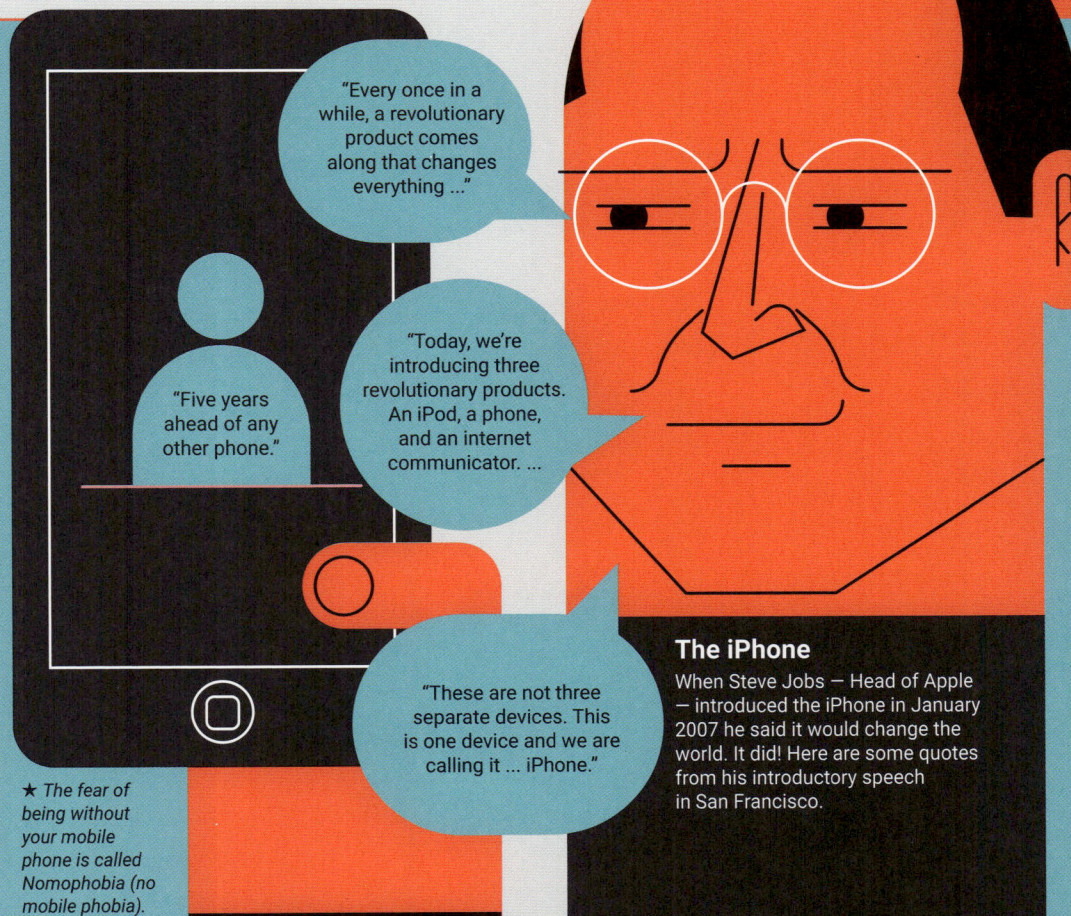

★ The fear of being without your mobile phone is called Nomophobia (no mobile phobia).

"Every once in a while, a revolutionary product comes along that changes everything ..."

"Five years ahead of any other phone."

"Today, we're introducing three revolutionary products. An iPod, a phone, and an internet communicator. ..."

"These are not three separate devices. This is one device and we are calling it ... iPhone."

The iPhone
When Steve Jobs — Head of Apple — introduced the iPhone in January 2007 he said it would change the world. It did! Here are some quotes from his introductory speech in San Francisco.

COMPUTERS

Try to imagine a day without a computer.* It's almost impossible, isn't it? Did you text your friends this morning? Did you look at YouTube or TikTok? Did you play video games on the bus going to school? In a relatively short period of time, computers have transformed our lives.

Remember that smartphones and tablets are computers, and that many other devices, like modern TVs and gaming consoles, contain computers.

First programs

The first computer program was written by the English mathematician Ada Lovelace. She was an associate of Babbage and wrote the program for his Analytical Engine. She is credited as the first computer programmer.

Ada Lovelace

Lovelace was the daughter of the famous English poet Lord Byron. Most women in the 1800s did not study maths and science but Lovelace had a good private education and excelled in both fields.

THE ANALYTICAL ENGINE

▶ Babbage designed an earlier device in 1822. It was called the Difference Engine, but it did not work.

The first computer

The first computer was planned by the English inventor and mathematician Charles Babbage in the 1830s. Known as the Analytical Engine, it was designed to carry out arithmetical calculations using instructions from punch cards and had a large memory. The machine was never completed and Babbage's contribution to computer science was forgotten until his notebooks were discovered in 1937.

Types of computers

Computers come in all shapes and sizes, from wearables and smartphones to giant supercomputers.

★ The latest exascale supercomputers, including Fugaku in Japan and Frontier in the USA, can make a billion billion calculations per second.

SUPERCOMPUTER

Supercomputers and mainframes

Supercomputers are big, expensive and fast. They are used for complex calculations. Mainframes are used to store large data bases and serve many users at the same time.

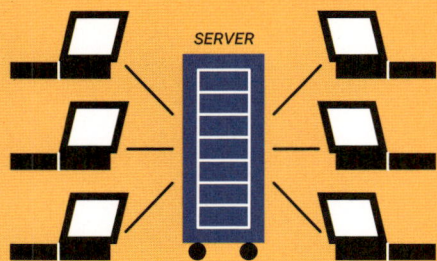

SERVER

Mid-range

Most mid-range computers are used as network servers. They have multiple processors, a large amount of RAM (random access memory) and large hard drives.

PCs

Personal computers are designed to be used by one person at home or in an office. They are relatively inexpensive.

Mobile computers

These are small, portable computers like smartphones, tablets and fitness trackers.

DESKTOP

SMARTPHONE

▶ Mobile computers are becoming cheaper and more powerful.

TABLET

Computer-ese

The computer world has given us some amazing new words.

Dead tree
A paper print-out of an electronic file.

Double geeking
Using two computers at the same time. Triple geeking is using three!

Word-of-mouse
Gossip or info spread on the internet.

Cluster funk
When many things on your computer go wrong at the same time.

Zen mail
An email that arrives with no text.

Meat space
The physical world, as opposed to the virtual or online world.

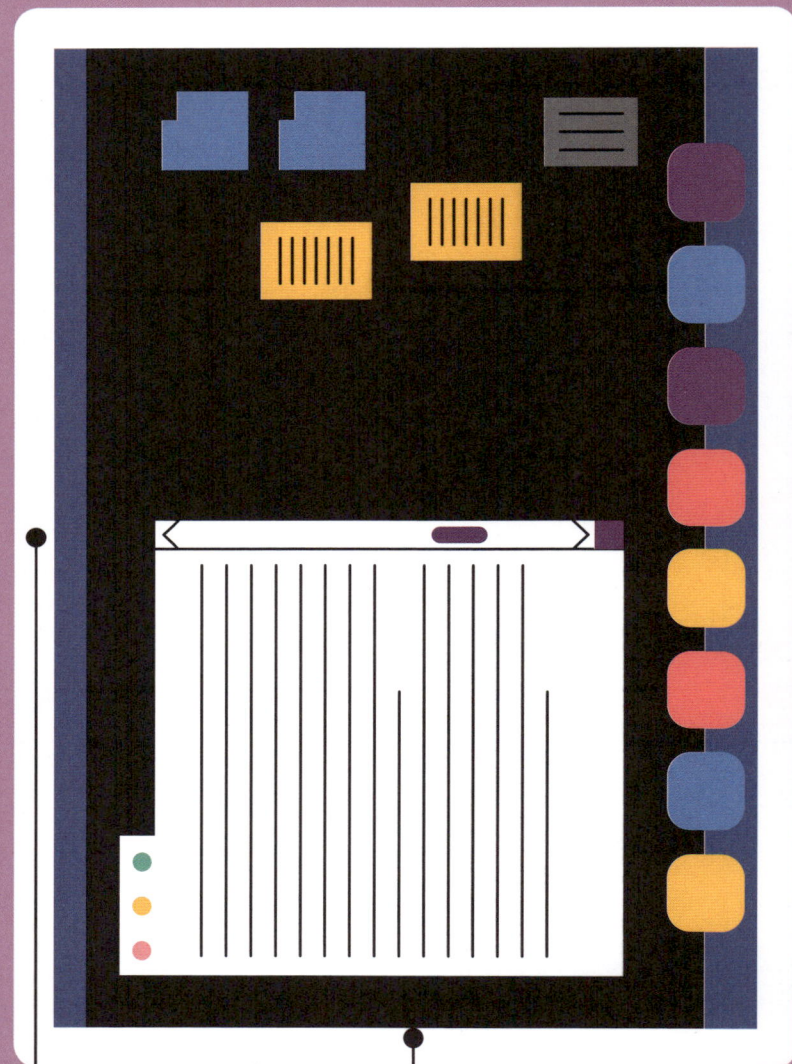

Camera
The round lens at the top of the screen is a built-in camera, or webcam. Used for video chats online.

Screen
Displays texts, pictures or videos so that the user can interact with the computer.

Inside a laptop

Laptops have all of the same components as a desktop computer, including a screen, keyboard, speakers, data storage, drives and pointing devices like a touchpad or trackpad. They have become the most popular type of computer and twice as many laptops are sold each year compared to desktops.

Hardware and software

Computer systems are made up of hardware and software. Hardware includes physical things like the keyboard, the monitor and the motherboard. Software includes all the programs stored on a computer's hard drive that tell the computer what to do.

★ Apps are simple programs for mobile phones and tablets.

Binary numbers

Computers use just two digits – 0 and 1 – to store and process data. This is called the binary numbering system. In everyday life we use the decimal numbering system which has ten numbers from zero to nine. Binary numbers are used in electronics and computer systems. Early computer systems had mechanical switches that turned on to represent 1, and turned off to represent 0. Modern computers still use binary code.

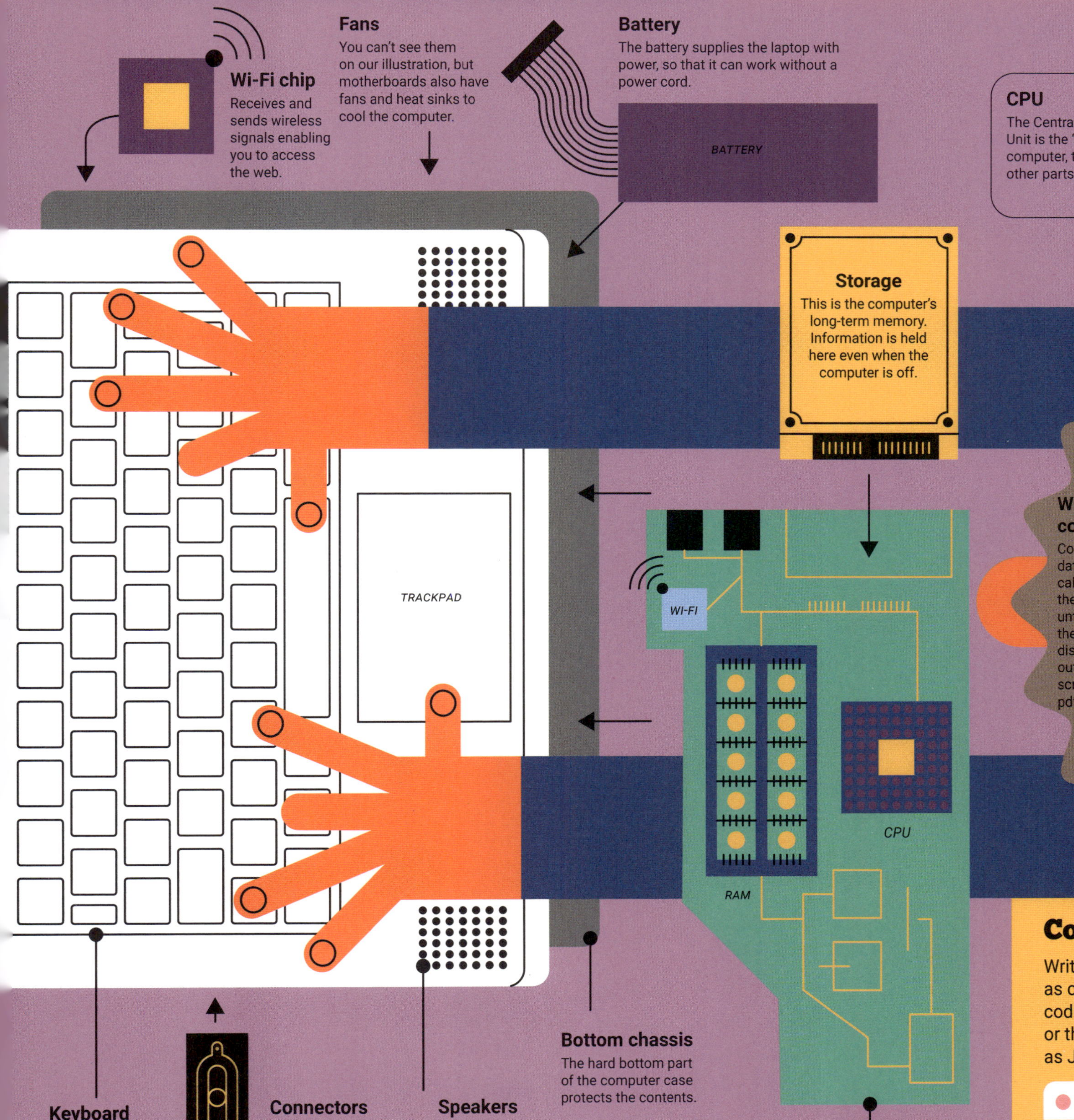

Wi-Fi chip
Receives and sends wireless signals enabling you to access the web.

Fans
You can't see them on our illustration, but motherboards also have fans and heat sinks to cool the computer.

Battery
The battery supplies the laptop with power, so that it can work without a power cord.

BATTERY

CPU
The Central Processing Unit is the "brain" of the computer, telling all the other parts what to do.

RAM
The Random Access Memory is a short-term storage unit that computers use while processing information.

Storage
This is the computer's long-term memory. Information is held here even when the computer is off.

TRACKPAD

WI-FI

CPU

RAM

What computers do
Computers take raw data in at one end; this is called input. They store the data in their memory until the user instructs them to process it. They display the results — or output — to the user on-screen (or as a print-out, pdf or other format).

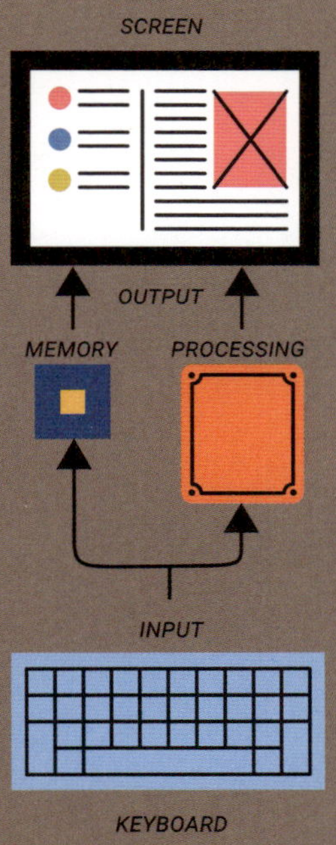

SCREEN

OUTPUT

MEMORY   PROCESSING

INPUT

KEYBOARD

Keyboard
The user taps on the letters, numbers and symbols on the keyboard to tell the computer what to do.

Connectors
Many laptops have connectors so you can plug in things like **USBs** or headphones.

Speakers
Speakers produce sound.

Bottom chassis
The hard bottom part of the computer case protects the contents.

Motherboard
Also called the mainboard, it it a hard circuit board that connects all the parts of the computer.

Coding

Writing instructions for computers is known as coding. There are hundreds of different coding languages, but most coders know two or three of the most widely used ones, such as Javascript, HTML and Python.

▶ In coding, an algorithm is a specific set of instructions for a job.

```
($) \/\/\/ ).() >
{ \/\/\/. \/\/\/\/ ()
{ \/\/\//>\/\/\/\/ (\/\/\/\/ )
```

THE INTERNET

The internet is a massive, open network of networks of connected computers all over the world. In just over 30 years it has revolutionised the way people live their lives and do business.

★ The internet weighs about 60 g (2 ounces).

▸ Every computer or device connected to the internet has a unique **IP address**.

▸ The internet has become the main source of information for millions of people, at home, at school and at work.

▸ Connections between big ISPs and networks carry huge amounts of data. They are linked by the internet backbone.

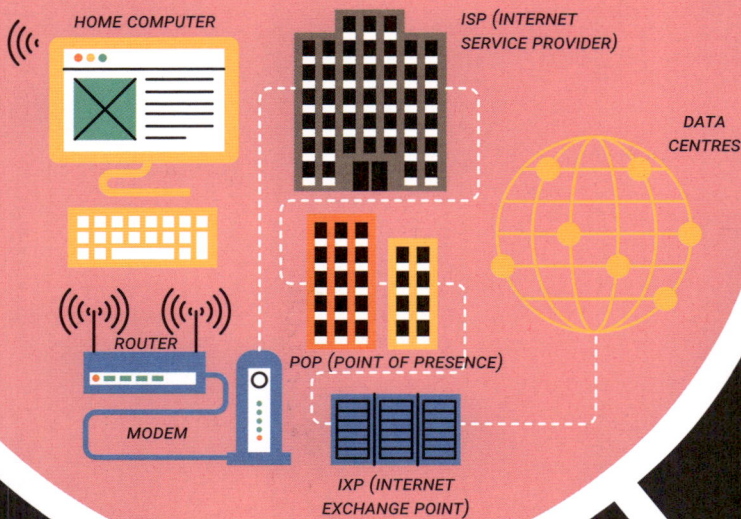

Structure of the internet

Most users access the internet from a computer or smartphone. These devices are connected to the internet through routers, modems or an **ISP** (internet service provider). They are connected to even larger networks and data centres.

HOME COMPUTER

ISP (INTERNET SERVICE PROVIDER)

DATA CENTRES

ROUTER

MODEM

POP (POINT OF PRESENCE)

IXP (INTERNET EXCHANGE POINT)

▸ The orange lines on the map represent undersea cables and the yellow dots are the cities they connect.

The physical internet

Some people say that the internet is a concept, or a series of connected networks and that it doesn't really exist physically. But it does have a physical infrastructure. The physical objects of the internet include routers, cables, antennae, internet exchange points and data centres.

▸ Internet use became widespread in the 1990s. In 1993 there were only 130 websites. By 1996 there were more than 100,000. In 2022 there were over two billion!

★ The first online takeaway food order was placed in 1994. It was for pizza.

Data packets

When you send a message over the internet it is broken into smaller pieces of data, known as packets. These travel separately and are reassembled when they arrive at destination.

SENDER

MODEM

RECIPIENT

▸ Each data packet holds about 1000 to 1500 bytes of information.

▸ Internet data is split into packets because this is the fastest and most efficient way to send it.

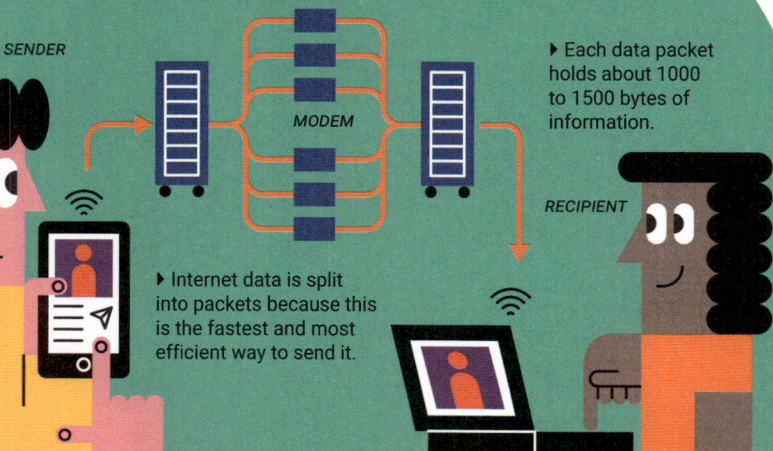

How did it start?

The internet grew out of decades of research by scientists in the United States, United Kingdom and France. As computer science developed in the 1950s and 60s, researchers looked for ways to connect their computers.

▸ The first message was sent over the internet on 29 October 1969. It went from UCLA to Stanford in California using the ARPANET.

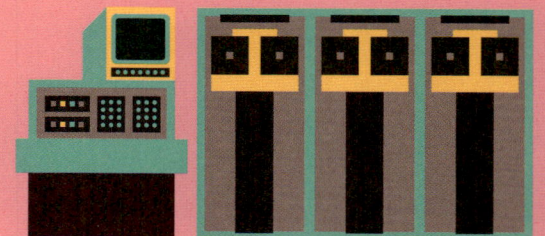

ARPANET (ADVANCED RESEARCH PROJECTS AGENCY NETWORK)

Internet fraud

Cybercrime is becoming more common and complex. **Phishing**, hacking and identity theft are three common online crimes designed to scam people out of money.

★ Phishing is the most common cybercrime.

★ More than 75% of cybercrimes begin with an email.

IDENTITY THEFT

Who owns the internet?

No one. Lots of people own or control parts of it, but no single person, company or government owns or controls all of it. The internet belongs to us all.

★ More than 330 billion emails are sent every day.

★ 99% of email users check their email every day.

Spam

About 85% of emails are spam, also known as junk mail. The internet is clogged with junk.

INBOX   SPAM

★ Spam filters are becoming more effective but there's a lot to block!

Are the Internet and the Web the same thing?

We often use the words web (WWW) and internet to mean the same thing but they are really quite different. The internet is the network of computers that the web runs on.

★ About two thirds of the global population is connected to the WWW.

★ The web is free and open to everyone. You don't have to pay a fee or ask anyone for permission to use it.

The WWW

The World Wide Web, also known as the WWW or simply the web, is a collection of webpages on the internet. They can be accessed using a web browser like Google Chrome or Safari.

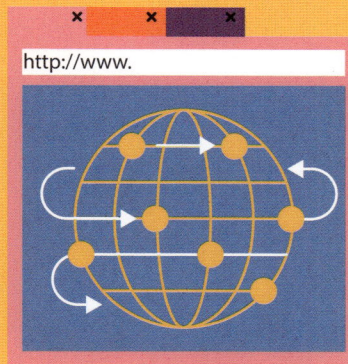

http://www.

▶ The web was invented by computer scientist Tim Berners-Lee in 1989. He set out to create a space for scientists to share data, but ended up inventing something much bigger.

Undersea cables

About 95% of global communications are carried by fibre optic cables. The rest are sent via satellite. Between continents, the cables run along the ocean floor. There are already about 1.2 million km (750,000 miles) of undersea cables in place, with more being laid every day.

★ If you think that the internet is in the cloud, think again. It's in the ocean!

★ The term Wi-Fi was invented as a play on words of Hi-Fi, which means "high fidelity." Wi-Fi does not mean "wireless fidelity" as many people claim.

★ The first email was sent by computer engineer Ray Tomlinson in 1971.

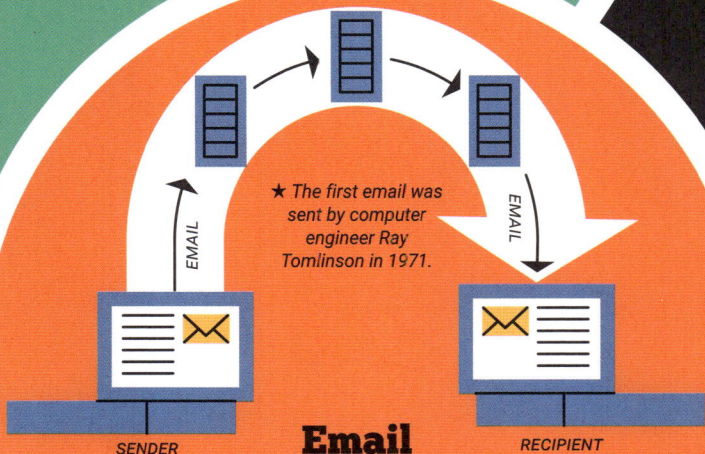

EMAIL

EMAIL

SENDER   RECIPIENT

Email

Electronic mail, or email, is a way of exchanging messages between computers and devices. Messages are sent according to rules, known as the Simple Mail Transfer Protocol (SMTP).

★ With more than 2.5 billion monthly users, Meta (previously known as Facebook) is by far the largest social media website.

Social media

Interactive websites that allow people to create and share information and ideas are known as social media. Meta, YouTube, Twitter, TikTok, Instagram and Pinterest are just a few of the sites that people use daily.

▶ Almost 4.5 billion (or 60%) of people in the world use social media. About 99% access social media sites using mobile devices like smartphones and tablets.

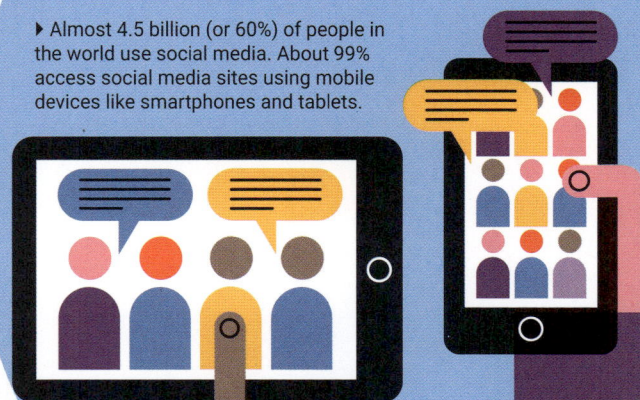

25

Avatars

An avatar is a digital version of yourself. You may already have an avatar if you play online games. But metaverse avatars are different because you will have just one that works in all the different virtual worlds you visit. It will be your metaverse identity.

▶ Several big fashion brands have already entered the metaverse. Many are designing clothes for avatars to wear.

★ Each segment of the metaverse is known as a platform. Metaverse avatars will be able to walk through all the different platforms.

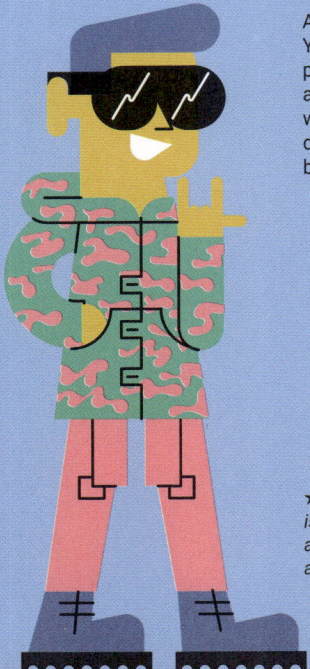

Snow Crash

The word "metaverse" was first used in a 1992 sci-fi novel by Neal Stephenson called *Snow Crash*. In the novel people use digital avatars of themselves to visit a virtual world.

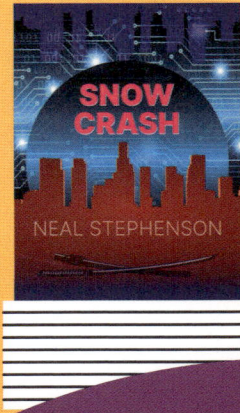

SNOW CRASH

NEAL STEPHENSON

▶ The metaverse will be made up of multiple interconnected virtual spaces, each with their own infrastructure, economy, communities and areas of interest.

★ Virtual reality is a key part of the metaverse experience so it's best if you wear a VR headset.

VR HEADSET

Working in the metaverse

During the Covid-19 pandemic people learned to work at home using the internet to connect with colleagues and bosses. In a metaverse future we may spend a lot of our working lives in virtual offices. Our avatars or holograms* will be able to hold meetings and even spend the working day in a virtual office.

▶ The metaverse will change existing jobs and create many new ones. Imagine, for example, a virtual mall with virtual customers being served by virtual assistants who are all working from home.

▶ Haptic gloves allow the wearer to have a realistic sense of touch in the metaverse.

WITM (WORKING IN THE METAVERSE)

★ A hologram is like a 3D photograph. With today's technology you can make a very realistic hologram of a person.

▶ Metaverse gaming also has play-to-earn games where players are rewarded in cryptocurrencies for their skills.

Games

Games are one of the most popular ways to enjoy the metaverse, especially now while the rest of the realm is still in its infancy. Metaverse games use tools such as VR, AR and AI, providing a much freer experience than traditional gaming.

★ In the future of metaverse gaming, players will be able to interact more with the games, immersing themselves more fully and even adding things to the games.

NFTS
Non-Fungible Tokens are virtual assets, such as art, trading cards, comics and games.

MIRRORWORLDS
A digital version of the real world with virtual equivalents of people, places and things.

AUGMENTED REALITY (AR)
Computer-generated images overlaid on the real world.

Metaverse jargon

WEB3
The next version of the internet. We are currently in the Web2 phase of the internet.

MIXED REALITY (MR)
An immersive experience with elements of virtual and augmented reality.

Ownership

Like the internet, no one owns the metaverse. It belongs to everyone. People who invest in the metaverse by helping to build it, such as software developers, artists, 3D modelers, game developers, users, investors and the like, will have a greater say about what it becomes than those who do not get involved.

Cryptocurrencies

A **cryptocurrency** is digital or virtual money. It isn't regulated by governments or banks like the physical currencies we use in the real world. In the metaverse people will use crypto tokens for shopping, trading and paying for what they want.

★ Bitcoin and Ethereum are two of the most popular cryptocurrencies.

BITCOIN

ZCASH

MONERO

ETHEREUM

★ There are more than 10,000 different cryptocurrencies and more than 300 million users around the world.

Shopping

People will be able to use their avatars to try on clothing, test armchairs and beds for size and even test drive cars. When they find the right product they will buy it and have it sent to them in the real world.

▶ People can also shop for virtual products to be used while they are in the metaverse, such as clothes for their avatars, for example.

★ Test driving a virtual car in the metaverse.

★ There are digital museums to visit in the metaverse with artworks on display.

Devices and gear

Although anyone with a computer or Smartphone can enter the metaverse, they will have a more limited experience than those who have invested in hardware like a VR headset and haptic gloves. Having the latest technologies, including the superfast 5G network and edge, spatial and cloud technology will also improve the experience.

Travel

Virtual travel will be so much easier than real-world travel. If you wanted to visit the Eiffel Tower, the Sydney Opera House and the Taj Mahal, you could do it all in one day!

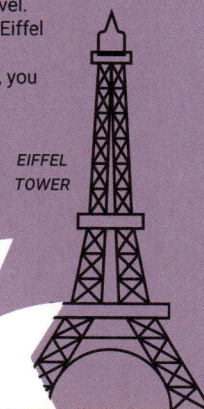
EIFFEL TOWER

SYDNEY OPERA HOUSE

THE METAVERSE

Metaverse is a vague term because it is completely new and still taking shape. It will consist of shared 3D virtual environments where people can go to work, meet up and have fun just as they do in the real world. It will be the new version of the internet.

★ Virtual concerts became popular during the pandemic. Ariana Grande's 2021 performance in the online video game Fortnite was attended by 78 million people!

▶ The metaverse will use a combination of technology, including virtual and augmented reality and artificial intelligence.

Entertainment

Virtual reality entertainment events with massive crowds of 3D avatars are already happening.

★ People "browse" the internet, but they will "live" in the metaverse.

Meeting people

The metaverse makes it easy to meet new people. It gives you access to users from all over the world. To meet them, you first choose a drop-off point in your preferred platform and enter it with your avatar. Drop-off points are crowded places, with new people popping up all the time. You can soon start making friends.

▶ In the metaverse a "greeter" is a person who introduces people to one another.

Catching up with distant friends

If you have a real-world friend who lives far away you can visit with them in the metaverse, with your avatar meeting theirs. You can also meet their friends and family, extending your social relationships even further.

TELEPORTING	TELEPRESENCE
To be instantly transported across space to a remote virtual or physical location.	The sensation of being in a place where you are not physically present. Lets you feel or appear present.
PERSISTENCE	**VIRTUAL REALITY (VR)**
The continuation of virtual life regardless of whether you are online or offline.	An immersive experience in a computer-generated (virtual) environment. Usually experienced with a digital headset.
EXTENDED REALITY (XR)	**DIGITAL TWINS**
A combination of augmented, virtual and mixed realities.	Real-life places that have been cloned in the metaverse for efficiency.

First satellites

The first satellite was called Sputnik 1. It was launched into orbit around the Earth by the Russians on 4 October 1957. A month later they launched Sputnik 2 which was the first spacecraft to carry a live animal into space. The animal was a dog named Laika.

★ Sputnik 1 was about the size of a basketball and weighed 83 kg (183 lb).

SPUTNIK 1

Where space begins

Space begins at about 100 km (62 miles) above the Earth's surface. The boundary is known as the Kármán line. Above it, satellites can circle the Earth without burning up or falling out of orbit.

★ The first American satellite, called Explorer 1, was launched in January 1958.

Telescopes

Like satellites, most space telescopes also orbit the Earth, but because they are monitoring deep space, they face away from our planet. Space telescopes get a crystal-clear view of the Universe because they are far above the rain clouds, light pollution and atmospheric distortions that affect telescopes on the ground.

★ Hubble has observed the planets in our Solar System and some of the most distant stars and galaxies in the Universe.

HUBBLE SPACE TELESCOPE

Hubble

The Hubble Space Telescope was launched into LEO in 1990 and is still going. Its findings have fundamentally changed the way we view the Universe.

The ISS

The largest spacecraft ever built circles our planet in LEO. The International Space Station (ISS) is larger than a football field and was assembled in space, module by module, starting in 1998. Travelling at 27,600 km/h (17,150 mph) and 400 km (250 miles) up, it completes an orbit of the Earth every 92 minutes.

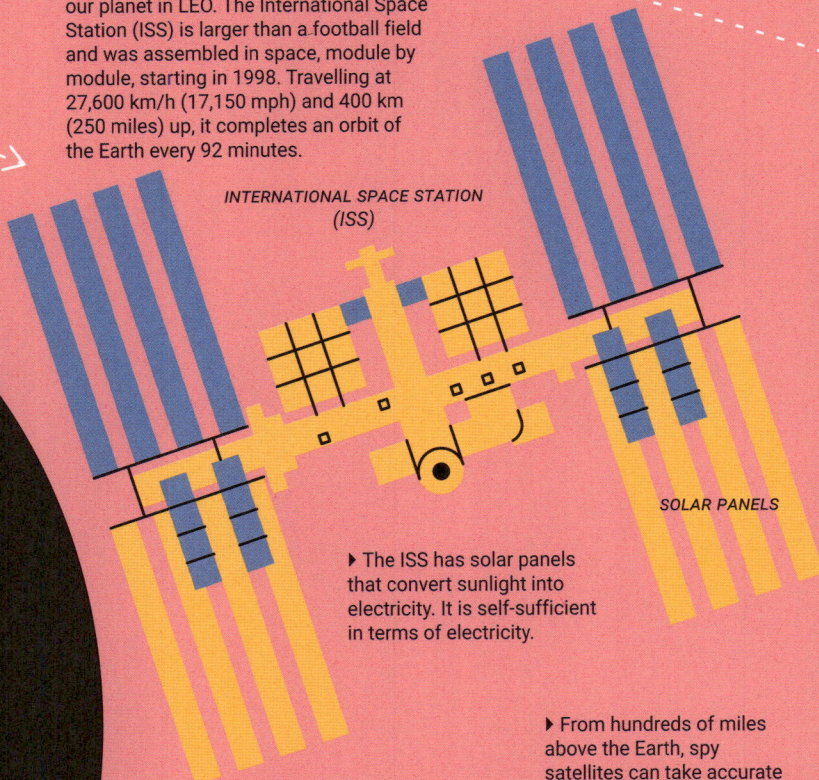

INTERNATIONAL SPACE STATION (ISS)

★ The ISS is the third brightest object in the night sky after the Moon and Venus. To see it, visit NASA's website for a list of sighting opportunities in your location.

SOLAR PANELS

▶ The ISS has solar panels that convert sunlight into electricity. It is self-sufficient in terms of electricity.

SATELLITES

Artificial satellites are communications systems that have been launched into orbit around the Earth. There are thousands of them and they do many different jobs. Some gather information about the weather, while others relay signals or keep an eye on conditions on Earth, such as volcanoes and forest fires. A few look away from the Earth into deep space.

▶ A satellite is something that moves around a larger object. Natural satellites include the Moon that orbits around the Earth, and all the other moons in space that circle their planets.

▶ From hundreds of miles above the Earth, spy satellites can take accurate photos of military bases and operations.

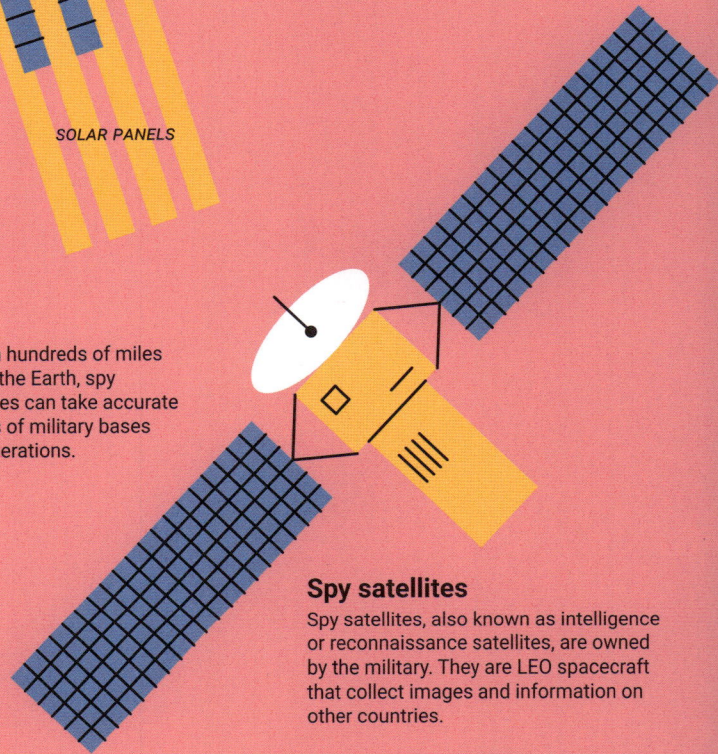

Spy satellites

Spy satellites, also known as intelligence or reconnaissance satellites, are owned by the military. They are LEO spacecraft that collect images and information on other countries.

LEO (LOW EARTH ORBIT)

▶ Sentinel-2A is one of a pair of polar orbiting EO satellites operated by the European Space Agency (ESA). They monitor things like vegetation, soil and water cover, inland waterways and coastal areas.

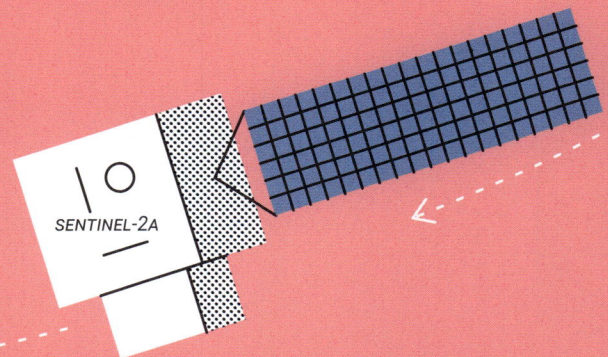

SENTINEL-2A

Earth observation satellites

Earth Observation (EO) satellites carefully monitor conditions of the Earth's physical environment. They provide images and information on a wide range of Earth science topics, including air quality, ocean temperatures, crop health and ice cap thickness.

Orbital pathways

Most satellites are located in **Low Earth Orbit** (LEO), which is between 200 and 2,000 km (124–1,242 miles) above Earth. A much smaller number are in Medium Earth Orbit (MEO), up to 35,800 km (22,300 miles) up. There are only a few satellites higher than that, in High Earth Orbit (HEO).

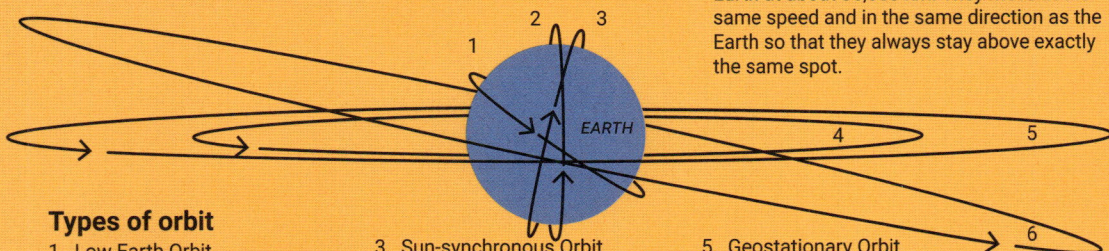

▶ Most satellites are in LEO because they are sent into space to observe the Earth. They can do this more efficiently if they are close.

▶ Geostationary (GEO) satellites orbit the Earth at about 35,800 km. They move at the same speed and in the same direction as the Earth so that they always stay above exactly the same spot.

EARTH

Types of orbit
1. Low Earth Orbit
2. Polar Orbit
3. Sun-synchronous Orbit
4. Medium Earth Orbit
5. Geostationary Orbit
6. Geosynchronous Orbit

GPS navigation

The Global Positioning System (GPS) is made up of more than 30 satellites circling the Earth. The satellites constantly send out signals which GPS receivers in your phone or car can pick up. If the receiver has signals from four or more of the satellites it can calculate where you are.

★ GPS is very precise. It can pinpoint your location to within a few feet.

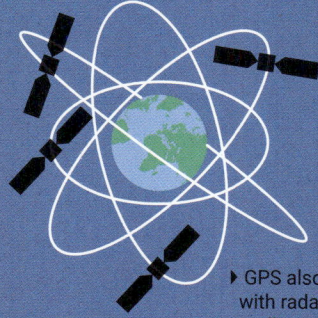

SATELLITES

YOU ARE HERE

▶ GPS also has ground stations with radars that check on the satellites to make sure they are where they should be.

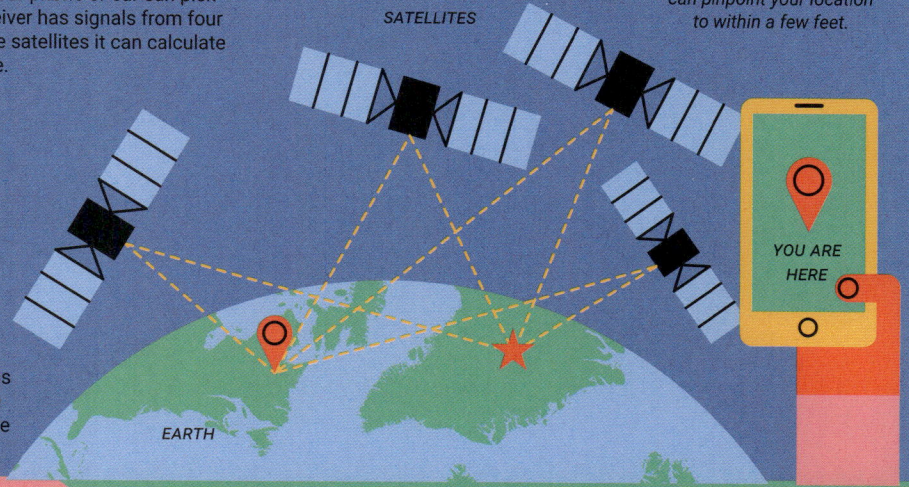

EARTH

James Webb Telescope

The most powerful space telescope ever built was launched on 25 December 2021. It will find the first galaxies that formed in the early Universe. This telescope orbits the Sun, not the Earth.

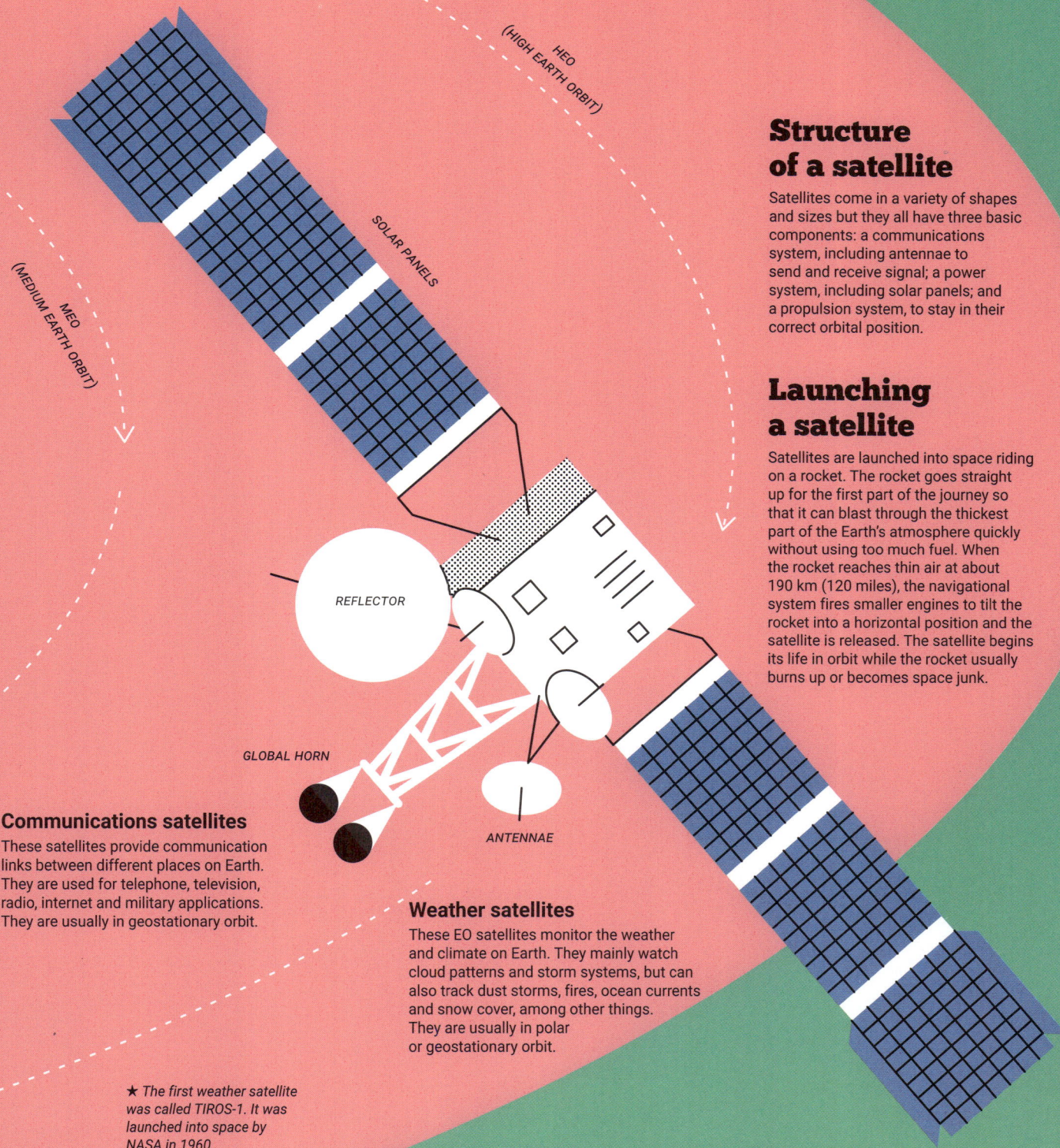

HEO (HIGH EARTH ORBIT)

MEO (MEDIUM EARTH ORBIT)

SOLAR PANELS

REFLECTOR

GLOBAL HORN

ANTENNAE

Structure of a satellite

Satellites come in a variety of shapes and sizes but they all have three basic components: a communications system, including antennae to send and receive signal; a power system, including solar panels; and a propulsion system, to stay in their correct orbital position.

Launching a satellite

Satellites are launched into space riding on a rocket. The rocket goes straight up for the first part of the journey so that it can blast through the thickest part of the Earth's atmosphere quickly without using too much fuel. When the rocket reaches thin air at about 190 km (120 miles), the navigational system fires smaller engines to tilt the rocket into a horizontal position and the satellite is released. The satellite begins its life in orbit while the rocket usually burns up or becomes space junk.

▶ The satellite sits in the top part of the rocket.

SATELLITES IN HERE

▶ Companies like SpaceX are building reusable launch rockets. This is cheaper and better for the environment.

★ Sometimes more than one satellite is launched from the same rocket. The record for the highest number launched at the same time is 143!

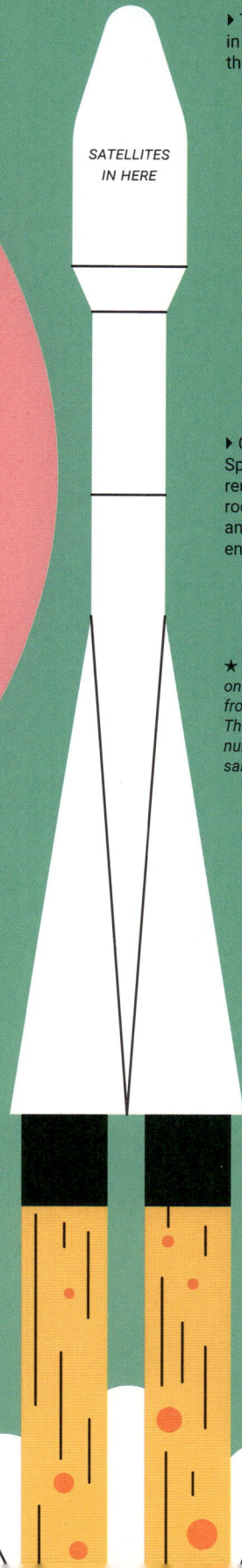

Communications satellites

These satellites provide communication links between different places on Earth. They are used for telephone, television, radio, internet and military applications. They are usually in geostationary orbit.

Weather satellites

These EO satellites monitor the weather and climate on Earth. They mainly watch cloud patterns and storm systems, but can also track dust storms, fires, ocean currents and snow cover, among other things. They are usually in polar or geostationary orbit.

★ The first weather satellite was called TIROS-1. It was launched into space by NASA in 1960.

Space junk

The Earth is now circled by an enormous amount of orbital debris, or space junk. It is made up of old satellites, launch vehicle stages that didn't burn up and leftovers from space missions. It travels at great speed, and even a small piece can seriously damage a spacecraft.

▶ In 2009, an out-of-use Russian spacecraft collided with and destroyed a U.S. satellite. The collision created more than 2,500 pieces of large and small pieces of space junk.

The technology of transport is about developing the best systems and devices to move people and cargo from one place to another. The latest technology is focused on new, smarter energy sources and vehicles that prevent greenhouse emissions, pollution and congestion. Speed, safety and affordability are also key.

TRANSPORT

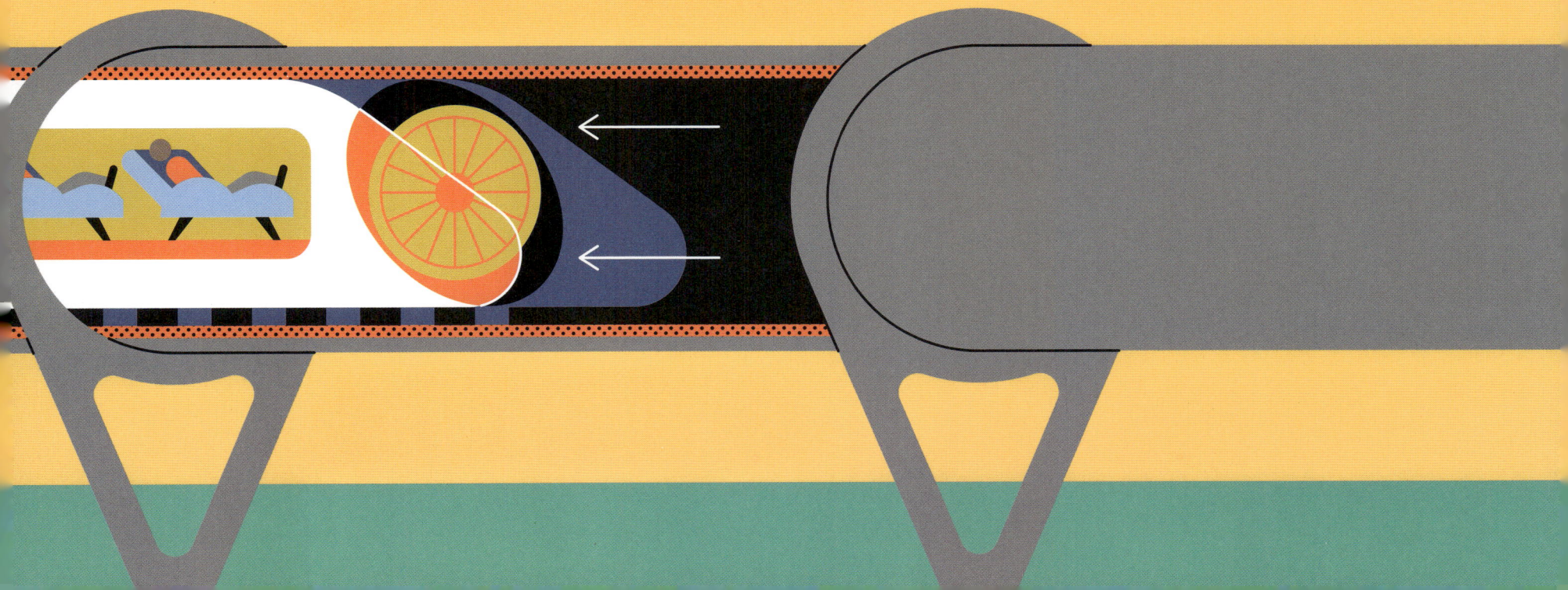

THE WHEEL

The wheel is an amazing piece of technology and its invention revolutionised human life. But on its own the wheel is of limited use. It is only when you make a hole in the centre and insert an axle, that the revolution begins.

The first wheel

The oldest wheel and axle ever used were on a potter's wheel, not a wagon. About 6,000 years ago a potter in ancient Sumeria first used a spinning disc on an axle to make a pot.

★ Adding an axle to the wheel is not a simple idea and it came relatively late. Cloth, rope, pottery, and musical instruments were all invented long before someone put an axle in a wheel.

▶ The first wheels were not used for transport, but for pottery, milling and irrigation.

▶ Several hundred years would pass before the wheel was added to a wagon.

★ The first wheels were solid blocks of stone with slices of tree trunk with holes cut in the middle.

SOLID WOODEN DISC

★ Wheels with spokes were invented in Anatolia (Turkey). They were light and fast, ideal for speedy travel.

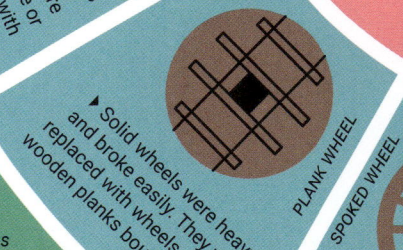

★ Solid wheels were heavy and broke easily. They were replaced with wheels made of wooden planks bound together.

PLANK WHEEL

SPOKED WHEEL

▶ Wheels with spokes were lighter. Rims made of wood — and later iron — made them sturdy.

Rollers

Before the wheel, people put heavy objects on sleds with smooth wooden runners and pushed them over the ground. Later, they placed the sled on trimmed round logs, or rollers, and rolled them along.

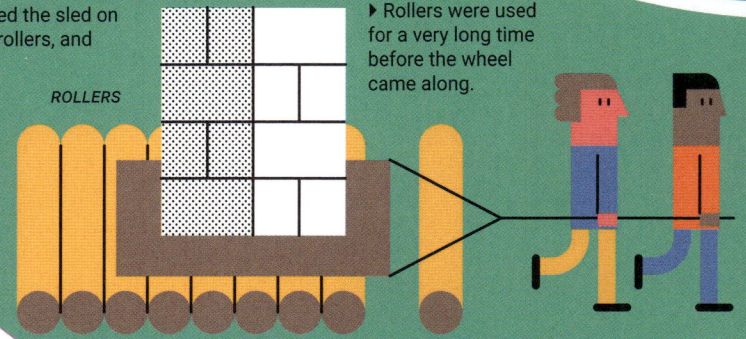

★ The ancient Egyptians used rollers to transport hefty limestone slabs from quarries to their pyramid-building sites.

ROLLERS

▶ Rollers were used for a very long time before the wheel came along.

Not very efficient

Rollers were slow and cumbersome because they had to be replaced as the object rolled forward. They were also hard work to push or pull!

Gears

Gears are wheels with teeth that mesh together. They transmit power from one part of a machine to another. Gears are used everywhere, from bikes and cars to clocks and can openers.

▶ The first gears were made of wood. Now they are made of plastic or metal.

MORE SPEED

MORE POWER

Increasing speed or power

When gears of different sizes are connected they increase speed or power (force). The larger wheel turns more slowly with greater power, while the smaller one spins more quickly, increasing speed.

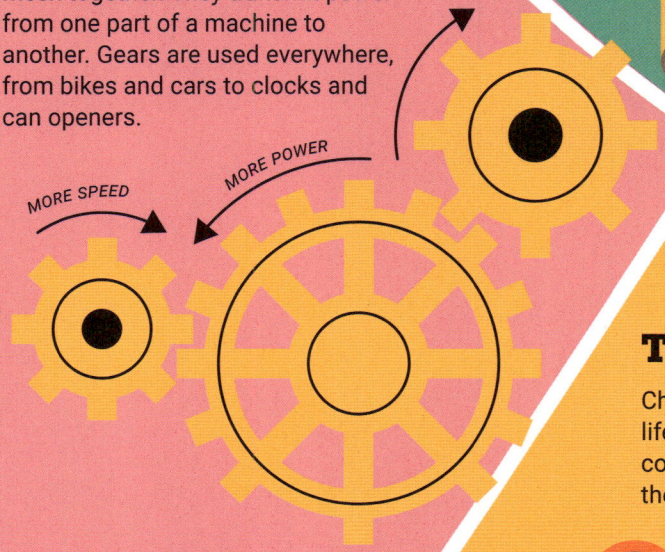

★ The ancient Greeks were using metal gears by about 100 BCE.

Transport

Chariots and carts were the first wheeled vehicles. They made life easier and better and the technology spread quickly. People could transport necessities like wood and food more easily and they could travel faster and further.

▶ The oldest wooden wheel ever discovered was found near Ljubljana, in Slovenia. It dates to about 5,200 years ago.

★ By about 5,000 years ago four-wheeled wagons were widely used in many parts of Europe.

CHARIOT WHEEL

▶ The two-wheeled chariot was used for war, hunting and sport.

Profound impact

Wheeled vehicles changed human society by increasing trade and travel. Roads were built and horses and other animals were domesticated and bred to pull carts and wagons.

★ At 210 metres (689 ft), the Ain Dubai is the tallest Ferris wheel in the world.

FERRIS WHEEL

Big wheels

Ferris wheels are huge wheels that rotate around a central axis. Passenger seats dangle from the outer rim. They move counter-clockwise and are powered by hydraulic motors.

A Chicago attraction

The world's first Ferris Wheel was erected in 1893 for the Chicago World's Fair. Built by George W. Ferris, it was meant to rival the Eiffel Tower which had been unveiled in Paris during the previous World's Fair in 1889.

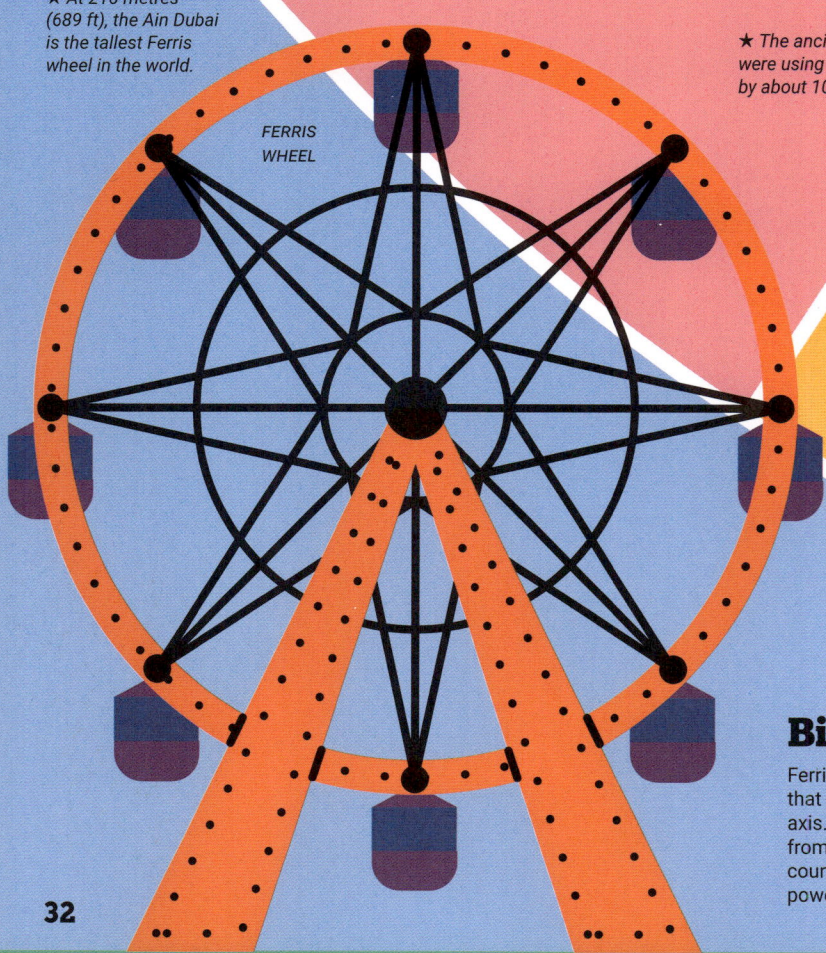

★ The first wheels with iron rims were on Celtic chariots from about 2,500 years ago.

TWEEL

Some modern tyres like the Tweel have little or no air. They don't go flat and can last longer.

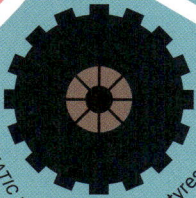

PNEUMATIC TYRE

STEEL WHEEL

▶ The first steel wheels were made for cars. They had solid rubber tyres that wore out quickly.

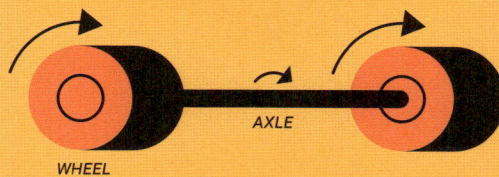

Pneumatic tyres are solid rubber or filled with air and provide a comfortable ride.

WHEEL — *AXLE*

▶ The axle must be in the centre of the wheel and at right angles to it. It needs to be smooth and thin to reduce friction, but sturdy enough to bear a load.

A simple machine

The axle runs through the centre of the wheel. Both spin in the same direction and complete one rotation in the same amount of time.

Other uses

Wheels are used in many ways other than for transport. In the past, waterwheels and windmills were used to pump water, grind grain into flour, cut wood and manufacture fabrics.

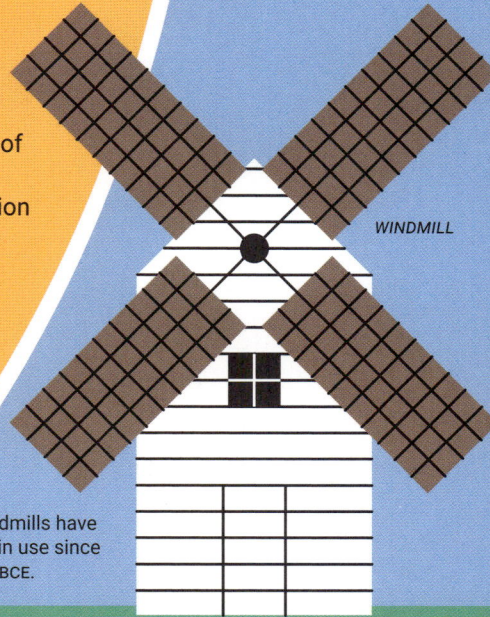

WINDMILL

▶ The spinning wheel is used to spin fibres into thread. It was invented in China or India more than 1,000 years ago.

SPINNING WHEEL

How wheels work

Wheels and axles work like simple machines. They reduce friction with the ground and provide leverage (by increasing force).

FORCE

▶ A cart with large wheels is easier to move because the wheels increase traction.

CART

▶ Pushing a heavy object over the ground is hard work because of resistance, or friction.

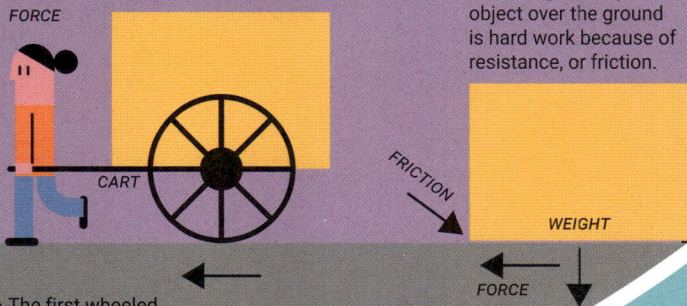

FRICTION

WEIGHT

FORCE

▶ The first wheeled vehicles date to around 5,500 years ago. They were wagons with four wheels.

▶ Windmills have been in use since 2000 BCE.

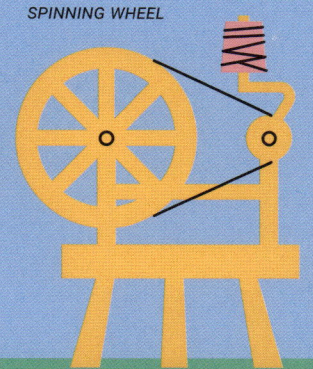

Windmills

Windmills are machines that convert wind power into energy. The large adjustable blades spin in the wind. They are attached to an axle that transfers the force of the wind down a shaft into a generator. The same technology is used today by wind turbines to generate electricity (see page 14).

Chairs with wheels

Wheelchairs do more than just move their users around. They give them independence and a happier, healthier life.

▶ Wheelchair-type furniture existed at least 1500 years ago. The first self-propelled wheelchair was invented in 1655 by a paraplegic clockmaker in Germany called Stephen Farfler.

WHEELCHAIR

So many ways to go!

In the 21st century almost all forms of transport have wheels, especially the ones that go on land. Cars, bikes, trucks and trains all roll on wheels. Many big rig trucks have 18 wheels!

SCOOTER

Clean vehicles

The majority of wheeled vehicles are powered by motors that burn fossil fuels. They pollute the air. Towns and cities encourage people to use self-powered vehicles, like bikes, skates and scooters.

Most popular vehicle

Cars are the most widely used vehicles in the world. There are almost 1.5 billion of them on the roads. Every year there are more.

BICYCLE

★ There are more than one billion bicycles in the world, half of them in China.

AUTOMOBILE

The wheelbarrow

This single-wheeled cart was already in use in China more than 2,000 years ago. It is ideal for carrying heavy loads and doesn't require an animal to move it along.

Wheels everywhere

Aeroplanes have wheels to land. Steering wheels, or ship's wheels, are used to control boats. Most engines have gears, or other types of wheels, to store or transmit energy.

▶ Even space vehicles have wheels! NASA's latest Mars Rover, called Perseverance, has six.

American wheels

Early peoples in the Americas did not develop the wheel for transport. They did not use wheeled vehicles until after Europeans arrived. However, they did make wheeled toys for their children.

WHEELBARROW

CARS

There's no doubt about it: cars changed the world. At the dawn of the 20th century there were just a few thousand cars, mainly in North America. Today there are almost 1.5 billion on roads around the globe.

Game changers

Cars gave people the freedom to move around, visiting places and working far from their homes. Roads multiplied, new industries blossomed, even new "takeaway" foods (like hamburgers) and leisure activities (like drive-in movies) appeared to cater for a newly mobile population.

▶ The Model T Ford, also known as "Tin Lizzie," was easy to operate and affordable. It was one of the first cars produced on an assembly line.

1769

STEAM CAR

Steam cars

The earliest cars were powered by external steam engines. French inventor Nicolas-Joseph Cugnot built the first one in 1769. They were popular in the 19th century but died out after the internal combustion engine was invented.

▶ Early steam cars weren't very convenient — it could take 20 minutes just to get one going!

The first modern car

Carl Benz's Motorwagen, patented in 1886, is generally considered the first modern car. It had three wheels and the engine mounted on the back.

★ Benz's wife Martha and their two sons took the world's first road trip when they drove 105 km (65 miles) from Mannheim to her hometown of Pforzheim and back.

1886

BENZ MOTORWAGEN

MODEL T FORD

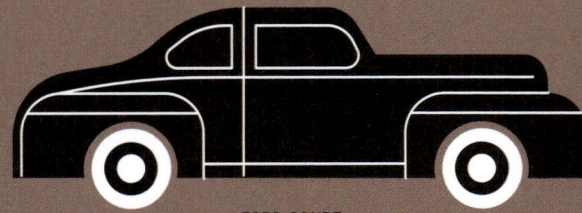

FORD COUPE

| 1900s | 1910s | 1920s | 1930s | 1940s | 1950s | 1960s |

OLDSMOBILE

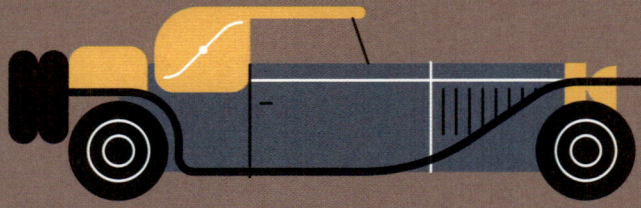

BUGATTI

CHEVROLET IMPALA

Electric cars

FRITCHLE ELECTRIC CAR

If you think electric cars are modern, think again! The first one was built in London in 1884. The first decade of the 20th century was the heyday of the electric car, before it was eclipsed by the discovery of cheap crude oil in Texas and the Model T Ford.

▶ Manufactured in the early 20th century, Fritchle cars were among the best.

▶ The Henney Kilowatt was introduced in 1959.

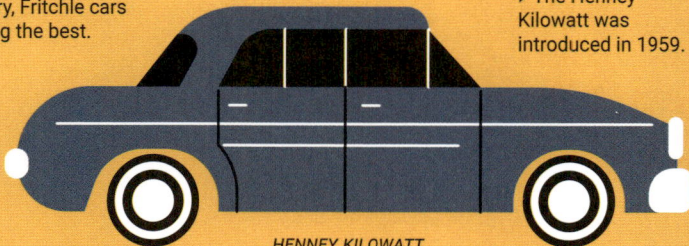

HENNEY KILOWATT

TESLA ROADSTER

▶ The Tesla Roadster claims to be the fastest car on the road.

Car tech timeline

1908 First Model T Ford
1912 Electric starters
1912 Ford assembly line starts rolling
1925 Cigarette lighters
1929 4-Wheel brakes
1930 Car radio
1934 Coil spring suspension
1949 Car keys
1951 Power steering
1953 Air conditioning
1958 Cruise control
1959 Seat belts
1960 Electric windows
1969 Intermittent windscreen wipers
1970 Clean Air Act
1975 Catalytic converter to reduce emissions
1981 Air bags and navigation units
1982 Electronic fuel injection
1984 CD players
1990 GPS sat nav
1992 Electromagnetic parking sensors
1994 On-board diagnostics in all new cars

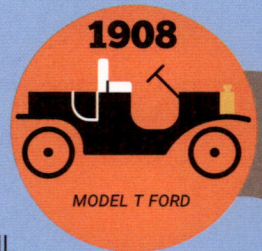

1908
MODEL T FORD

1949
CAR KEYS

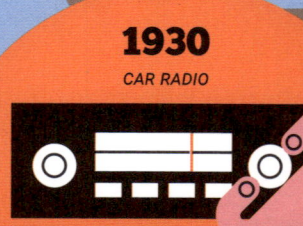

1930
CAR RADIO

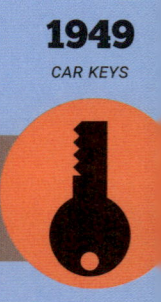

The internal combustion engine

The invention of the internal combustion engine was a big step forward. It led to the rise of the modern car.

SPARK PLUG

COMBUSTION CHAMBER

PISTON

The 4-stroke engine

The 4-stroke combustion engine uses four distinct piston strokes (intake, compression, power and exhaust) to complete one operating cycle.

▶ The internal combustion engine was invented in Europe in the 1860s and 1870s by Etienne Lenoir and Nicolaus Otto.

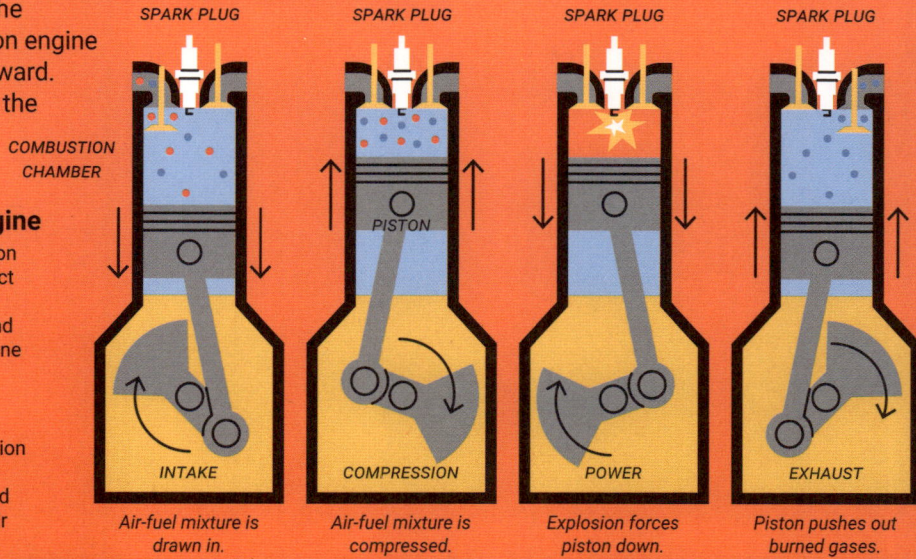

INTAKE
Air-fuel mixture is drawn in.

COMPRESSION
Air-fuel mixture is compressed.

POWER
Explosion forces piston down.

EXHAUST
Piston pushes out burned gases.

Flying cars

Long dreamed of, flying cars have still not become a reality. Many prototypes have been built over the years but none has taken off commercially — yet!

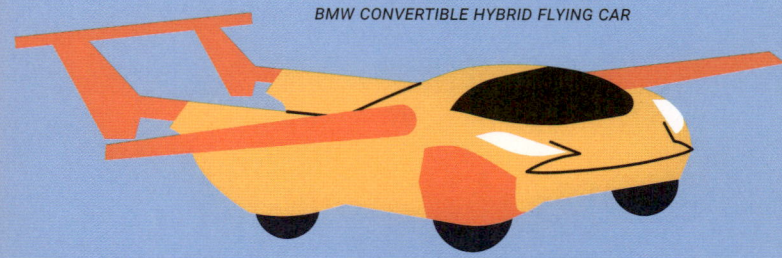

BMW CONVERTIBLE HYBRID FLYING CAR

▶ A BMW convertible hybrid flying car recently completed a successful test flight between two London airports. It had a cruising speed of 170 km/h (105 mph) and a range of 1,000 km (600 miles).

FORD MUSTANG

TOYOTA PRIUS

ALFA ROMEO QUADRIFOGLIO

1970s / **1980s** **1990s** **2000s** **2010s** **2020s**

FORD TAURUS

BMW X3

PORSCHE HYBRID

The first hybrid car was built by Dr Ferdinand Porsche in 1898.

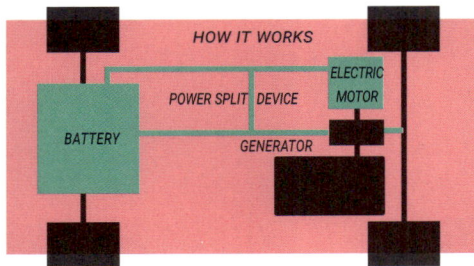

HOW IT WORKS

POWER SPLIT DEVICE

ELECTRIC MOTOR

BATTERY

GENERATOR

Hybrid cars

Hybrid cars use more than one type of power. They have an internal combustion engine and an electric motor and can switch from one to the other as required. They pollute less than traditional petrol or diesel cars. Modern hybrid cars became widespread from 1997, with the release of the Toyota Prius.

1997 Modern hybrid cars become popular
2001 Bluetooth
2002 Parking cameras
2003 Automatic parking
2010 Driver assist

2018 Mobile phone as key
Near future Self-driving cars

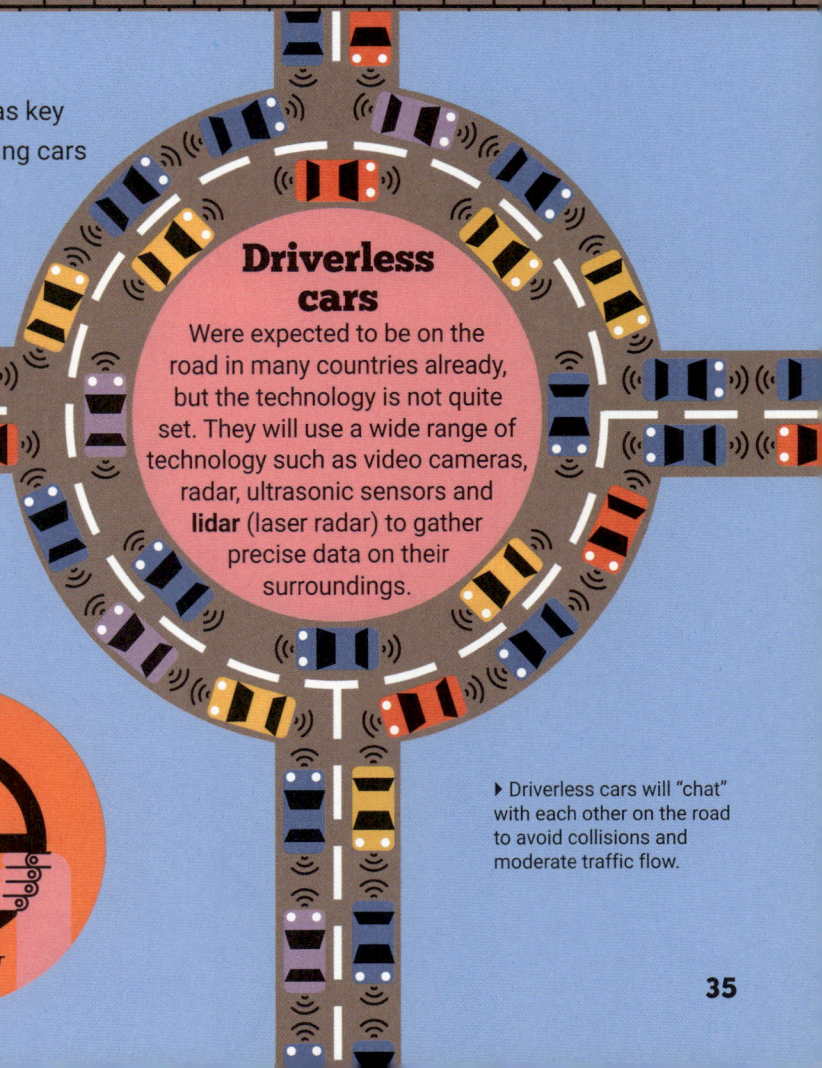

1959
SEAT BELTS

2010

DRIVER ASSIST

Driverless cars

Were expected to be on the road in many countries already, but the technology is not quite set. They will use a wide range of technology such as video cameras, radar, ultrasonic sensors and **lidar** (laser radar) to gather precise data on their surroundings.

▶ Driverless cars will "chat" with each other on the road to avoid collisions and moderate traffic flow.

35

THE JET AGE

Jet airliners can fly more people further, faster and in greater comfort than any other type of aeroplane. Although the jet engine was invented in 1939, it wasn't used for commercial travel until 1952. Over the next several decades advances in engine design increased fuel efficiency, speed and safety. The jet engine changed the way people travel for work and pleasure, making the world a smaller place.

▶ The first commercial jet service was flown by BOAC between London and Johannesburg in May 1952.

TURBINE

AEOLIPILE

STEAM

FIRE

HERO OF ALEXANDRIA

★ The aeolipile was a very simple type of steam engine.

Hero's engine

The origins of the jet engine date back more than 2,000 years to when the ancient Greek engineer Hero of Alexandria invented the aeolipile.

Invention

Modern jet engines were invented at about the same time in Germany and the UK. Two men — Hans von Ohain in Germany and Frank Whittle in Britain — working independently, developed the first operational turbojet engine in the 1930s.

Frank Whittle
Royal Air Force officer Frank Whittle invented the gas-turbine engine that powered the first British jet. The first flight was in 1941.

FRANK WHITTLE

Hans von Ohain
German physicist and engineer Hans von Ohain designed the world's first jet engine, the He 178. It made its first flight on 27 August 1939.

HANS VON OHAIN

How jet engines work

Jet engines have a fan with blades that spin at high speed at the front to take in air. The air passes to a compressor and is then sent to the combustion chambers where it is sprayed with fuel. An electric spark lights the mixture. The burning gases expand and blast out through the nozzle exhaust at the back of the engine, creating the thrust that propels the aircraft forwards.

▶ Rockets are also propelled by a type of jet engine. They burn their fuel very quickly, providing the huge thrust needed to lift a rocket through the Earth's atmosphere into space.

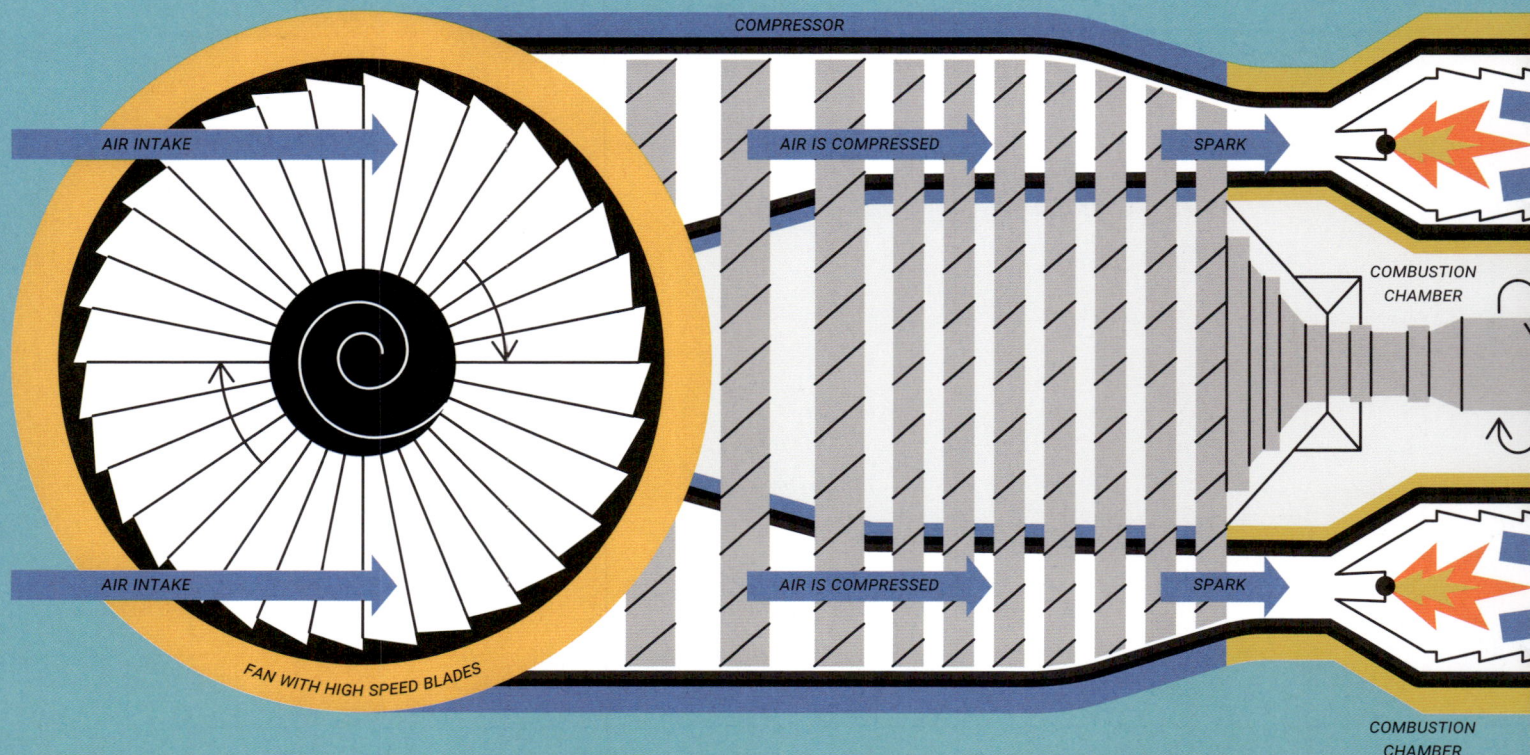

COMPRESSOR

AIR INTAKE

AIR IS COMPRESSED

SPARK

COMBUSTION CHAMBER

AIR INTAKE

AIR IS COMPRESSED

SPARK

FAN WITH HIGH SPEED BLADES

COMBUSTION CHAMBER

★ The NASA/USAF X-15 was the fastest jet fighter ever made. It flew at five times the speed of sound. It was cancelled in 1968.

▶ The Messerschmitt Me 262 was the first jet fighter. It was produced in Germany at the end of World War II.

MESSERSCHMITT

Jet fighters

Modern fighter planes have aerodynamic shapes and powerful engines to fly at supersonic speed. They are very high-tech, with radars and infrared sensors to detect enemy missiles and radar, and onboard computers and software to fly and fight effectively.

GLOSTER METEOR

▶ The Gloster Meteor was the only British jet fighter used in World War II.

FLIGHT ROUTES

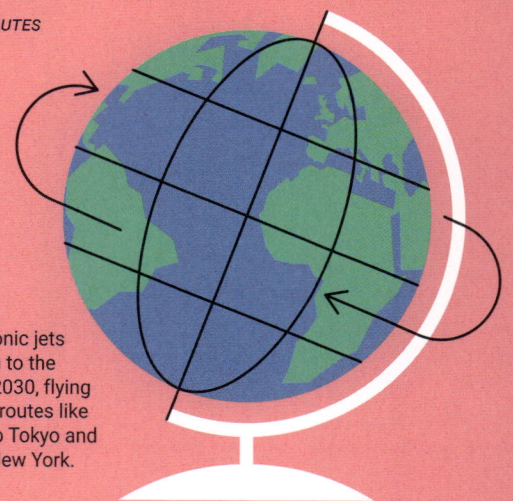

▶ Supersonic jets will return to the skies by 2030, flying business routes like London to Tokyo and Paris to New York.

Air traffic

The Covid-19 pandemic hit air travel particularly hard, interrupting decades of rapid growth. The industry recovered quickly and soon returned to pre-pandemic growth patterns.

Long-haul travel

The first jet airliners took off in the 1950s. They sliced hours off travel times and ushered in the "jet age." Ticket prices fell and more people could afford to travel to far-off destinations. Soon more people were travelling by air than by train.

★ In 1935 a flight from Brisbane to London took about two weeks, with up to 43 stops! By 1947 the same trip could be done in four days. In 2025 a nonstop flight between Sydney and London will take just 19 hours.

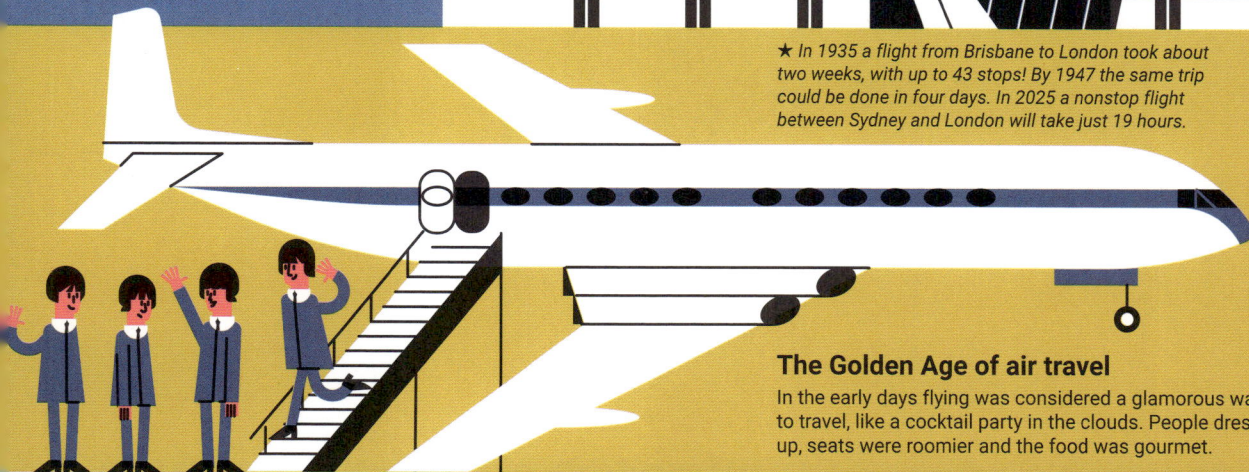

The Golden Age of air travel

In the early days flying was considered a glamorous way to travel, like a cocktail party in the clouds. People dressed up, seats were roomier and the food was gourmet.

Commercial jetliners

During the pandemic a large number of older jetliners were retired. They have been replaced by younger, more fuel-efficient aircraft with lower CO_2 emissions. Today the Boeing 737 and the Airbus A320 jostle to be the most widely used commercial passenger jet.

BOEING 747 OR JUMBO

AIRBUS A380

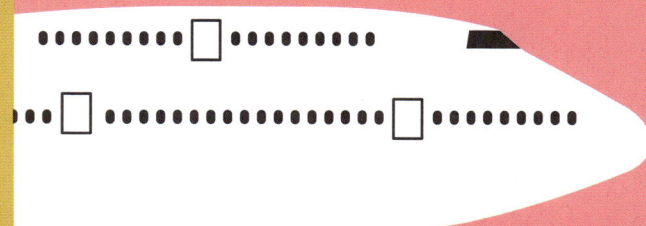

★ The Airbus A380 was the largest passenger jet ever built.

▶ It is the hot air blasting through the nozzle exhaust duct that propels the aircraft forwards at great speed.

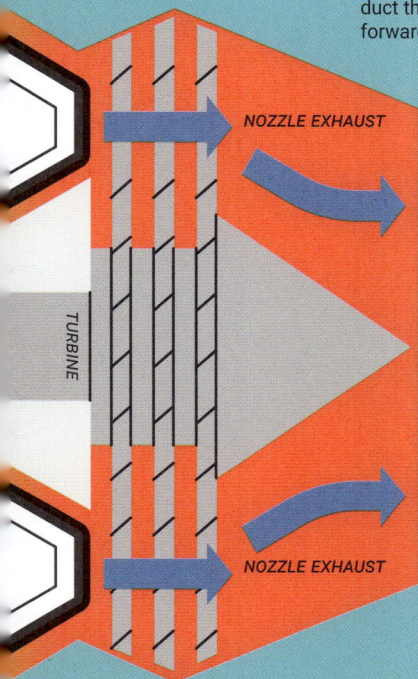

NOZZLE EXHAUST

TURBINE

NOZZLE EXHAUST

Supersonic aircraft

Supersonic aeroplanes fly faster than the speed of sound. When an aircraft exceeds the speed of sound it creates a very loud bang, called a sonic boom.

★ The speed of sound is 1225 km/h (761 mph).

★ Sonic booms are unpleasant. They startle people, wake them up and can even cause light damage to property.

What causes the boom?

As an aircraft flies along its engines give off sound waves. If the plane travels faster than these waves it compresses some at its nose, creating a shock wave that makes the boom when it hits the ground. New supersonic jets will be shaped in a way that keeps the sound waves apart, preventing the sonic boom.

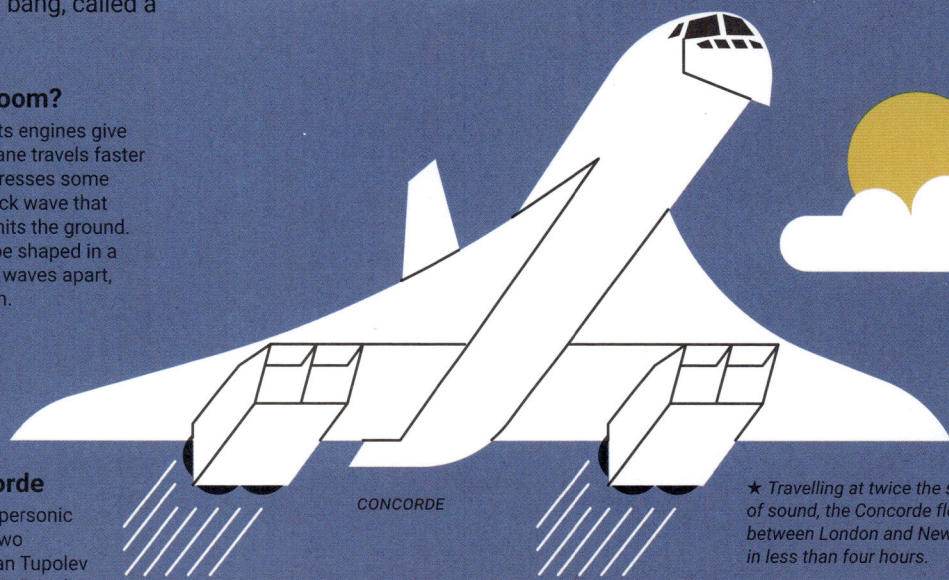

Tupolev and Concorde

There have been many supersonic military aircraft, but only two passenger jets: the Russian Tupolev Tu-144 and the joint Franco-British Concorde. Both went out of business.

CONCORDE

★ Travelling at twice the speed of sound, the Concorde flew between London and New York in less than four hours.

Meals in the air

Food technologists work hard to make those little trays of airline food taste good. Inside the cabin at high altitude our sense of taste is different. Most flavours, including sugar and salt, seem less intense. But others, such as curry, become stronger. It's a balancing act to get it right!

▶ Engineers are experimenting with new shapes: wide airfoil-shaped bodies and high-lift wings can greatly improve fuel efficiency.

★ In a normal flight year, airlines serve more than one billion inflight meals.

Sustainable air travel

Air travel is the most damaging way to travel for the environment. Emissions from airplanes are responsible for about five per cent of global warming. Aeroplanes emit a lot of CO_2 but they also release other gases and water vapour high in the atmosphere where it is most damaging.

Zero-emission jets

Engineers are designing cleaner, quieter planes that burn low-carbon or carbon-free fuels. Some large airlines have committed to net zero by 2050. Some hope to use all-electric or hydrogen engines. We don't have the technology yet, but we soon will have.

★ Some people are going on "flight diets," cutting the number of times they fly each year to reduce their carbon footprint.

TRAINS

Trains were invented over 200 years ago but they are still relevant. Trains have a much lower carbon footprint than road or air transport. They are an efficient way to transport heavy, bulky things like machinery, chemicals and metals.

▶ Train tickets were invented in 1836. Each ticket was printed by a custom-made printing machine.

ADMIT ONE

N° 1289822

▶ The Penydarren steam train took the world's first railway journey in 1804. It carried 10 tonnes of coal, five wagons and 70 men over 14.4 km (9 miles) at an average speed of 3.9 km/h (2.4 mph).

First trains

The first steam trains were built in England in the early 1800s. They carried goods, but were soon used to transport people too.

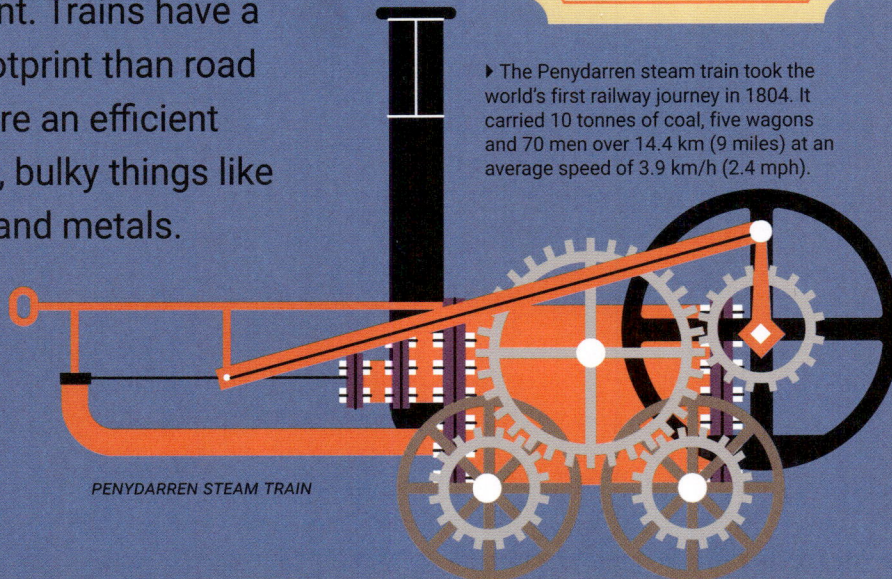

PENYDARREN STEAM TRAIN

Biometric train tickets

Ticketing can be slow and expensive, so many rail companies are experimenting with biometric tickets. Passengers can use an app on their phone which has their fingerprints or scans of their iris to pay for tickets and go through gates.

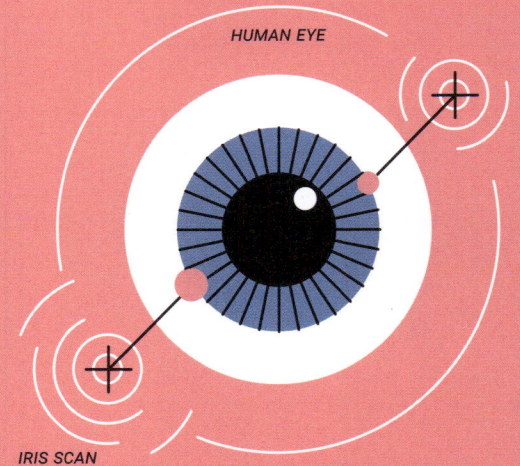

HUMAN EYE

IRIS SCAN

SLEEPERS

RAIL CLIPS

RAILS

BALLAST

Steam trains

These trains burn coal in a firebox. This makes water in a tank produce steam which drives pistons that power the wheels.

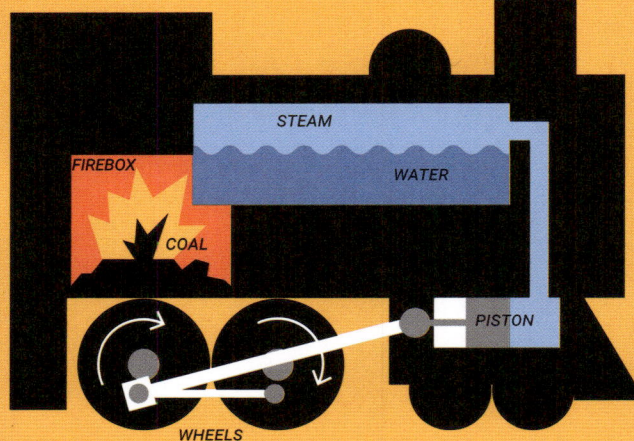

STEAM

WATER

FIREBOX

COAL

PISTON

WHEELS

▶ Steam trains were gradually phased out in most parts of the world in the middle of the 20th century.

★ The Magnificent Mallard set the record for the fastest steam train in 1938 doing 202 km/h (126 mph).

Electric trains

These trains are powered by electric motors. Some get electricity from overhead cables while others collect power from a "live" rail in the tracks. Electric trains are fast, clean and quiet.

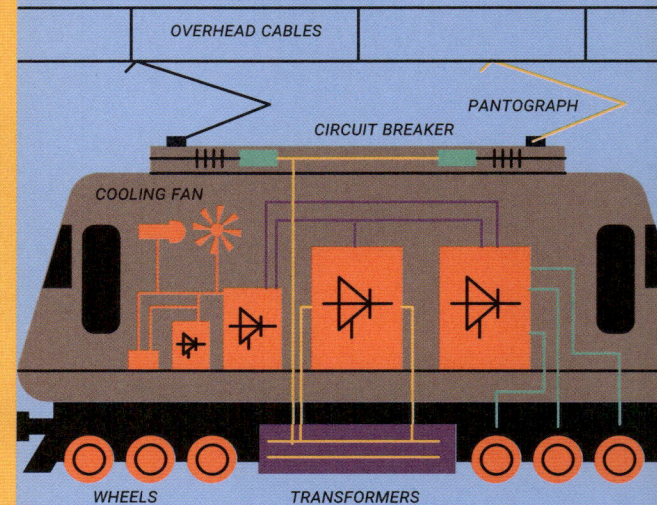

OVERHEAD CABLES

PANTOGRAPH

CIRCUIT BREAKER

COOLING FAN

WHEELS

TRANSFORMERS

▶ Building the electric tracks is expensive, but once in place electric trains are cleaner and cheaper to run than diesel.

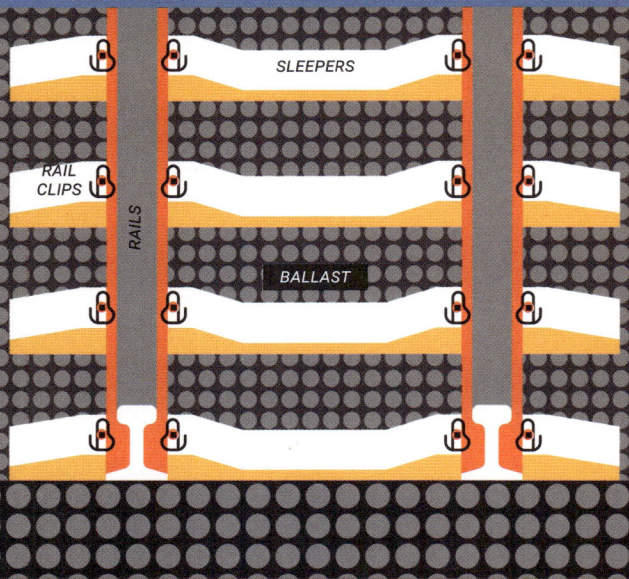

Railway tracks

The earliest rails were made of wood, but they wore out quickly. They were soon replaced by cast iron and then steel. Most modern railways use welded ribbon rails supported by sleepers laid over crushed stone ballast (see above).

Environmentally friendly

With the exception of walking or biking, travelling by train is the most environmentally friendly way to go. A comparison of train travel with air and road journeys in Europe showed that trains release just 14 grams of CO_2 per passenger mile, compared with 285 grams when travelling by air and 158 grams when going by car.

▶ Electric trains are better for the environment than diesel trains, and they are also much quieter. New train technology will make them even more efficient and environmentally friendly.

★ Travelling by train on the Eurostar between London and Paris reduces CO_2 emissions by 90% when compared to flying the same route!

The Hyperloop

The Hyperloop is a very fast train-like transport system where floating passenger pods speed along inside an almost airless tube. It will travel at speeds as fast as 1220 km/h (720 mph). The Hyperloop is still at the project stage and various technologies are being tested.

★ Some Hyperloop projects use maglev technology while others use similar aerodynamic concepts.

▶ Hyperloop trains will run inside vacuum tubes built underground or resting on pylons above ground. They will operate on busy routes between large cities.

Diesel-electric trains

Most modern diesel trains have electric motors. The burning of diesel fuel powers pistons that drive the wheels. These trains have become more efficient but they still pollute more than fully electric trains.

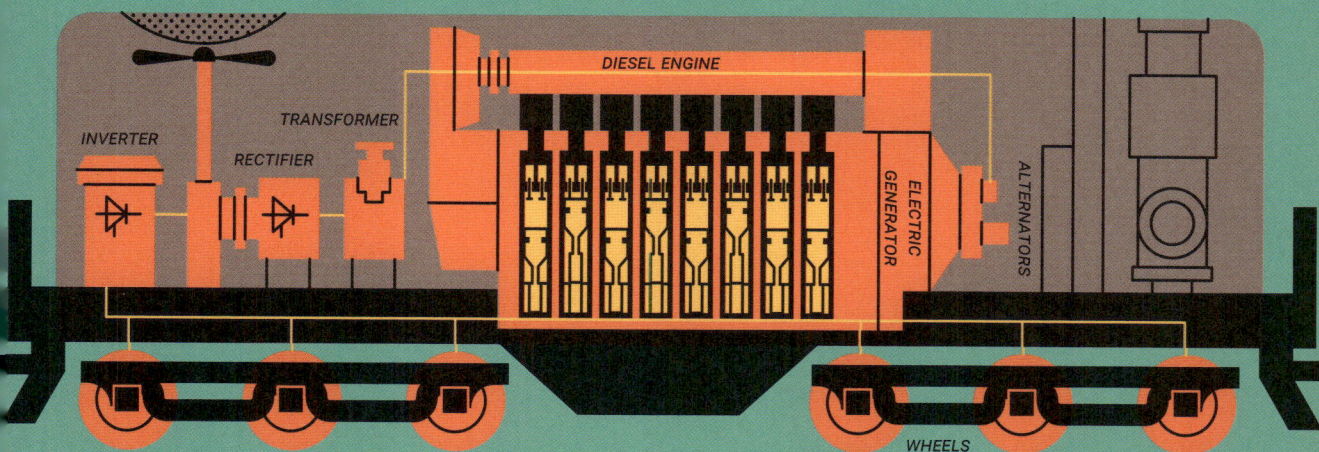

INVERTER
TRANSFORMER
RECTIFIER
DIESEL ENGINE
ELECTRIC GENERATOR
ALTERNATORS
WHEELS

▶ Diesel trains are still widely used in many parts of the world, especially on less busy or remote routes where the cost of electrifying the tracks is very high.

Amazing train facts

THE WORLD'S OLDEST SURVIVING STEAM TRAIN is called "Puffing Billy." Built in 1813—14, it is now on display in the Science Museum in London. It inspired the composer Edward White to write a piece of music called *Puffin Billy* which has become a children's classic.

THE LONGEST STRAIGHT RAILWAY IN THE WORLD runs across the Nullabor Plain in Australia for 478 km (almost 300 miles) between Adelaide and Perth.

THE WORLD'S LONGEST TRAIN runs 700 km (435 miles) across Mauritania, in Africa, from the coast into the mountains of the central Sahara Desert. The train is 2.5 km (1.55 miles) long and transports iron ore.

THE HIGHEST TRAIN IN THE WORLD is the Qinghai-Tibet Railway between Golmud and Lhasa. At its highest point it reaches an altitude of 5,072 m (16,640 ft). The locomotives are turbocharged and the carriages have an oxygen supply for each passenger. There is also a doctor on board in case people have altitude sickness.

THE WORLD'S LONGEST DIRECT TRAIN JOURNEY runs 9,289 km (5,772 miles) between Moscow and Vladivostok in Russia. It crosses eight time zones and takes about a week. It makes 142 stops and passes through 87 towns and cities.

Bullet trains

The first high-speed trains started operating in Japan in 1964. They travel at speeds up to 320 km/h (200 mph). France followed suit and launched its first TGV service between Paris and Lyon in 1981.

▶ China now runs the largest network of high-speed trains. In Europe, high speed trains cross borders, delivering fast, clean and comfortable international travel.

▶ Maglev trains use two sets of magnets, one to push them up off the tracks and the other to propel them along.

Maglev trains

Maglev means "magnetic levitation" and these trains travel above the tracks, without touching them. With no friction, they are faster, quieter and smoother than any other trains.

Moving platforms

Proposals for moving passengers from high-speed trains to local trains include moving platforms. High-speed trains will approach a local train on the outskirts of a city. They will slow and run alongside the local train while passengers transfer. This means high-speed trains won't waste time going into city centres to drop off passengers.

LOCAL TRAIN
BULLET TRAIN

▶ Planned first Hyperloop routes include Los Angeles to San Francisco, Mumbai to Chennai and Mexico City to Guadalajara.

★ The fastest trains in the world are the Maglevs that run in Japan and China. They have been clocked at speeds above 600 km/h (372 mph).

STEAM
RECLINING PASSENGER SEATS
FAN

▶ A powerful fan at the front of the hyperloop will transfer any air in the tube to the back of the train to minimise friction and increase speed.

Speeding up

30 mph	Stephenson's Rocket (1829)	(50 km/h)
130 mph	First Shinkansen (Bullet train, 1964)	(209 km/h)
357 mph	Fastest conventional rail train TGV	(574.8 km/h)
372 mph	Fastest maglev train	(602 km/h)
659 mph	Fastest subsonic passenger jet	(1,049.29 km/h)
760 mph	Hyperloop	(1,223.1 km/h)

▶ Hyperloop trains will have reclining seats so that passengers are comfortable during the extreme acceleration at the start of the journey.

▶ Hyperloop trains will be powered by fully electric engines. Those running on pylons above ground may have solar panels to generate their own electricity.

SPACE TRAVEL

Space exploration thrives on new technology. From Moon trips and reusable rockets to Mars colonies and FTL travel, the role of technology in space is both essential and mind-blowing.

EXOPLANET

STAR

★ In 2021 a team of hologram doctors was beamed up to the International Space Station to examine the astronauts.

▶ An exoplanet is a planet that orbits a star outside our Solar System.

FTL space travel

Human space travel is hampered by distance. With current technology, we just can't go fast enough. We need to be able to travel faster then light (FTL) to visit deep space. Einstein said that nothing can travel faster than light, but not all scientists agree.

★ Most scientists don't believe that FTL travel is possible. Even if it does exist, they are not sure that humans could survive it.

Distant Voyagers

In 1977 NASA launched two space probes: Voyager I and Voyager II. They are still travelling. Both have now left the Solar System and are travelling in interstellar space. They have flown further than any other human spacecraft.

VOYAGER I

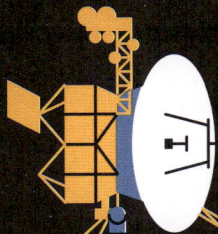

★ Both Voyagers are still functioning, beaming back information to Earth. Their 1970s technology has far exceeded everyone's expectations.

Exploring our Solar System

Our Solar System has eight planets and more than 200 moons. Robotic spacecraft have landed on two of the planets (Venus and Mars) and deliberately crashed into two more (Jupiter and Saturn). One probe landed on Saturn's largest moon, Titan, in 2005. There have been many robotic missions to our Moon, but only 24 people have travelled beyond low Earth orbit, 12 of whom have walked on the Moon.

DRAGONFLY PARACHUTE LANDER

Dragonfly

Dragonfly is a NASA space mission that will explore Saturn's moon Titan. Due to launch in 2027, the robotic probe will be like a mobile space lab examining the surface of Titan for signs of life.

1. Dragonfly will float down to Titan using a parachute.

2. The probe will take off and land vertically as it moves around Titan.

3. Dragonfly will take samples, examine them, and send the results back to Earth.

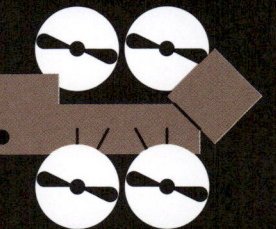

4. Visiting dozens of sites, it will build up a picture of overall conditions on Titan.

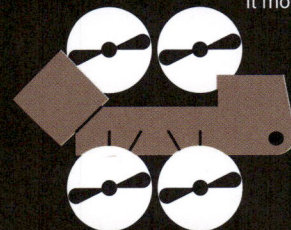

Colonising Mars

The first colony on Mars is likely to be ready by the end of this century. Several uncrewed spaceships have already landed on the planet. Space companies are now trying to develop spaceships that can not only land, but also relaunch and return to Earth.

▶ Mars has no oxygen so settlers will live underground or inside space domes, which will also protect them from the extreme cold.

★ With current technology, a one-way trip to Mars takes about nine months. Scientists are trying to develop new propulsion systems to reduce the travel time.

▶ Titan is the largest of Saturn's 83 moons. It is the only moon in the Solar System that has clouds and a dense atmosphere. It also has liquid water on its surface.

THE VIEW FROM THE FLIGHT DECK

MARS COLONY

THE LONG
WAY ROUND

SHORTCUT

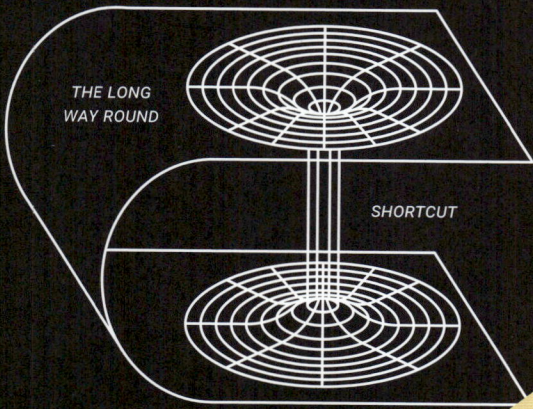

▸ Wormholes are common in sci-fi novels and films. They are like holes or bridges in spacetime that would allow us to take shortcuts across immense distances.

Interstellar traveller

In 2017 astronomers in Hawaii spotted a cigar-shaped object hurtling through the sky. They named it Oumuamua, pronounced oh-moo-uh-moo-uh (which means "a messenger from afar arriving first" in Hawaiian). It is the first object ever discovered from beyond our Solar System. It may be a comet or an asteroid, but some scientists think it may be an alien spacecraft.

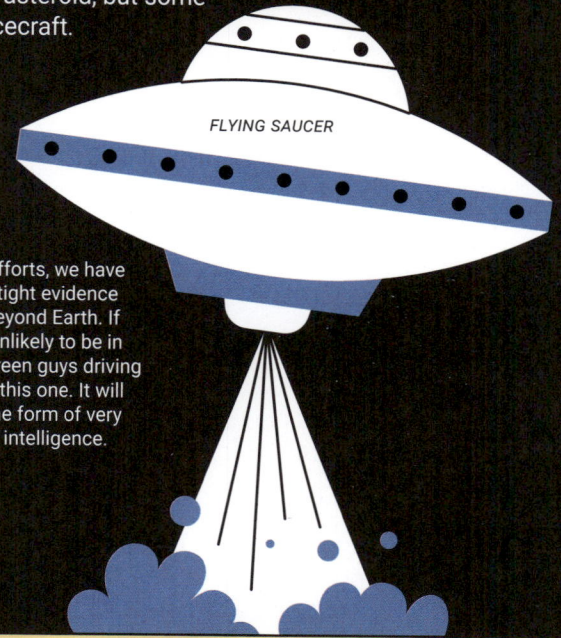

FLYING SAUCER

Artemis

The goal of the Artemis Space Program is not only to put humans back on the Moon, but also to establish a long-term presence there. If all goes according to plan, by 2025 people – including the first woman and the first person of colour – will walk on the Moon.

Alien visitors

Despite our best efforts, we have never found watertight evidence of intelligent life beyond Earth. If it does exist, it is unlikely to be in the form of little green guys driving flying saucers like this one. It will most likely be some form of very advanced artificial intelligence.

EARTH

MOON

▸ The illustration shows the journey that Artemis 1 made from Kennedy Space Center in the USA to the Moon and back.

Reusable rockets

New rockets like SpaceX Falcon 9 have been developed with first stages that return to Earth after launch and can be reused.

▸ The SpaceX Starship may be used for space tourism. It is designed to carry up to 100 passengers.

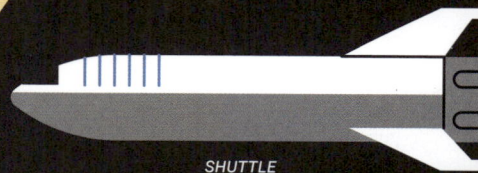

SPACEX
STARSHIP

Rockets and spacecraft

NASA has built its most powerful rocket ever, called the Space Launch System (SLS) to launch the Orion crew vehicle into space. Artemis 1 was an uncrewed dry run. Artemis 2 will carry a crew into Earth orbit, while Artemis 3 will land crew on the Moon.

★ The Artemis Program also includes Gateway, a space station that will orbit the Moon, providing support for craft coming and going to the surface of the Moon, as well as acting as a launchpad for trips to Mars.

SHUTTLE

Rockets

Rockets are used to launch spacecraft into Earth orbit and beyond. Big rockets heading for space have two stages stacked inside their cylindrical shells. The first stage has several engines to thrust the spacecraft through Earth's thick atmosphere. When the first stage drops off, the smaller second stage ignites and continues the journey.

IS SPECTACULAR!

SHUTTLE

SPACEX STARSHIP

▸ Above: Here you can see the relative sizes of a Space Shuttle rocket (retired in 2011) and the more recent SpaceX Starship.

Industrial technology has to do with the design and development of products, many of which are used in domestic settings. Robotics are key in industry, with more robots used in manufacturing than in any other field. On the home front, high-tech houses are set to be the next big thing.

INDUSTRIAL & DOMESTIC

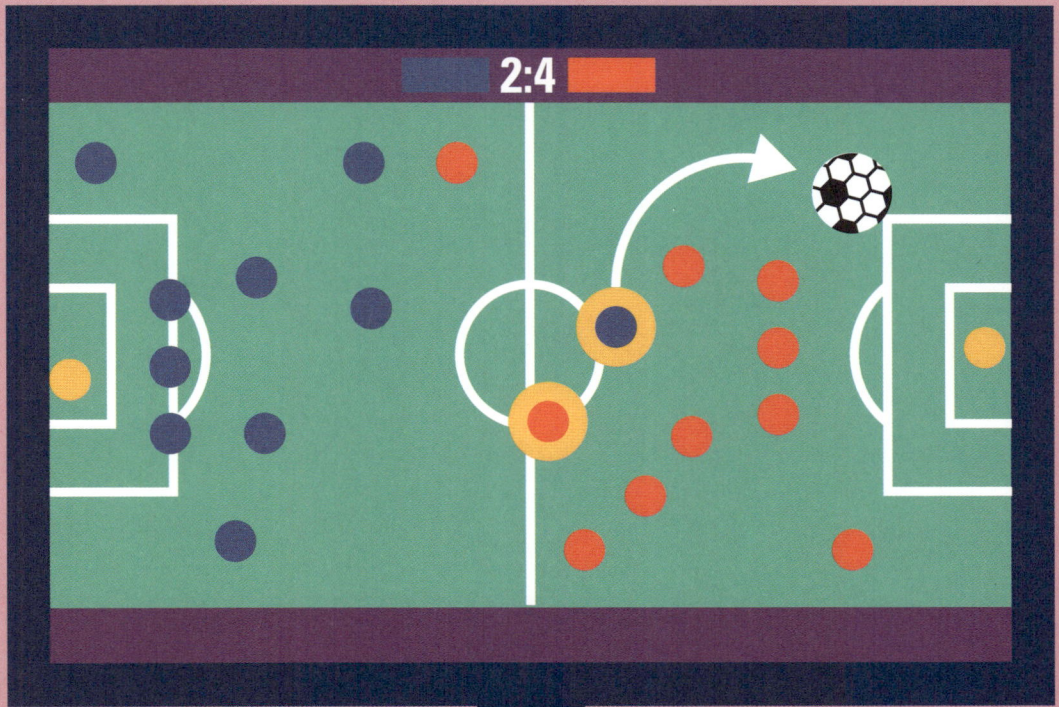

ROBOTS

A robot is a machine that can be programmed to work on its own. Most robots are controlled by computer and carry out very specific tasks with speed and precision. Huge advances in robot design, engineering and operation have made robotics the field of the future.

▶ In 1739, French inventor Jacques de Vaucanson made people laugh with a mechanical duck that seemed able to eat corn, digest it, and "eliminate" it!

Automata

Robots have been around since ancient times, but they weren't called "robots" until the 20th century. Early robot-like machines were known as automata, and they did incredible things to amaze and entertain people.

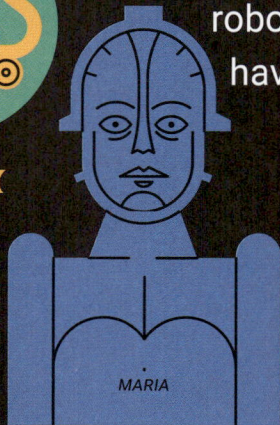

MARIA

★ Fritz Lang's 1927 silent movie Metropolis featured a humanoid robot called Maria.

Types of robots

When you hear the word "robot" you might think of an android that looks and acts like a human but in a stilted, mechanical way. In reality, most robots look like machines.

Robotic teachers

In the future, classrooms may be led by robots. This would free up human teachers to help students on a one-to-one basis. Robots can also help by planning lessons, grading student papers and communicating with parents about their progress.

▶ In China, hundreds of kindergartens use a small robot called KeeKo to tell stories, ask questions and react with facial expressions.

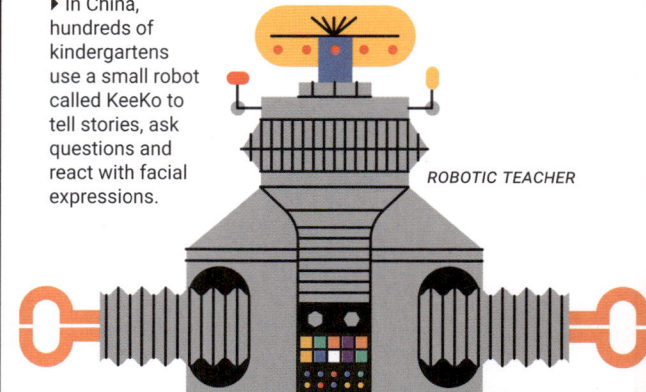

ROBOTIC TEACHER

Industrial robots

This is by far the most common type of robot. Millions of them are used in factories around the world, mainly on assembly lines, where they do repetitive tasks more precisely than humans can.

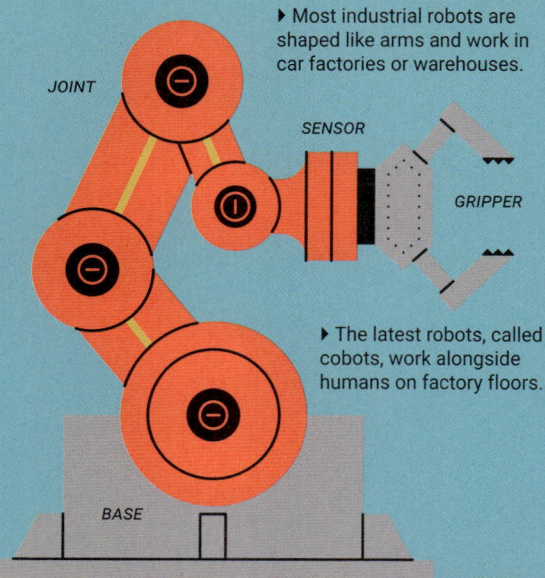

▶ Most industrial robots are shaped like arms and work in car factories or warehouses.

JOINT

SENSOR

GRIPPER

▶ The latest robots, called cobots, work alongside humans on factory floors.

BASE

Space robots

Space robots come in all shapes and sizes. They assist astronauts on spacecraft, but also work on their own to collect samples, measure things and assemble and fix equipment.

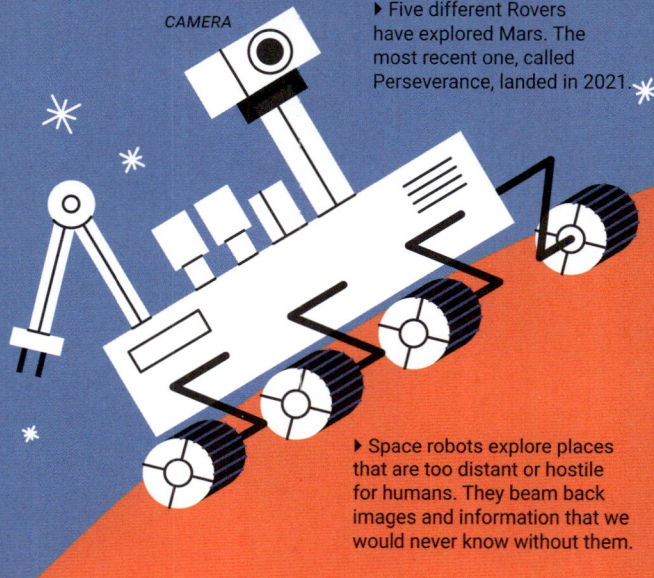

CAMERA

▶ Five different Rovers have explored Mars. The most recent one, called Perseverance, landed in 2021.

▶ Space robots explore places that are too distant or hostile for humans. They beam back images and information that we would never know without them.

Unsafe zone robots

Robots are used in war zones and during terror attacks to identify and dismantle bombs. They can also help find survivors after a disaster, such as an earthquake or nuclear accident.

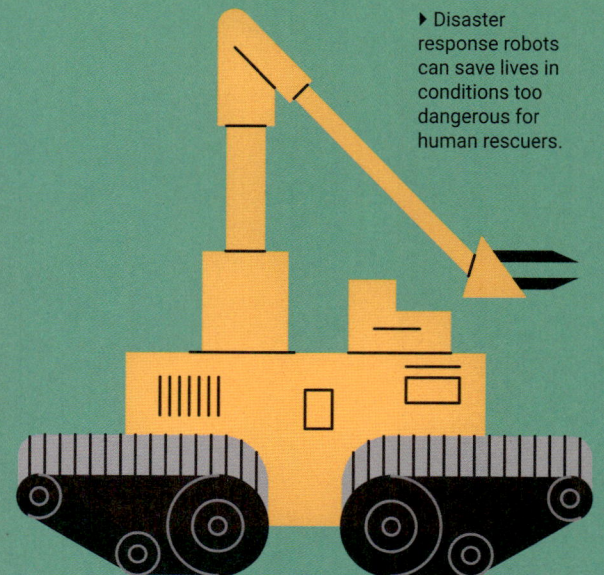

▶ Disaster response robots can save lives in conditions too dangerous for human rescuers.

Robotics

Robotics is a mix of science, engineering and technology that revolves around designing, building and using robots. It is a fast-growing sector with huge potential for the future in many different fields.

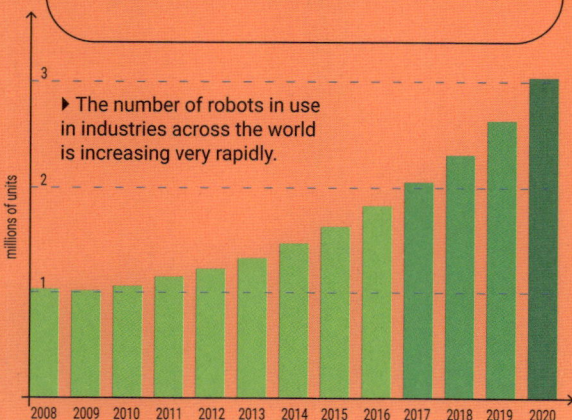

▶ The number of robots in use in industries across the world is increasing very rapidly.

millions of units

2008 2009 2010 2011 2012 2013 2014 2015 2016 2017 2018 2019 2020

Consumer robots

These are robots you can buy and use for fun (see also Toys, above) or to help with tasks and chores in the home. They can provide 24/7 security, clean floors, mow lawns and help organize your day, among other things.

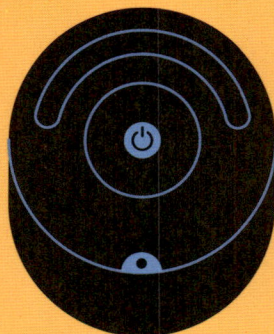

ROBOTIC VACUUM CLEANER

▶ Home robots are increasingly operated remotely using smartphones and smartwatches.

ROBOTIC LAWN MOWER

Drones

Drones are aircraft without a human pilot on board. They are usually controlled by a person on the ground but can also be flown by in-built computers. They were developed by the military to spy on places that are too dirty or dangerous for piloted flights.

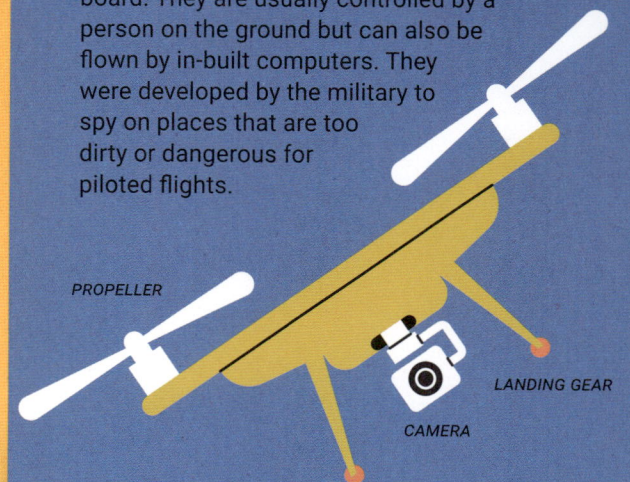

PROPELLER

LANDING GEAR

CAMERA

▶ Most drones are now used in industries like agriculture, construction, insurance and law enforcement.

▶ People enjoy flying drones for fun and the market for consumer drones has skyrocketed.

Toys

There are all sorts of robotic toys, from rowdy models with flashing lights that are all about fun, to educational types that can teach children coding and other skills. Many of the best have a companion app to control them.

FURBY

▸ Launched in 1998, Furbies were the first robotic toys to become wildly successful.

▸ Many robotic toys have built-in games to teach things like colours, numbers and shapes.

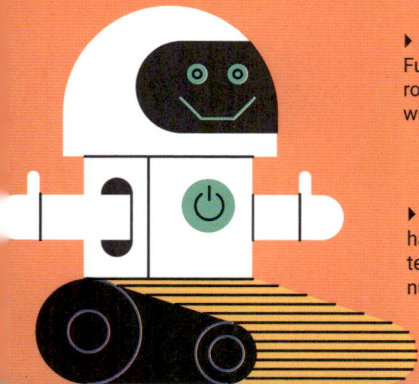

▸ In Japan, robots are already widely used in nursing homes, offices and schools.

Carers

Social robots may soon be used as carers to assist the elderly or people with disabilities at home. They can help with everyday tasks like cleaning and preparing food, as well as calling for help in case of emergency.

Social robots

These robots can interact with humans and other robots. Many social robots resemble humans, or are cute and friendly. Social robots can provide companionship to people who live alone or watch over children and young people when parents are busy or at work.

Medical robots

Skilled surgeons use robotic systems to operate. They make tiny incisions and are very precise, leading to fewer infections and faster healing. See pages 72–73 for more detailed information.

▸ Robots also help diagnose illness and do routine nursing, such as taking blood pressure and monitoring vital signs.

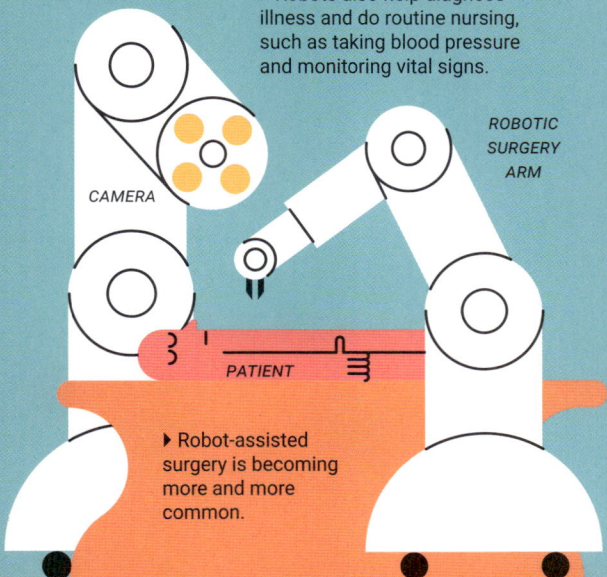

CAMERA

ROBOTIC SURGERY ARM

PATIENT

▸ Robot-assisted surgery is becoming more and more common.

Humanoids and androids

Humanoid robots are built in the shape of human beings and usually have a head, a body, two arms and legs and feet (although some have a base with wheels). They are made of metal and you would not mistake one for a real person. **Androids** are also robots but they are made to look as life-like as possible. Until recently, androids were the stuff of science fiction but some new androids look amazingly real.

HUMANOID ROBOT

Android anchor

In 2018 Nippon TV "hired" a robo-journalist called Erica Aoi. She became the world's first robotic news anchor.

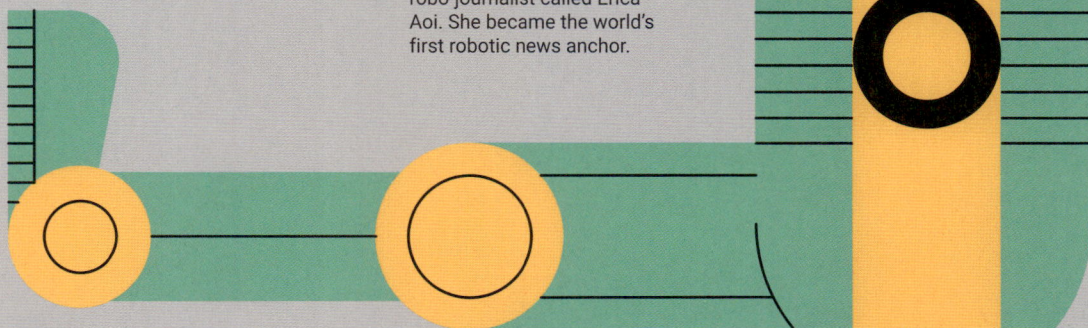

▸ Studies show that robotic pets stop people feeling lonely and make them happier, just like real animals do.

Robotic pets

Dogs, cats and birds are the most common animals to be kept as robotic pets. They look and behave like the real thing, but don't need feeding and can be switched off when not required.

ROBOTIC DOG

★ Leonardo da Vinci designed and probably built a humanoid robot in the form of a knight in 1495.

DIGITAL ASSISTANT

★ Millions of digital assistants like Alexa and Siri are now in use.

Virtual assistants

Many of us now use digital assistants in our homes and daily lives. Amazon's Alexa or Apple's Siri are two of the most widely used. They can respond to commands, provide information and help control other connected devices.

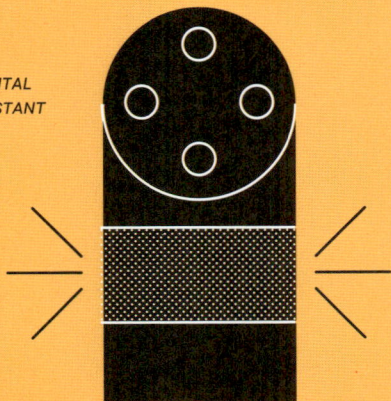

SMART FACTORIES

Smart factories use a range of technologies, including **AI**, the **IoT**, **big data analytics** and cloud computing to constantly collect and analyse data from every part of the production process. Everything is digitised and connected, from concept and design to production and delivery of products. Smart factories plan for problems before they arise and take action to prevent them.

▸ Engineers use Augmented Reality to see and test products in a virtual environment before making prototypes.

The four industrial revolutions

Instead of just one industrial revolution beginning in England in the 1760s, we now count four major periods of change in technology, economy and society.

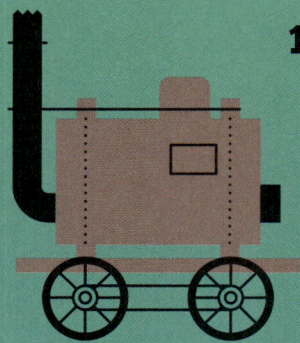

1760s

First industrial revolution
Water and steam power are used to mechanise production. Industry replaces agriculture as the mainstay of the economy.

1870s

Second industrial revolution
Revolves around the discovery of electricity, gas and oil and the invention of the combustion engine. Production of steel and chemical-based products begins. The telegraph and telephone revolutionise communications.

1950s

Third industrial revolution
Nuclear fuel emerges as a new source of energy. Electronics, telecommunications and computers enter factories and homes. Robots are used in industry. Space exploration and biotechnology emerge.

2000s

Fourth industrial revolution
Internet use explodes, connecting people and businesses across the globe. Access to processing power, storage capacity and knowledge is unprecedented. Advances in AI, robotics, 3D printing and many other fields revolutionise everything.

Ideas and design

In a smart factory, people work in teams to discuss and design the best version of the product they want to make. They use many different technologies to visualise the product and also to check out the competition and forecast marketing strategies and profitability.

Quality control

When the product is finished it goes into quality control where computerised machines check it thoroughly to make sure it conforms to safety and quality standards.

▸ It is much less costly to catch a problem while products are still in the factory. Recalling faulty goods from the market is expensive and embarrassing.

Packaging

After quality control, the products head for packaging where machines carefully wrap them and seal them inside cartons.

▸ Goods packaged in a smart factory include labels and barcodes that allow warehouses and shops to keep track of them until they reach their final destinations.

3D printing

A product is developed on-screen and then made using 3D printing. The process is still too expensive for mass production but it is perfect for testing.

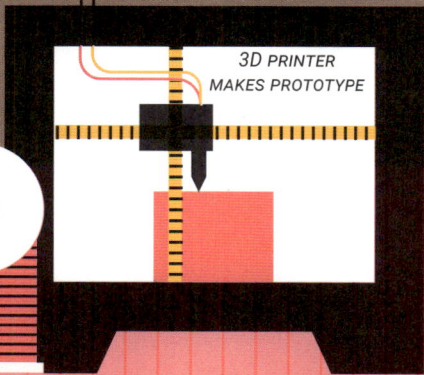

3D PRINTER MAKES PROTOTYPE

Making prototypes

After design, prototypes (advance samples) of the product and the tools that will be needed to produce it are made. Often 3D printers are used to prepare several slightly different versions of the product and the production line to see which ones look and work the best.

★ Smart factories cut costs, save time and reduce wastage.

▶ This factory is making a robotic toy dog for use in homes and schools to help children learn and relax.

The IoT

The Internet of Things (IoT) is a network of physical objects ("things"), that have software, sensors and other technologies so that they are all connected 24/7. They exchange information constantly. Smart factories use the IoT so that they always know if, for example, they have enough raw materials or if there are problems in the warehouse or delays with shipping. They can manage all these things ahead of time, keeping production on track.

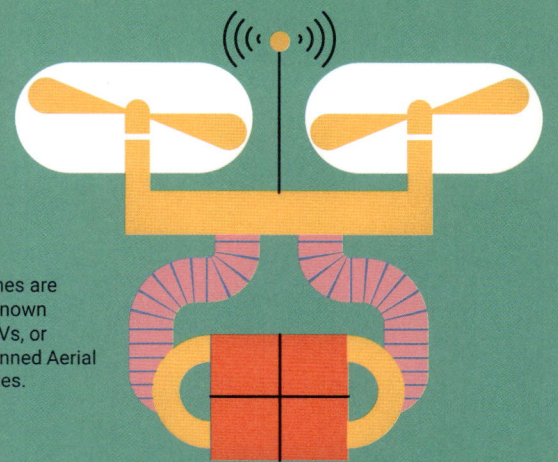

FACTORY CONNECTED TO THE IoT

Assembly

When a product has been fully tested, raw materials are ordered, machines are programmed and production begins.

Machine learning

Machines in smart factories are programmed to adjust and adapt the production line without waiting for commands from humans.

▶ Sensors on factory equipment are constantly collecting data.

▶ Drones are also known as UAVs, or Unmanned Aerial Vehicles.

Warehouse

Packaged products pass to a smart warehouse which is controlled by a management system that oversees work by picking machines and AGVs (automated vehicles such as forklifts and pallet carts).

▶ The same smart warehouse will also manage the ordering and arrival of raw materials or components used to make the products.

Drone delivery

Drone technology has surged in the last five years and a handful of companies are spearheading the move to using them for rapid delivery. They are ideal for delivering urgently-needed goods, such as medicines, but also for getting that book into your hands just 30 minutes after you read a review.

Shipping

Smaller smart factories often outsource their shipping to external companies. These companies are also smart and provide constant feedback to the factory on the whereabouts and delivery status of goods.

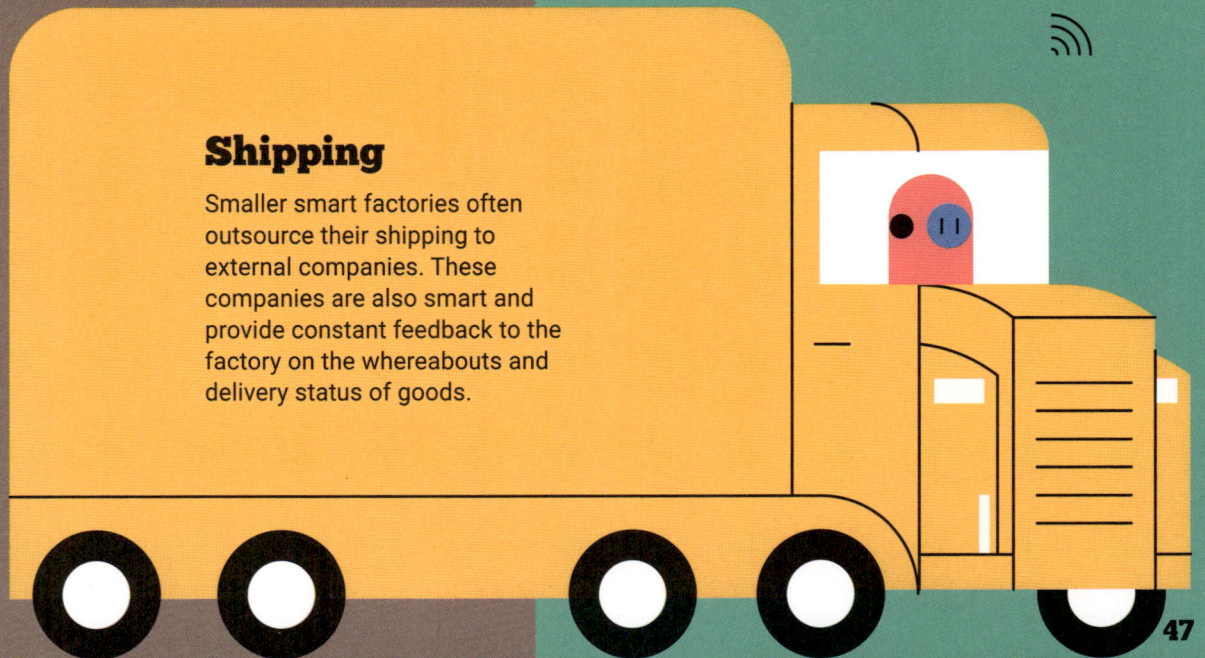

CINEMA & TV

New technology has radically changed how people watch films and TV. Here we take a look at the technologies that have helped cinema and TV to evolve over time.

Camera obscura

Camera obscura is a Latin phrase that means "dark room." It is a room or box with a hole cut in one wall. When light passes through the hole it projects an upside-down image of the outside world onto the wall opposite the hole. This simple technology is the basis of the photographic camera.

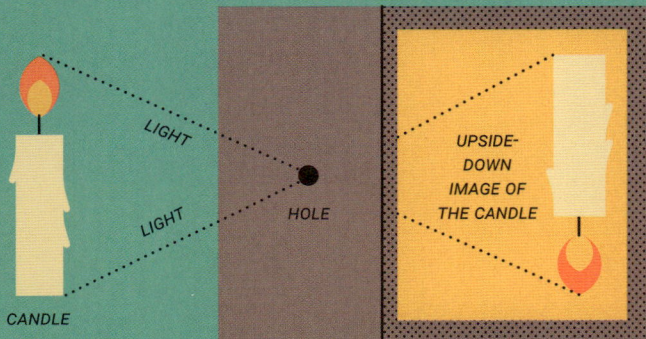

LIGHT

LIGHT

CANDLE

HOLE

UPSIDE-DOWN IMAGE OF THE CANDLE

CAMERA OBSCURA

★ The camera obscura was known in ancient China and Greece over 2400 years ago.

Before cinema

Photography was born when inventors added lenses and mirrors to the camera obscura and discovered how to print the images they made. But for film one important element was still missing: movement!

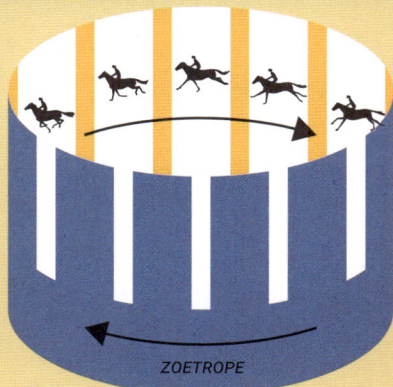

ZOETROPE

The zoetrope

This was one of several devices invented to add movement, or animation, to photos. It consists of a drum with slits in the side and pictures inside. When you spin the drum and look through the slits, it seems like the pictures are moving.

Films for one

The kinetoscope was a forerunner of classic movie projectors. It had strips of film with sequences of images running in front of a light to create the illusion of movement. Only one person at a time could view the films.

KINETOSCOPE

▶ The kinetoscope was invented in 1891 by Thomas Edison and one of his assistants William Dickson.

The Lumière brothers

French brothers Louis and Auguste Lumière invented an early movie camera and projector and became the fathers of the silver screen. Their first film, called *Workers Leaving the Lumière Factory*, is recognised as the first movie.

★ The Lumière brothers were inventors and manufacturers of photographic equipment. They sent a team of tech workers around the world to show people how to use their new moving-picture camera and projector.

AUGUSTE

LOUIS

LUMIÈRE PROJECTOR

Film

In the 20th century motion pictures were shot on celluloid, or film. Movies were made up of a long strip of celluloid divided into images, or "frames," with perforations (holes) on the sides so it could be fed through a projector.

Film projectors

Celluloid film was wound onto reels (spools). Traditional movie projectors had two reels. The one at the top held the unseen film that slowly unwound into the projector. A strong light from behind projected its images through a lens onto the big movie screen. The film was then wound onto the second reel.

The top reel holds the film being fed into the projector.

TOP REEL

The shutter flashes each frame three times to reduce flicker.

The gate holds the film flat.

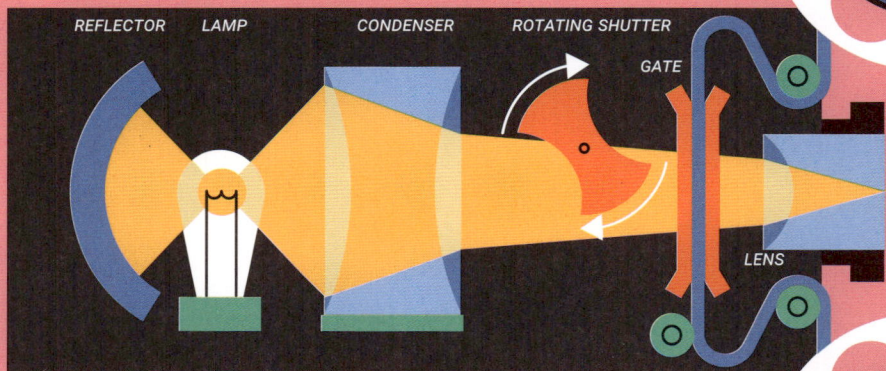

REFLECTOR   LAMP   CONDENSER   ROTATING SHUTTER

GATE

The lens focuses the light onto the screen.

LENS

A very bright lamp shines a light through a condenser onto a rotating shutter.

A mechanism pulls the film forwards one frame at a time (24 times per second).

★ Celluloid was a synthetic material similar to plastic. It was highly flammable.

The bottom reel receives the film from the projector.

BOTTOM REEL

▶ New celluloid films were very high quality, but after a lot of screenings scratches and marks appeared and the quality declined.

The digital revolution

The film industry changed very rapidly in the first decades of the 21st century. Filmmakers began shooting films on digital cameras, which was much cheaper and easier then shooting on film. Editing and distribution also became quicker and simpler. New technology also changed the way people watched movies. It was no longer necessary to go to a cinema; you could download a film onto your smart TV, laptop or mobile phone.

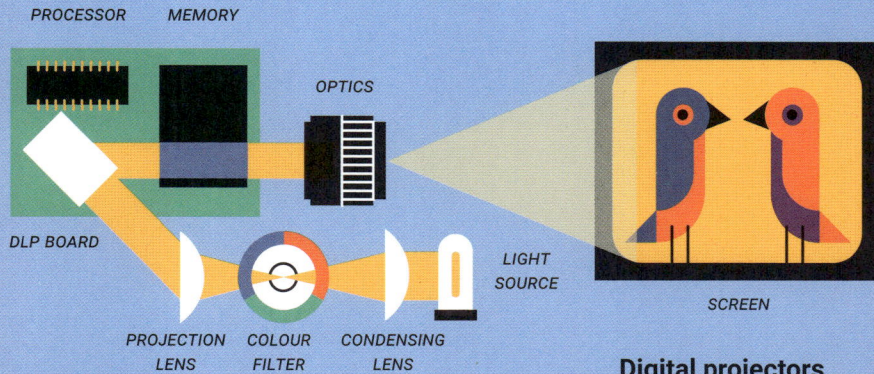

PROCESSOR   MEMORY

OPTICS

DLP BOARD

PROJECTION LENS   COLOUR FILTER   CONDENSING LENS   LIGHT SOURCE

SCREEN

▶ The switch to digital cinema began at the end of the 20th century and was complete by about 2010.

Digital projectors

There are two main types of digital cinema projector technologies: Micromirror projectors and LCD projectors.

Distribution

Before cinemas went digital, film companies spent a lot of money making copies of the heavy, cumbersome reels of film and sending them by courier to movie theatres. When physical film disappeared, distribution also went digital with films sent on DVDs or hard drives, or via the internet or special satellite links.

★ The first movie theatre opened in 1905 in Pittsburgh, USA. It had 96 seats and was called the Nickelodeon.

Television

Television took off in Europe and the Americas in the 1950s. It transformed the way people spent their free time, how they learned about political events, and even how they shopped.

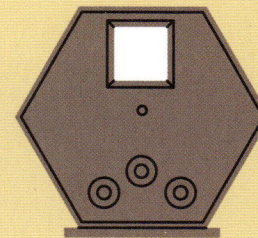

OCTAGON 1928

Evolution of TV

Television was invented in the 1920s, with the first demonstration of true TV taking place in 1927. It became popular and widespread in the 1950s and then evolved rapidly decade by decade. Colour was introduced in the 1960s, followed by cable in the 1970s, VCRs in the 1980s and high-definition displays in the late 1990s. Today, viewers are just as likely to watch on mobile phones, laptops and tablets as on an actual TV set.

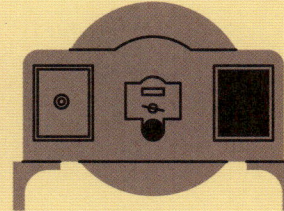

BAIRD 1930

▶ The first TVs had aerials (antennae) to pick up programmes from broadcasting stations.

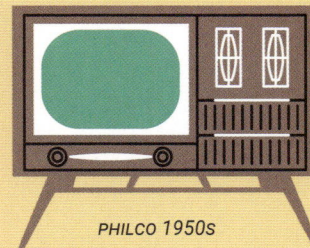

PHILCO 1950S

Smart TVs

Today, TV sets are all connected to the internet and as well as offering traditional broadcasting media like TV and radio, they can be used to access streaming services, online gaming and social media, in the same way as a smartphone, tablet or computer.

TV WITH ANTENNAE 1970S

▶ Smart TVs are a mix of the technology found in computers, televisions and set-top boxes (cable boxes)

REMOTE CONTROL

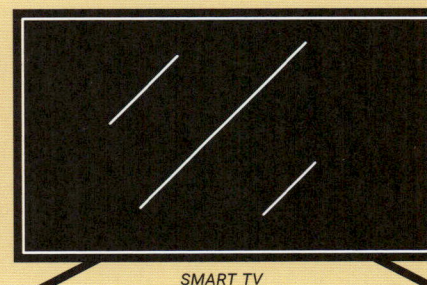

SMART TV

★ In 1950 just 20% of American homes had a TV. By the end of the decade 90% owned one. The 50s and 60s are known as "the golden age of television."

HIGH-TECH HOMES

Technology has the potential to transform our homes, making our lives healthier, more comfortable and greener. The smart home can be controlled by an app on your phone. Here you can see some of the features you might expect to find.

Bedrooms

The centrepiece of this room is the smart bed which monitors your sleep quality, giving you a daily report. It regulates temperature, keeping you snug through the night and the seasons. It also remakes itself every morning.

The kitchen

Smart kitchen devices help store and prepare food and deal with leftovers and waste. Depending on how high-tech you want to go, you could have a robotic chef and any number of smart, connected appliances.

Cleaning

Floors are kept clean by robotic vacuum cleaners. New models can also be set to mop hard floors. Robotic window cleaners make life simpler. External windows on upper floors can be cleaned easily by setting the robot on the outside window and letting it do its job.

Security

A smart security system keeps the house safe, with cameras to monitor outdoor spaces and facial or other recognition systems to let people in. It also detects gas and water leaks and power surges, and warns of dangerous pollution levels, so that you can take action before problems occur.

The basement

The basement is connected to the rest of the house and fitted with sensors to detect intruders or flooding. If there is plenty of space, you might install a home gym with fitness wearables and connected equipment. Alternatively, there might be a home cinema, or both.

▸ The roof is covered with photovoltaic solar panels that convert light into electricity.

▸ Plan your outfit for the day by virtually trying on clothes in a smart mirror from the comfort of your bed.

SMART MIRROR

★ *If waking up is hard, you may want a Clocky — an alarm clock that runs around the room until you catch it to turn it off!*

7:00 AM

SMART BED

CLOCKY

▸ Smart refrigerators check inventory and propose shopping lists. They can even check best-by dates and order more food.

VOICE CONTROL

▸ Smart rubbish disposer can be programmed to sort waste into the correct recycling bins.

SMART SELF-CLEANING OVEN

▸ Motion sensors are positioned at entrances. They are programmed to activate floodlights, trigger alarms, and even call the police.

INTERNAL LIFT

GARAGE DOOR

▸ Smart garage walls will have computer screens to plan your route and check weather and traffic conditions.

COMPUTER

▸ Cars are all fully electric and are automatically recharged every evening.

▸ Wealthy homes may have internal lifts. One to lower the car into a basement garage every night, and another to whisk passengers up to the upper floors.

Bathrooms

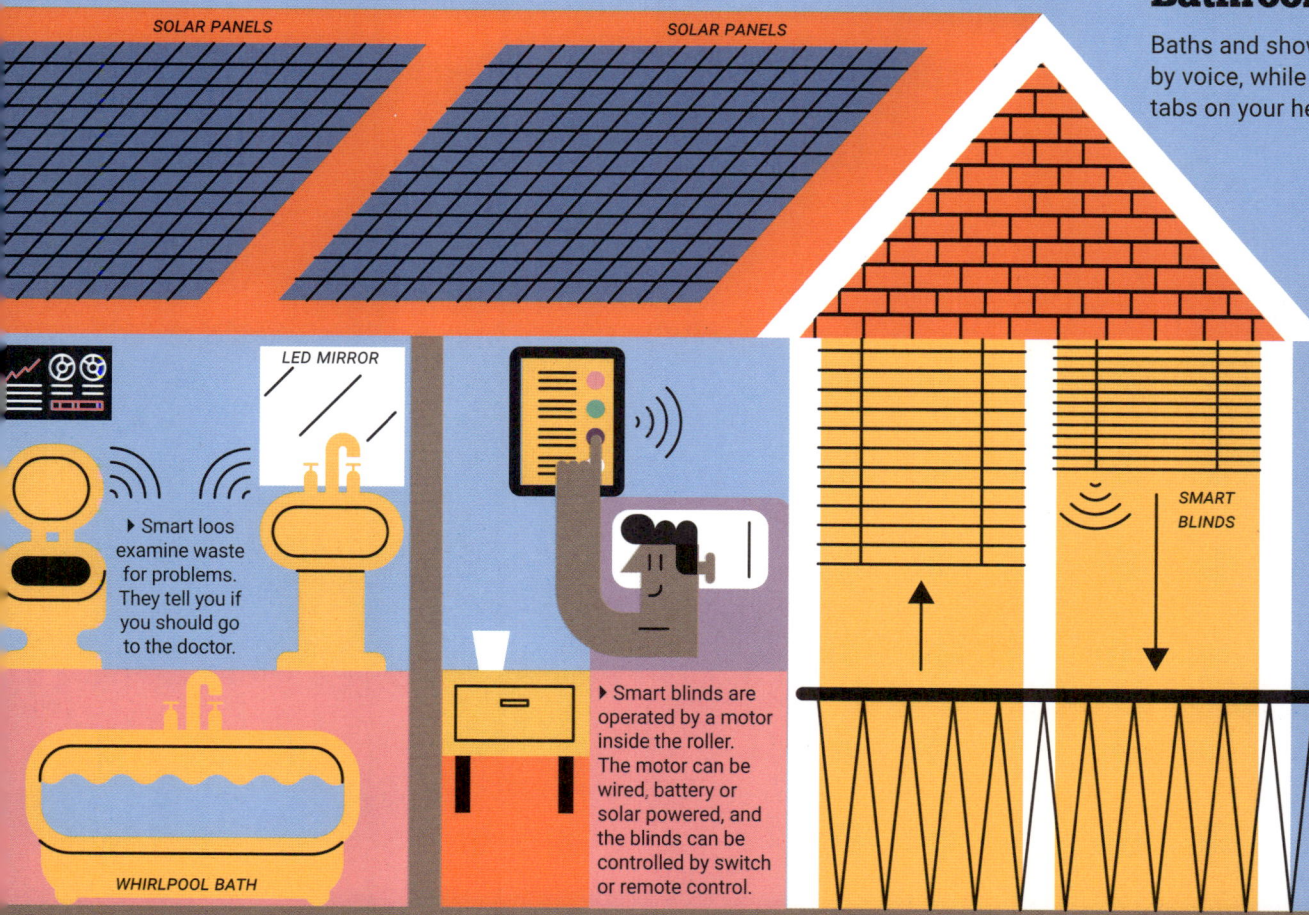

Baths and showers are controlled by voice, while smart loos keep tabs on your health.

SOLAR PANELS

SOLAR PANELS

TURBINE

LED MIRROR

▶ Smart loos examine waste for problems. They tell you if you should go to the doctor.

WHIRLPOOL BATH

SMART BLINDS

▶ Smart blinds are operated by a motor inside the roller. The motor can be wired, battery or solar powered, and the blinds can be controlled by switch or remote control.

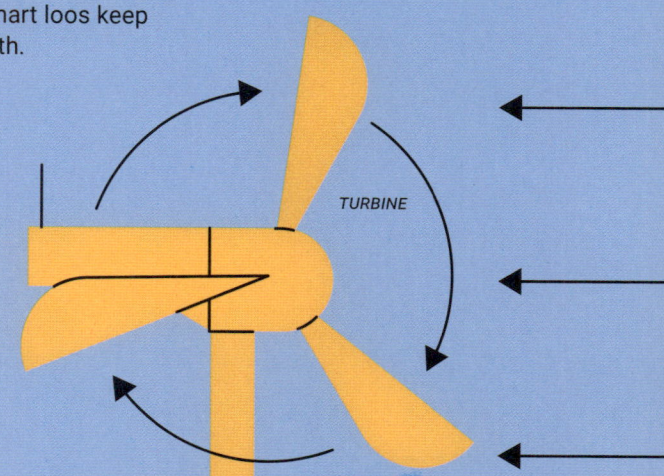

Energy

If your house is located in an exposed, windy area, a wind turbine in your back yard could generate enough electricity to power your house and all its appliances.

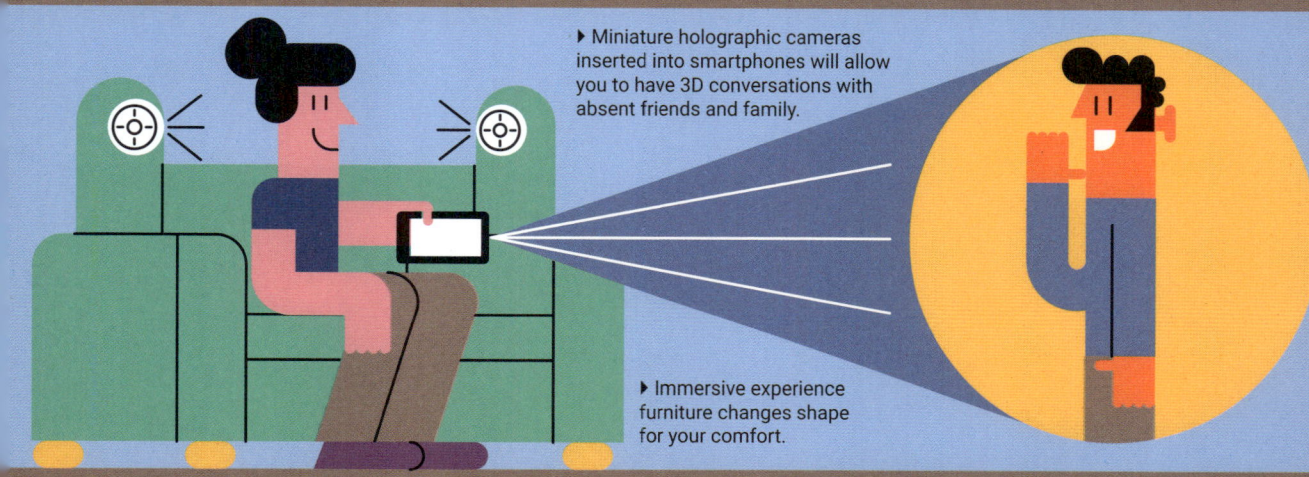

Heating

Household heating is provided by low-carbon air or ground source heat pumps. Houses with outdoor space can use ground source (geothermal) heat pumps which transfer heat from the ground to your radiators or underfloor heating. They also heat water.

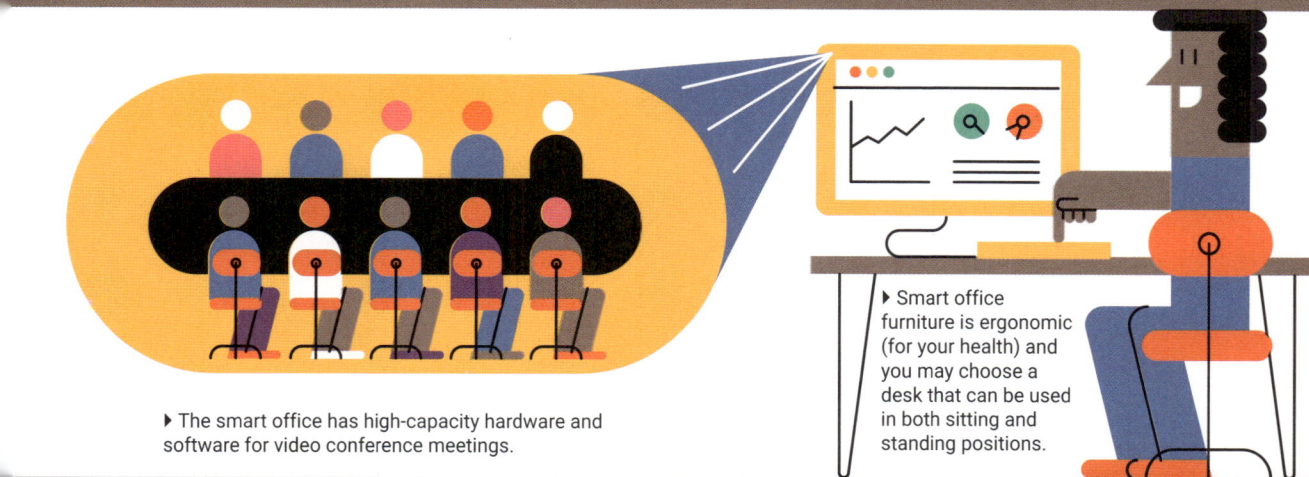

▶ Miniature holographic cameras inserted into smartphones will allow you to have 3D conversations with absent friends and family.

▶ Immersive experience furniture changes shape for your comfort.

▶ The smart office has high-capacity hardware and software for video conference meetings.

▶ Smart office furniture is ergonomic (for your health) and you may choose a desk that can be used in both sitting and standing positions.

Smart home office

WFH (Working From Home) will become the norm for most office workers. They will only go to the office one or two days a week. The rest of the time they work from a well-equipped, smart, home office.

Living rooms

Living rooms are full of high-tech features, including wall-size video screens, virtual reality artwork, a holographic telephone and voice controlled lighting, heating and cooling.

TOYS & GAMES

Toys frequently reflect the latest trends in technology. Video games are often the first places we see new tech like **artificial intelligence** (AI), and **virtual** and **augmented reality** (VR/AR).

Silly putty

The weird gooey toy called Silly Putty is made mainly of silicone and colouring. It was invented by accident during World War II by scientists who were trying to make synthetic rubber.

▶ Silly Putty belongs to a group of compounds called non-Newtonian fluids because it doesn't behave like normal fluids such as water.

World's oldest toy

Spinning tops are one of the oldest toys. They have been found on archaeological sites dating back at least 6,000 years.

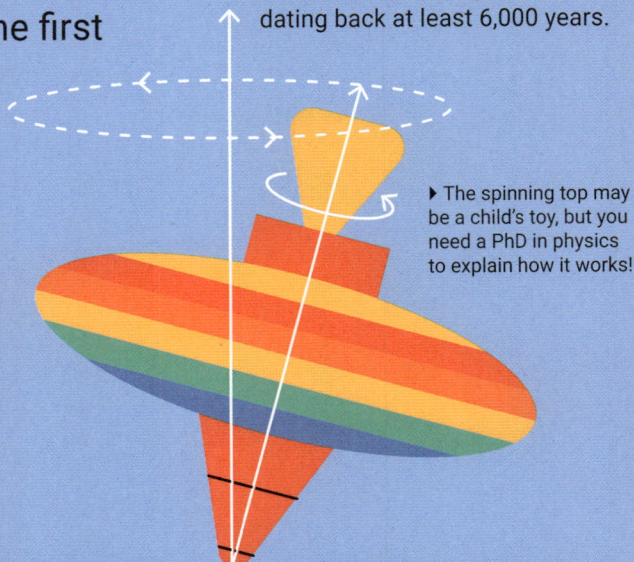

▶ The spinning top may be a child's toy, but you need a PhD in physics to explain how it works!

Donkey Kong

Platform games like *Donkey Kong* by Shigeru Miyamoto took off in the 1980s. Nintendo still releases new *Donkey Kong* games more than 40 years after its original release in 1981.

The first video games

The video games we play today are descended from games like *Space Invaders* that were very popular in the 1970s and 1980s. Back then, people didn't have computers at home, so they went to amusement arcades and played on large machines in cabinets.

ARCADE GAME

★ The first video game was invented in 1958 by a physicist called William Higinbotham. It was a simple game called Tennis for Two. Players used a controller to bat the ball back and forth.

Esports

Esports (electronic sports) are a high-growth area in video games. Individual players and teams battle it out for victory during these competitive events. Prizes are rich and the prestige of winning brings funding from sponsorship, endorsements and team salaries. By 2028 esports are expected to be part of the Olympics.

★ Esports have made video games into spectator events with millions of people tuning in to watch the annual League of Legends World Championships.

Virtual pets

Electronic pets became popular in the 1990s when robotic toys like Furby and Tamagotchi were first released. Tamagotchi (1996) is a handheld digital pet that owners raise from egg to adult.

★ The first Furby was the hit of the holiday season in 1998. It could open and close its eyes and spoke its own language. New-model Furbies are far more interactive and are still very popular.

Rubik's cube

This mechanical brain-training puzzle has to be turned until the colours on all six sides are the same. The average person takes three hours on their first attempt. Really smart cubers can do it in less than 10 seconds. An AI system in California has learned to solve it in one second!

★ With over 400 million copies sold, Rubik's cube is one of the best-selling toys in the world.

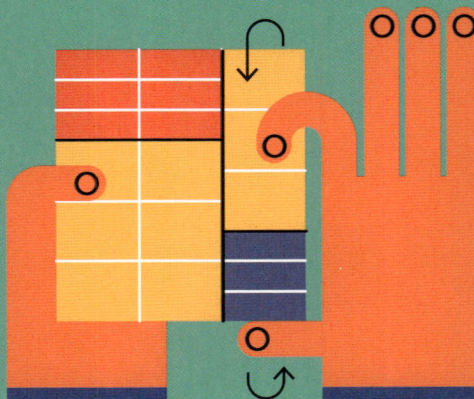

Amazing facts

Playstation 2 is the best-selling games console. It is closely followed by Nintendo DS.

By 2024 an estimated 3.3 billion people will play video games.

The average age of gamers is 37.

Gamers have faster reaction times than those who don't play. They also develop better decision-making skills under pressure.

Game Boy

Game Boy was not the first handheld console but it quickly became the best-known and most widely used after its release in 1989. Production ceased in 2003.

★ In 2021 studies showed that about 45% of gamers are girls and women.

AI car racing

Car racing sets have been popular for 50 years. The most recent models have AI cars that can swerve to avoid obstacles and stay on track. Players use remote controllers to run the cars over the tracks.

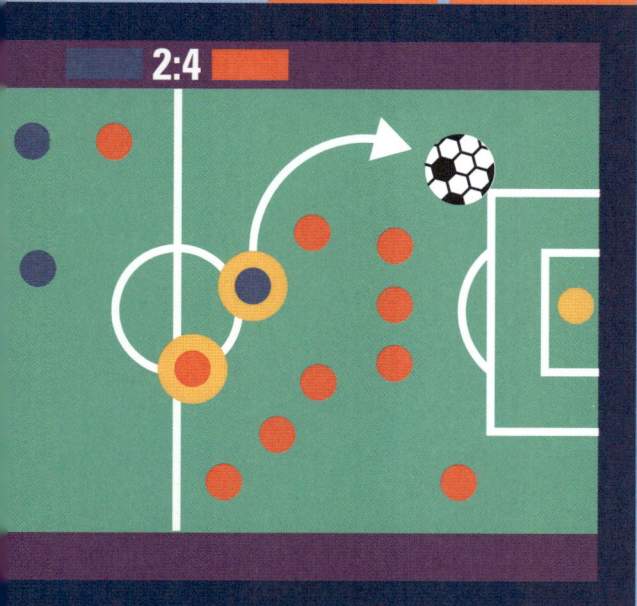

The future

The future of video games is bright with experts expecting to see a huge expansion of cloud-based games and streaming becoming more popular than computers and consoles.

★ Many gamers scoff at the idea of the metaverse being something new. They have been congregating in online communities for years.

▶ Robotics kits and apps focus on building and coding to create models that kids can play with. They are educational toys.

Embracing the future

Forward-thinking toy companies are not afraid of new technology. Companies like Lego have embraced it and built toys that combine traditional building skills with apps and virtual reality.

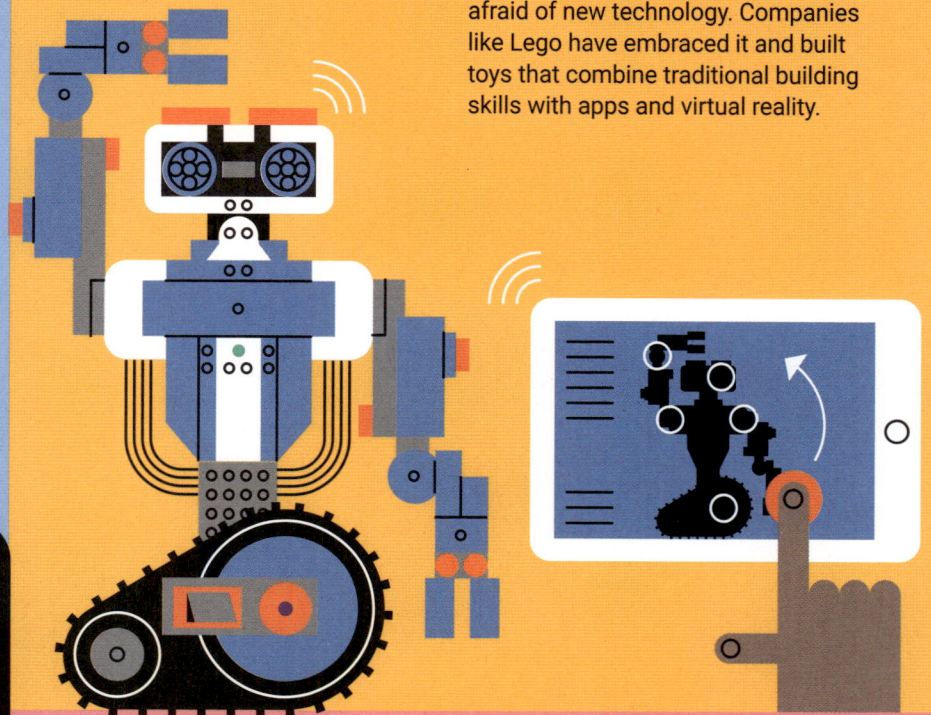

★ Tetris was the first video game played in space, by Russian Cosmonaut Aleksandr A. Serebrov in 1993.

★ In 1997 an IBM computer called Deep Blue beat the world chess champion Garry Kasparov in just 20 moves.

Top-selling video games

1. **Minecraft** (2011)
Over 280,000,000 copies sold

2. **Grand Theft Auto V** (2013)
Over 150,000,000 copies sold

3. **Tetris** (2006)
Over 100,000,000 copies sold

4. **WII Sports** (2006)
Over 83,000,000 copies sold

5. **PlayerUnknown's Battlegrounds** (2017)
Over 70,000,000 copies sold

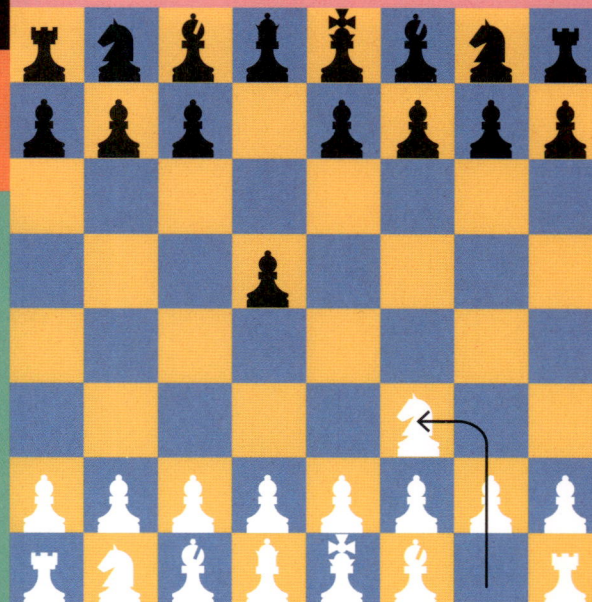

Online chess

People have been playing chess for almost 1500 years, but in the 1980s they began playing against computers. By the end of the decade chess players, including some **Grandmasters**, began losing to computers. Today the best chess engines can beat most grandmasters at every game.

Nowadays you can play against computers online. You can also play against other people by logging into any of the many online chess sites.

Construction technology is used in the design, development and conservation of buildings and structures like bridges and tunnels. Materials are the components used to create these structures and many of the other objects we use in daily life. Recent technology in these fields has a strong focus on sustainability and recycling.

MATERIALS & CONSTRUCTION

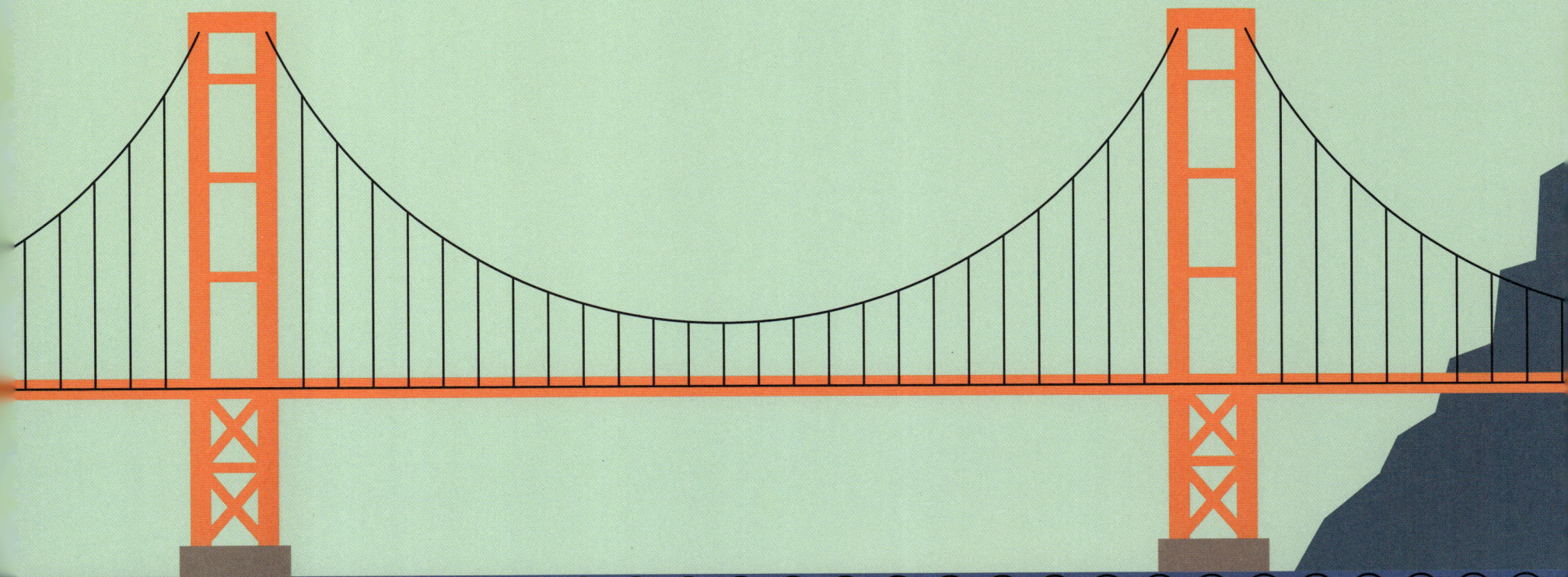

PLASTICS

Plastics have transformed everyday life. They are inexpensive, lightweight, strong and longlasting and we use them to produce a wide array of useful products. However, there are huge concerns about how plastics are made and how their disposal is managed. We urgently need more high-tech solutions to produce plastics from renewable, biodegradable resources and to reuse and clean up the plastics that currently clog our oceans.

The age of plastic

The widespread use of plastic took off after World War II. In 1950, global plastic production was 1.5 million tonnes. By 2020, it was 35 million tonnes! By 2050 it is estimated that plastic production will quadruple.

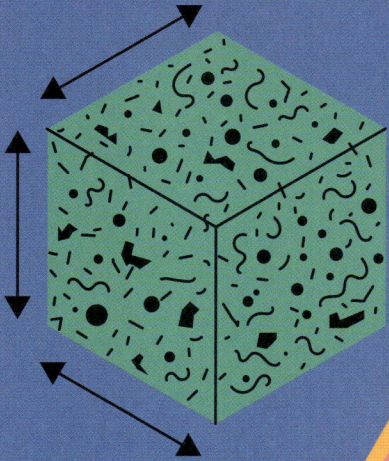

▶ In 2020 less than 10% of the plastic produced globally was recycled. More than 20% was simply discarded with no attempt to manage it. The rest was incinerated or ended up in landfill.

First plastics

Plastic is a synthetic material, which means that it is made by people and does not occur in nature. In 1907 Leo Baekeland invented Bakelite, a type of plastic that was tough, heat resistant and ideally suited for mass production.

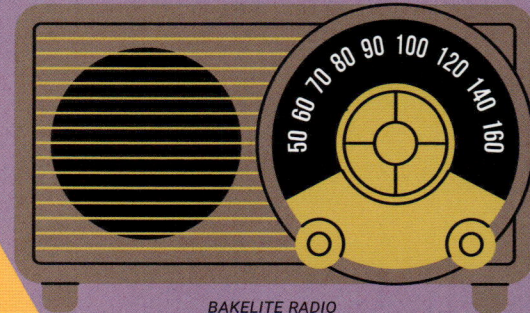

BAKELITE RADIO

▶ Chemicals are usually added to plastics to make them suitable for their end use. These chemicals are often toxic.

Life cycle of plastic

Almost all plastic is made from fossil fuels. These are non-renewable resources that increase greenhouse gases. Ideally, plastic should be made from renewable resources and correctly recycled.

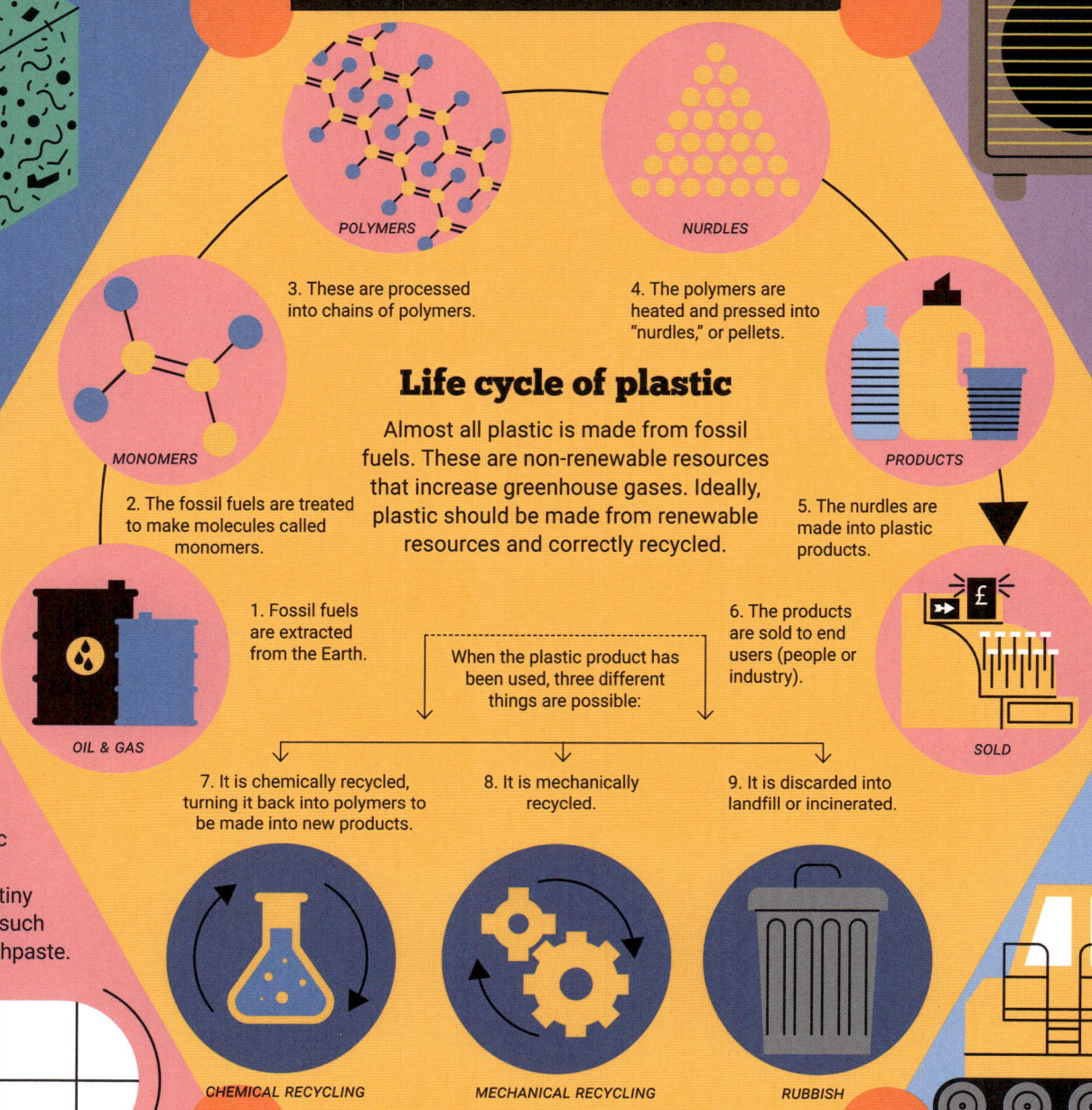

POLYMERS

NURDLES

MONOMERS

OIL & GAS

PRODUCTS

SOLD

1. Fossil fuels are extracted from the Earth.

2. The fossil fuels are treated to make molecules called monomers.

3. These are processed into chains of polymers.

4. The polymers are heated and pressed into "nurdles," or pellets.

5. The nurdles are made into plastic products.

6. The products are sold to end users (people or industry).

When the plastic product has been used, three different things are possible:

7. It is chemically recycled, turning it back into polymers to be made into new products.

8. It is mechanically recycled.

9. It is discarded into landfill or incinerated.

CHEMICAL RECYCLING

MECHANICAL RECYCLING

RUBBISH

Microplastics

Microplastics are tiny beads of plastic, less than 5 mm (0.02 inches) long. Some come from larger plastic objects like water bottles as they break down. The rest are tiny particles added to cosmetics, such as soap, face creams and toothpaste.

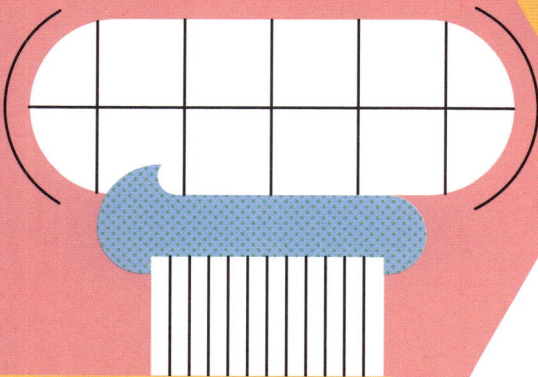

MICROPLASTICS IN TOOTHPASTE

★ Adding microplastics to cosmetics has been banned in many countries.

▶ Have you ever noticed tiny specs of stuff in your toothpaste? They are microplastics.

Landfill

Fossil fuel plastics should not be sent to landfill. They take hundreds of years to decompose and leak toxic pollutants into the soil and water as they break down.

Plastic pollution

Our oceans are heavily polluted with plastic. When plastic is not recycled it ends up in rivers that drain into the sea. Old fishing nets, lines and ropes also increase the amount of plastic in the sea. Marine plastic kills wildlife and contaminates our food sources.

★ Every year over a million seabirds and 100,000 marine animals die from plastic pollution.

★ More than a million plastic bags are thrown away every minute.

▶ There are five huge, swirling patches of plastic in our oceans. The Pacific Garbage Patch is the largest, at around 1.6 million sq km (620,000 sq mi), or three times the size of France.

Types of plastics

There are different types of plastic, each with its own properties and uses. They are divided into seven categories.

PET 1

1. Polyethylene terephthalate Water bottles, jars, caps.

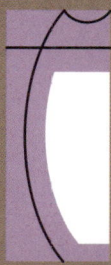

HDPE 2

2. High-density polyethylene Grocery bags, shampoo bottles.

PVC 3

3. Polyvinyl chloride Mainly used in construction.

LDPE 4

4. Low-density polyethylene Bread bags, rubbish bags.

PP 5

5. Polypropylene Yoghurt containers, hangers, straws.

PS 6

6. Polystyrene Toys, take-away packaging.

Other 7

7. Other Nylon, baby bottles, CDs.

▶ Bioplastics still need to be disposed of carefully. They must be recycled and reused, not dumped in landfill where they produce greenhouse gases.

Bioplastics

Plastics can be made from renewable resources such as plants and algae. These types of plastic are more expensive to produce but they are better for the environment. Although bioplastics break down more easily, many of them contain toxic chemicals.

Single-use plastics

Single-use plastics are designed to be used just once then thrown away. They include things like plastic bags and bottles, food wrappers, straws and coffee cups.

★ *Make an effort to avoid using single-use plastic. If you can't avoid it, be sure to recycle as much of it as possible.*

STRAWS

WATER BOTTLES

▶ If not recycled, single-use plastics don't break down, they break up into tiny pieces, or microplastics.

Aerospace plastics

The first aircraft had wooden frames. The next generation was made of metal, but metals are heavy and require a lot of energy to fly. Plastic is light, strong and cheap to produce, making it the material of choice for many parts of modern aeroplanes.

WINGS

▶ Plastic is used in the wings, fuselage, interior wall panels, luggage compartments, instrument panels, doors and more.

▶ Carefully managed aerospace plastics are good for the environment. Lighter aircraft can fly further using less fuel and leaving fewer emissions.

Recycle, reuse, cleanup

We need to make and manage plastics more efficiently. Scientists want the companies that sell plastic to be responsible for taking it back and recycling or reusing it. Meanwhile environmental organisations like The Ocean Cleanup need support as they work to clear away excess plastic.

Innovative solutions

Scientists have discovered more than 50 species of **plastivores**, or organisms that eat plastic. They are mainly bacteria and fungi but there are also a few insects capable of turning plastic into energy. Researchers are studying their digestive systems. If they can mimic the way they work, they may be able to design a perfect plastic-biodegradation system.

▶ The river current turns the wheel that powers the conveyor belt of junk up inside the rubbish gobbler. Solar panels provide extra energy when required.

MR TRASH WHEEL

Mr Trash Wheel

Mr Trash Wheel is a rubbish-gobbling vessel moored in Baltimore Harbor in the USA. Powered by water currents and solar panels, Mr Trash Wheel intercepts rubbish that flows from the city into the river and then out into the ocean. First installed in 2014, there are now four rubbish-gobblers at work in the harbour.

★ *The Ocean Cleanup aims to clear away 90% of floating ocean plastic by 2040.*

RECYCLING

Humans produce a lot of rubbish. Rich countries make more than poor ones, but as lower-income regions catch up they also create huge quantities of refuse. In most places the waste we produce is not well managed. We need to do better, and innovative technological solutions can help.

Landfill

Rubbish that isn't recycled is either burned in giant incinerators or taken to landfill sites (rubbish dumps) where it is buried. Incineration produces fumes that add to air pollution. Landfills can also damage the environment if they are not properly managed.

BULLDOZER

LANDFILL

▶ The bottom and sides of a landfill need to be lined to avoid leakage of toxic liquids into the soil and water. When full, the landfill needs to be sealed to stop gases escaping into the air.

★ In rich countries food wastage is mainly caused by careless shopping habits.

Food for thought

1. About one-third of all the food produced worldwide is wasted.

2. All that wasted food would be enough to feed two billion people, or more than twice the number of hungry people in the world.

3. Every piece of food that ends up in landfill produces about four times its own weight in greenhouse gases.

4. There are apps to connect people with surplus food to those who need it. Users upload a photo and description and people living nearby can claim the food before it goes to waste.

5. New software for supermarkets and restaurants can predict 50% more accurately how much produce they will need to buy for their clients, helping them to slash food wastage.

6. New technology connects cafes, supermarkets and restaurants with unwanted food to local shelters, after-school programmes and other nonprofit organisations that feed hungry people.

Getting it sorted

Household waste is picked up and taken to sorting facilities where it is separated it into different types, such as paper and cardboard, metal, glass, plastic and general rubbish. Each type is then sent to specialist plants to be recycled into new products. Here you can see what happens in a typical sorting facility.

REMOVAL BY HAND OF NON-RECYCLABLE THINGS

2. Paper products are spun to the top

Cardboard and paper floats to the top as it passes over spinning discs. It is separated and recovered. Meanwhile containers drop to the bottom and are also recovered.

★ Recycling one aluminium can saves enough energy to power a TV for three hours.

★ Plastic drinking straws can not be recycled. It's best to choose paper straws, or none at all.

RUBBISH TRUCK

1. Rubbish is picked over manually

Recovery methods differ, but usually mixed waste is sorted first by hand to remove things that are too bulky or clearly not recyclable. These are incinerated or sent to landfills.

Turning plastic into fuel

As we have seen (pages 56–57), plastic is a serious problem for the environment. New technology is being developed that can turn plastic into gasoline, diesel fuel and other high-value items. Scientists are looking for low-cost, environmentally friendly ways to do this.

▶ About 99% of plastic is made from chemicals that come from fossil fuels.

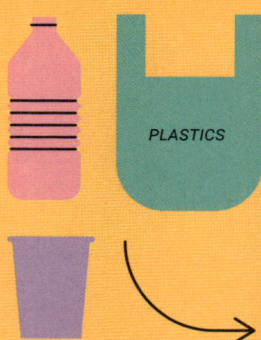

PLASTICS

FUEL

E-waste

E-waste includes unwanted electrical items, such as mobile phones, computers, kitchen appliances and electrical tools. Each one contains a variety of materials and often requires careful disassembly and processing before the parts can be recycled or safely discarded.

★ E-waste is increasing sharply. Currently, less than 20% of it is recycled.

E-WASTE RECYCLING BIN

▶ E-waste articles should not be put in landfill as they do not break down and often release toxic chemicals. They should be placed in special e-waste recycling bins.

Disassembly robots

Big tech companies are tackling the problem of e-waste by collecting more of their old devices and using new technologies to recover more materials from them. Apple has made three robots — called Daisy, Dave and Taz — to disassemble iPhones and recover materials, including **rare earth elements** (REE).

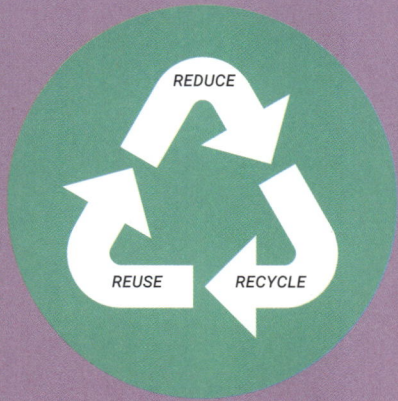

The three Rs

The three environmental Rs — Reduce, Recycle and Reuse — are meant to remind us to reduce waste and to reuse and recycle as many resources and products as we can.

Throw-away fashion

Some people now regularly buy a lot of very cheap clothing, wear it once or twice, then throw it away. Even well-made, longlasting clothing is usually not recycled and ends up being burned or in landfill.

★ The fashion industry is responsible for 10% of greenhouse gas emissions.

★ Polyester takes 200 years to decompose.

FAST FASHION

Fast fashion

Fast fashion brands copy the latest trends from the catwalk, producing cheap versions very quickly. They use low-quality materials like polyester (made with petroleum) and toxic dyes. Because the clothes need to be very cheap, these fashion brands often don't pay their workers living wages or they employ children.

★ Only 13% of clothing and footwear is recycled.

★ Recycling just one plastic bottle saves enough energy to power a 60-watt light bulb for up to six hours.

★ Germany, South Korea, Austria, Belgium, Slovenia, Sweden and Switzerland all have recycling rates above 50%.

★ The average recycling rate among OECD countries is about 35%.

★ Germany leads the world in waste management. In 2021 about 70% of all the waste produced in Germany was recycled. Just thirty years earlier, only 3% was recycled. Then the government made a huge effort with policies and education to reduce landfills and recycle more, with excellent results.

3. Magnets remove metal

Powerful overhead magnets are used to extract metal objects. Electromagnets can be used to separate out aluminium cans.

4. Glass is crushed

Items made of glass are crushed or broken, then cleaned and sorted by colour for reprocessing.

5. Optical scanners

In some plants, optical scanners using infra-red light or air jets are used to separate different kinds of plastics.

New stuff from old

Recycled materials are made into a huge variety of new products, from paper, kitty litter and clothing to footwear, rugs and art.

▶ Some materials, like glass and metals, can be recycled an infinite number of times. Others, like paper and plastic, can only be recycled a few times.

How you can help

We can reduce the amount of waste we produce and recycle more. Here are some ideas for what you can do to help.

Buy recycled paper
It uses 30% less energy to produce compared to new paper. It releases 40% less greenhouse gases, produces 50% less waste water and results in 40% less solid waste. It also uses 100% fewer trees!

Glass
Glass is 100% recyclable. It does not decompose and should not end up in landfill. Make sure it goes in the recycling bin.

Learn local recycling guidelines
Recycling differs from place to place. Read your local council guidelines and follow them. Find drop off centres for batteries, printer toners and other things that need specialist recycling.

Batteries
We use a lot of them — in toys, phones, clocks, remote controls and more. Batteries contain toxic chemicals and need to be recycled separately. Find out where batteries are collected in your area and make it your job to take all your household's batteries to the collection point.

Don't wish-cycle
Find out exactly what you can and can't recycle in your area. Don't put stuff in the recycling if you know it can't be recycled. For example, in many places single-use plastic bags are not recyclable (however much you may wish that wasn't so). It will just end up contaminating the whole bin so that everything ends up in landfill.

Building a skyscraper

Once the foundations are laid, construction workers create a large steel frame. Sections of prefabricated frame are lifted into place by cranes and bolted together. When the frame is ready the external cladding is applied. The interiors are added last.

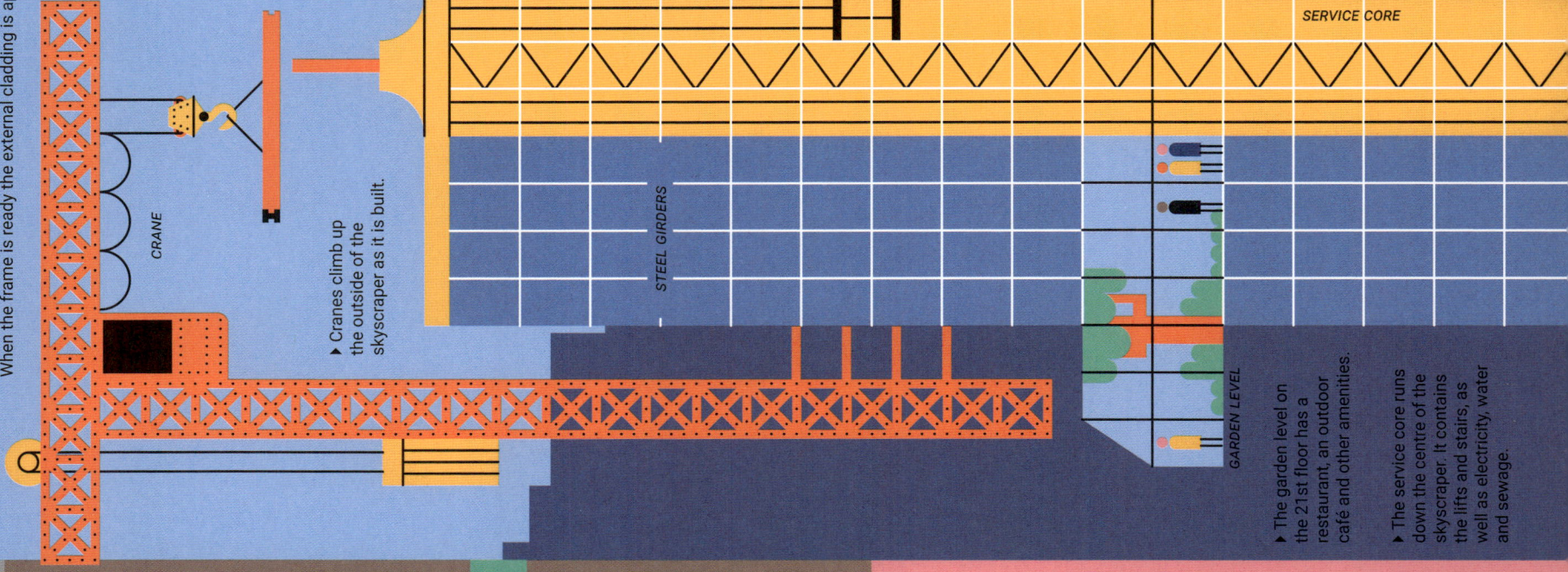

▶ Most skyscrapers have a skeletal frame of vertical columns and horizontal girders. The exterior walls don't provide any support, they just enclose the spaces.

LOAD-BEARING COLUMNS RUN DOWN THE BUILDING

SERVICE CORE

STEEL GIRDERS

CRANE

▶ Cranes climb up the outside of the skyscraper as it is built.

GARDEN LEVEL

▶ The garden level on the 21st floor has a restaurant, an outdoor café and other amenities.

▶ The service core runs down the centre of the skyscraper. It contains the lifts and stairs, as well as electricity, water and sewage.

Lifts

Skyscrapers wouldn't be possible without lifts that haul people and things up and down the tall buildings. The American inventor and industrialist Elisha Otis built the first steam-powered safety lifts in the 1850s. Electric lifts were introduced towards the end of the 19th century and they made really tall buildings possible.

LIFT SHAFT

SHAFT DOOR

CAR

LIFT ATTENDANT

COUNTER-WEIGHT

ROPES

★ The first Otis lift had a safety brake. If a rope broke, a spring made a wooden frame snap out against the sides of the lift shaft to stop the car from falling. This made lifts less dangerous and people became more willing to use them.

★ In 1902 the Otis company pioneered a gearless, traction electric lift and buildings above 50 floors began to appear.

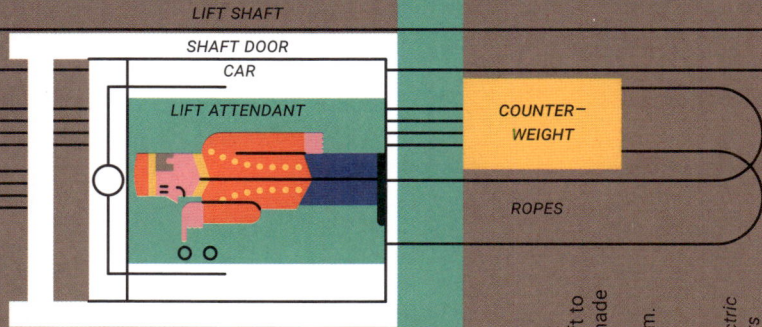

Skyscraper snippets

THE EMPIRE STATE BUILDING in New York was the first building with more than 100 floors (It has 102). Opened in 1931, the Art Deco landmark was the world's tallest building for 39 years, until it was eclipsed by the first World Trade Center in 1970.

THE MILE-HIGH ILLINOIS was a proposal by American architect Frank Lloyd Wright for a skyscraper over one mile (1.6 km) tall. Wright described the building in 1956: It would have 528 floors, 76 lifts, 100,000 occupants, 15,000 parking spaces and 100 helicopter landing pads. It would be twice as tall as the Burj Khalifa, the world's current tallest building. It was never built.

THE JEDDAH TOWER in Saudi Arabia is an unfinished skyscraper designed by American architect Adrian Smith, who also designed the Burj Khalifa. When finished, it will be the tallest building in the world and the first ever to stand more than one km (3,281 ft) tall.

NEW IDEAS for unconventional tall buildings include **Floating skyscrapers** that are tied to asteroids orbiting around the Earth. **Earthscrapers** have been designed like upside-down pyramids that plunge 65 stories into the ground. There are even projects for **Oceanscrapers** built using the rubbish that currently mars our oceans. These buildings would be 500 metres (1,640 ft) wide and home to 20,000 people. Most of the structure would be underwater, like an iceberg.

SKYSCRAPERS

Taller, slimmer, sustainable (or not), with stunning shapes or built of unusual materials – skyscrapers have not gone out of fashion. They create space for offices and homes in crowded cities, but they are also symbols of wealth and power.

★ Cities with a lot of skyscrapers have dynamic skylines that are especially striking from afar at night.

The first skyscrapers

The first skyscrapers were built in Chicago and New York in the 1880s when engineers began using internal metal frames as the main support structure for their buildings.

▶ The Home Insurance Company Building in Chicago is generally considered the first skyscraper. It was built in 1885 (and demolished in 1931). It had ten floors and was designed and built by William Le Baron Jenny.

Coping with nature

Very tall buildings have to be designed and built to cope with high winds, lightning, earthquakes, extremes in temperature, and more.

Earthquakes

Skyscrapers in earthquake-prone regions like Japan and the west coast of North America have special technology that protects them and their inhabitants against damage during earthquakes.

Reinforced lift shafts.

Fire-resistant building materials.

Birdcage interlocking steel frame.

Surrounded by open areas where people can assemble.

Lightning

Most skyscrapers are topped with a lightning rod. It is made of highly conductive material such as copper and is connected to a wire that runs all the way down to the ground so that the electric current is safely dispersed.

Foundations are sunk into rock, not clay. Rubber shock absorbers are added to stop tremors reaching the building.

EARTHQUAKE PROOFING MEASURES
Computer-controlled weights on the roof reduce movement.

LOBBY AND SHOPS

UNDERGROUND PARKING SPACE

CONCRETE PILLARS

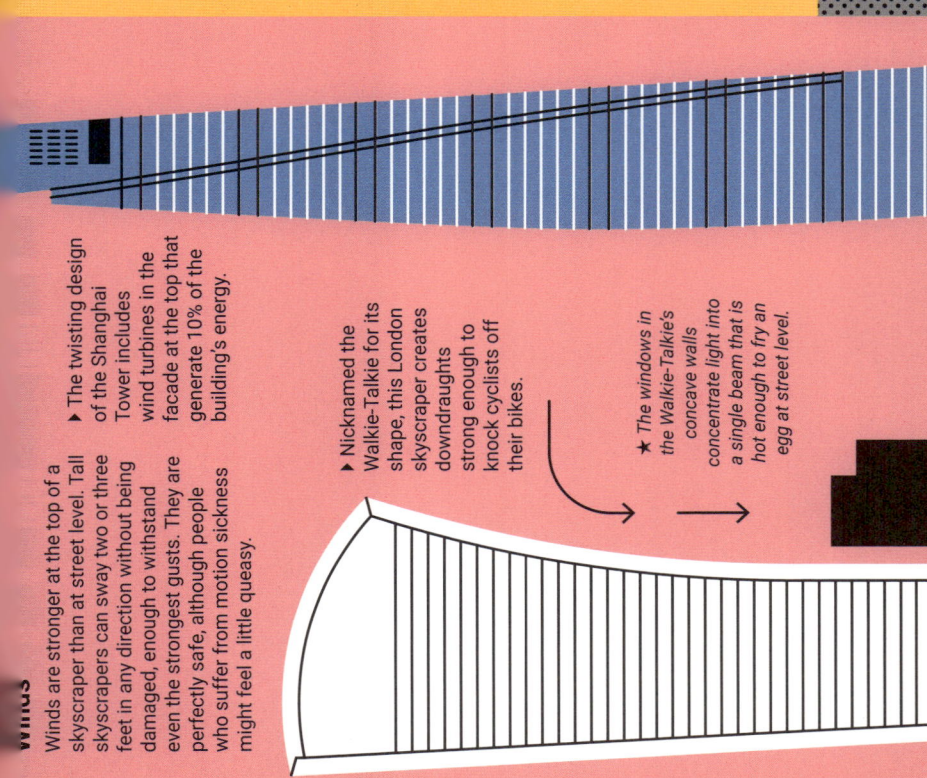

► The ceiling on the ground floor is often higher than the other floors. Sometimes a striking, light-filled atrium is added to welcome people as they enter the building.

▶ Strong foundations are fundamentally important. They are usually made of concrete columns buried deep into the earth. The pillars support the full weight of the building.

Winds

Winds are stronger at the top of a skyscraper than at street level. Tall skyscrapers can sway two or three feet in any direction without being damaged, enough to withstand even the strongest gusts. They are perfectly safe, although people who suffer from motion sickness might feel a little queasy.

▶ The twisting design of the Shanghai Tower includes wind turbines in the facade at the top that generate 10% of the building's energy.

SHANGHAI TOWER

▶ Nicknamed the Walkie-Talkie for its shape, this London skyscraper creates downdraughts strong enough to knock cyclists off their bikes.

★ The windows in the Walkie-Talkie's concave walls concentrate light into a single beam that is hot enough to fry an egg at street level.

WALKIE-TALKIE

Size, shape and design

A conventional skyscraper is a tall, rectangular building, often tapering at the top. But designers are constantly looking for taller, more unusual shapes and cutting-edge designs are often astonishing.

★ The Burj Khalifa in Dubai was the world's tallest building in 2022. It is 830 metres (2,722 ft) tall.

★ The lifts in the Taipei 101 are among the fastest in the world. It takes just 30 seconds to get to the top.

★ Architects dream of 3D-printing skyscrapers. There are many plans but no buildings yet.

★ The Aldar Headquarters in Abu Dhabi is the world's first circular skyscraper. Opened in 2010, it has won many awards for its futuristic design.

★ Construction of the twisting Diamond Tower in Jeddah, Saudi Arabia, is on hold. When complete, it will be one of the tallest residential buildings in the world.

★ The distinctive shape of the 30 St Mary Axe skyscraper in the city of London caused it to be nicknamed "The Gherkin" even before it was built.

ALDAR HQ

DIAMOND TOWER

THE GHERKIN

3D PRINTED SKYSCRAPER (PROJECT)

TAIPEI 101

BURJ KHALIFA

Types of bridges

While bridges come in all shapes and sizes, they are mostly variations on six basic types.

ARCH BRIDGE

These bridges have an arch in the centre and abutments (supports) at either end that hold it in place. The weight is spread evenly across the arch. These are strong bridges.

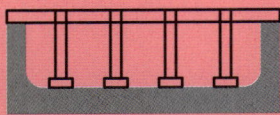

BEAM BRIDGE

Beam bridges are the simplest, oldest and cheapest type. They consist of a horizontal beam supported by piers at each end. Longer beam bridges also have pillars under the deck.

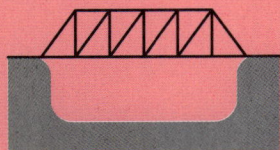

TRUSS BRIDGE

Truss bridges have inter-connecting triangular structures that make them very strong. They are light and can be installed in precarious places, for example in high mountain passes.

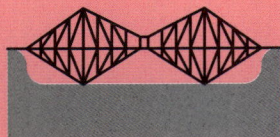

CANTILEVER BRIDGE

A cantilever is a long projecting beam or girder supported at only one end. Cantilever bridges are built using two cantilevers that meet in the middle of the bridge. They are good for longer bridges.

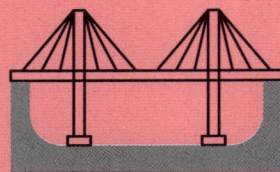

CABLE-STAYED BRIDGE

Cabled-stayed bridges have one or more towers with cables, or stays, connected to the deck of the bridge that support it.

SUSPENSION BRIDGE

In a suspension bridge the weight of the deck is supported by cables. The main cables are attached to towers at each end. They can span long distances and are often built over water.

Golden Gate Bridge

The iconic Golden Gate Bridge spans the mile-wide (1.6-km) strait between San Francisco Bay and the Pacific Ocean. Because the bridge stands in an area prone to earthquakes, it has been extensively refitted to withstand even very large seismic events (tremors).

★ Each of the 500 vertical hangers on the bridge is strong enough to hold a weight of 227,000 kg (500,000 lb).

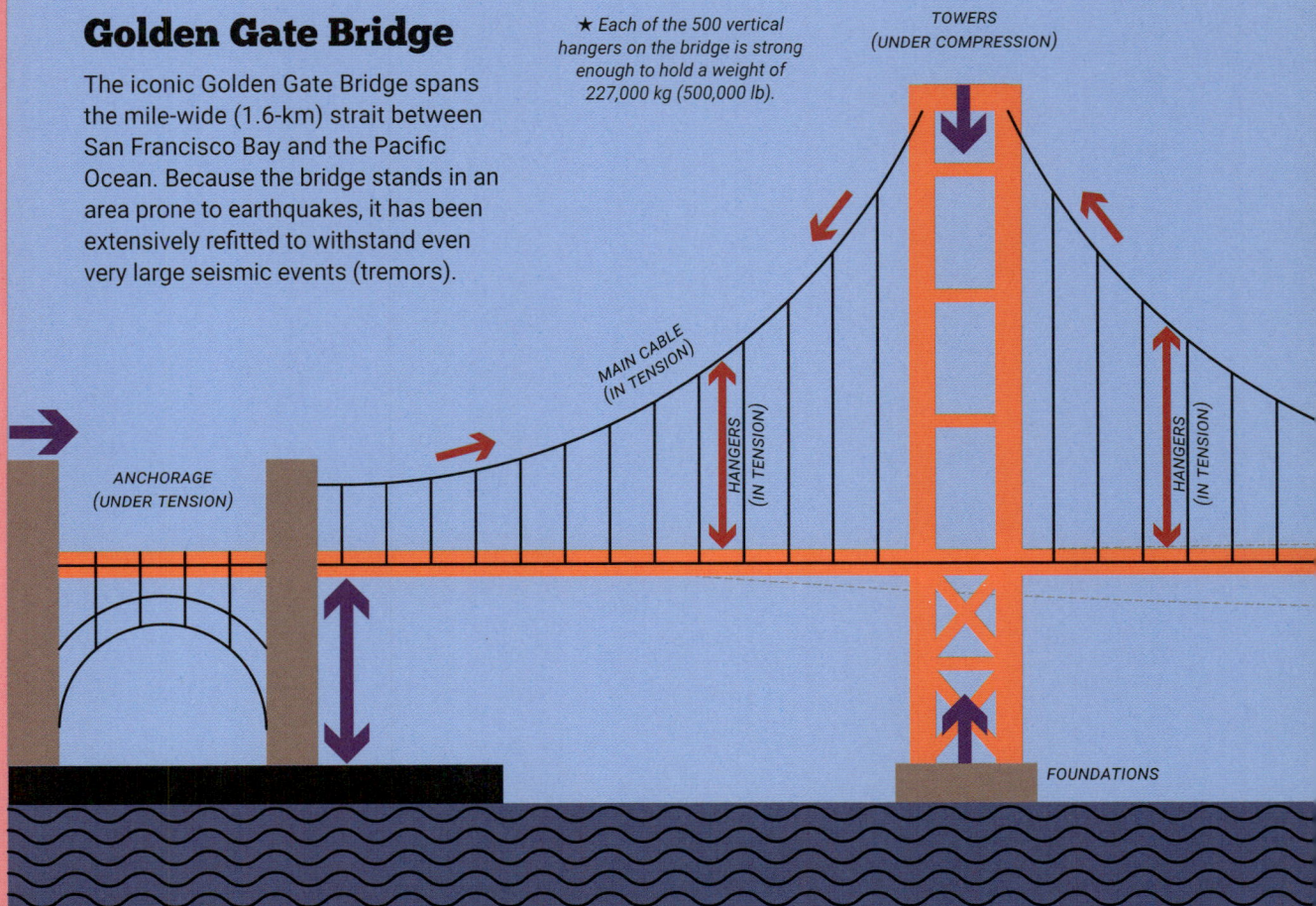

TOWERS (UNDER COMPRESSION)

MAIN CABLE (IN TENSION)

HANGERS (IN TENSION)

HANGERS (IN TENSION)

ANCHORAGE (UNDER TENSION)

FOUNDATIONS

BRIDGES

Bridges connect two places by soaring over an obstacle, allowing safe passage where none existed before. They often become iconic symbols of towns and cities, and landmarks that are a source of civic identity and pride.

Drawbridges

The Tower Bridge across the River Thames in London is a mixed suspension and bascule bridge. Bascule bridges, also known as drawbridges, have a section that can be raised or lowered to let boats and other river traffic through. Opened in 1894, the Tower Bridge has become a symbol of London.

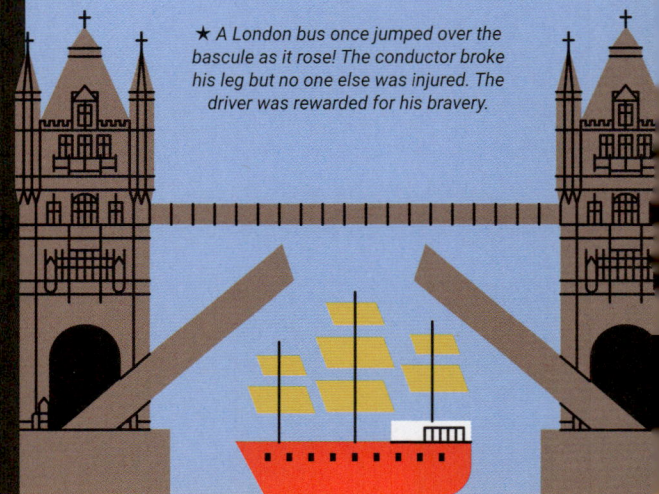

★ A London bus once jumped over the bascule as it rose! The conductor broke his leg but no one else was injured. The driver was rewarded for his bravery.

The highest bridge in Europe

The Millau Viaduct in southern France is a fine example of a cable-stayed bridge. Designed by French engineer Michel Virlogeux and British architect Norman Foster, it combines superb engineering with extraordinary elegance.

"Impossible to build"

The Millau Viaduct is a motorway bridge over the Tarn Valley. It is regarded as an outstanding engineering achievement. When the project began, some said it would be impossible to build. Made of concrete and steel, the viaduct has won many awards for structural engineering.

★ The viaduct has seven concrete piers supporting a superstructure of 16 steel roadway sections. It has six carriageways all held in place with 154 steel cable stays.

★ The tallest pylon of the Millau Viaduct is higher than the Eiffel Tower.

Longest span

Suspension bridges are measured by the length of the longest span. The Golden Gate was the longest in the world when it was built in 1937, but it is now ranked 18th. The Akashi Kaikyō Bridge in Japan now has the longest span: 1,991 metres (6,532.2 ft).

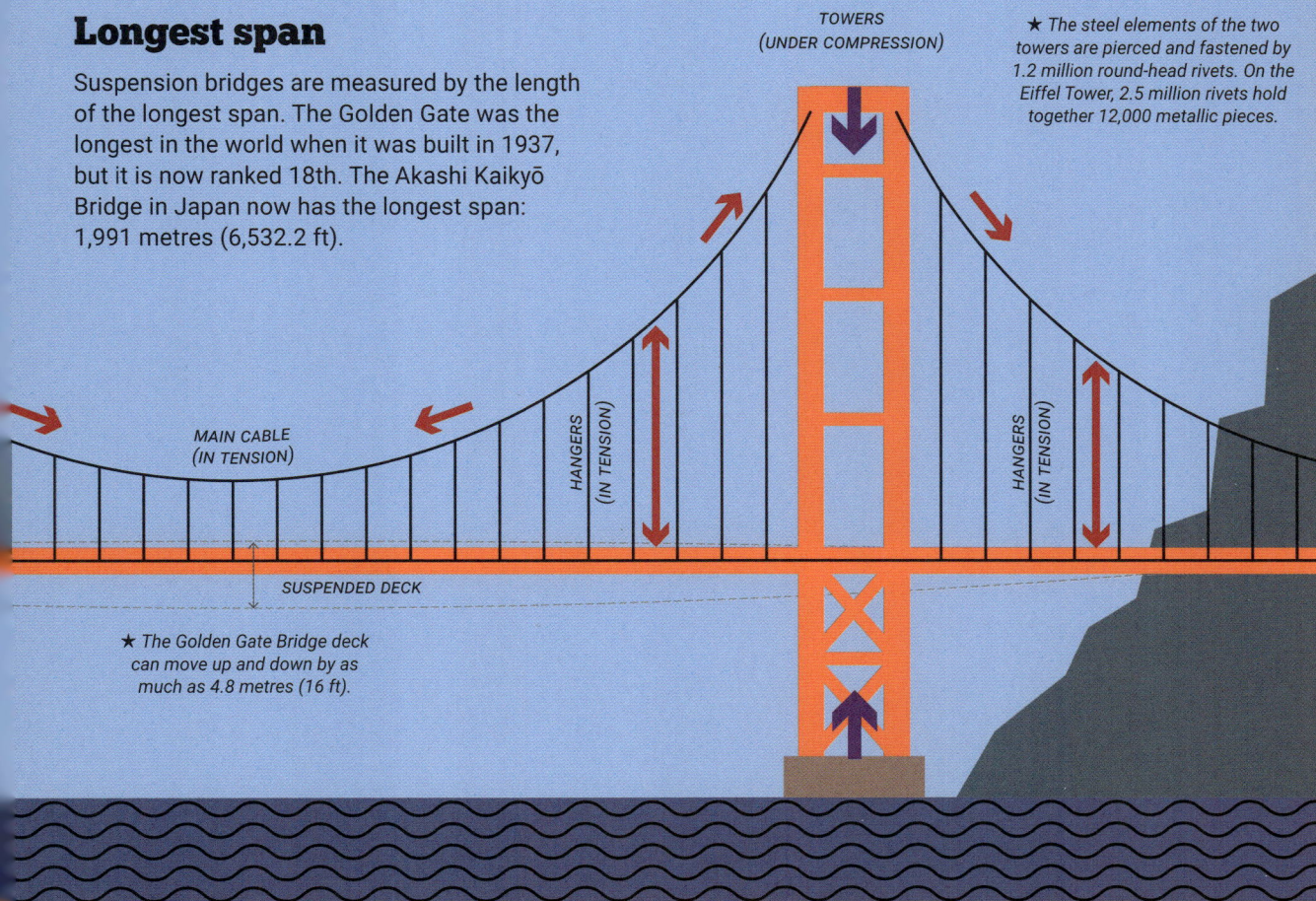

TOWERS
(UNDER COMPRESSION)

★ The steel elements of the two towers are pierced and fastened by 1.2 million round-head rivets. On the Eiffel Tower, 2.5 million rivets hold together 12,000 metallic pieces.

MAIN CABLE
(IN TENSION)

HANGERS
(IN TENSION)

HANGERS
(IN TENSION)

SUSPENDED DECK

★ The Golden Gate Bridge deck can move up and down by as much as 4.8 metres (16 ft).

The Golden Gate in numbers

Name	Golden Gate Bridge
Date of inauguration	May 27, 1937
Bridge length	2,737 m (1.7 miles)
Bridge width	27.4 m (90 ft)
Traffic lanes	6 + 2 sidewalks
Daily traffic	110,000 vehicles
Tower height above water	227.4 m (746 ft)
Main cable diameter	0.92 m (36 in)
Main cable length	2,332 m (7,650 ft)
Number of hangers	500
Diameter of hangers	5 cm (2 in)

▶ Suspension bridges are designed to move more than other bridges. But when 300,000 walkers started crossing the Golden Gate Bridge to celebrate its 50th anniversary, the steel cables stretched, pulling the towers inwards and lowering the deck by around two metres (7 ft). IThe bridge was quickly evacuated.

Forth Bridge

This cantilever railway bridge across the Firth of Forth is a symbol of Scotland. Built in 1890, it was the first major structure in Britain to be made of steel.

Sydney Harbour Bridge

Known as the "coat hanger" by locals, the Sydney Harbour Bridge is a world-famous symbol of this vibrant Australian city. It opened in 1932 and is the tallest steel arch bridge in the world. The bridge carries two railway lines, an eight-lane highway, a cycleway and a pedestrian walkway.

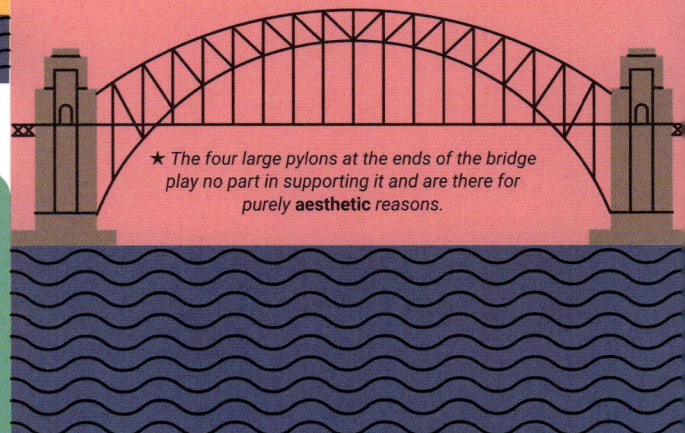

★ The four large pylons at the ends of the bridge play no part in supporting it and are there for purely **aesthetic** reasons.

Haoshang Bridge

The Haoshang Bridge in Leshan, China, is a moon bridge, which is a highly rounded arch bridge for pedestrians. Built in an antique style, it has three elegant arches and perfect, harmonious symmetry.

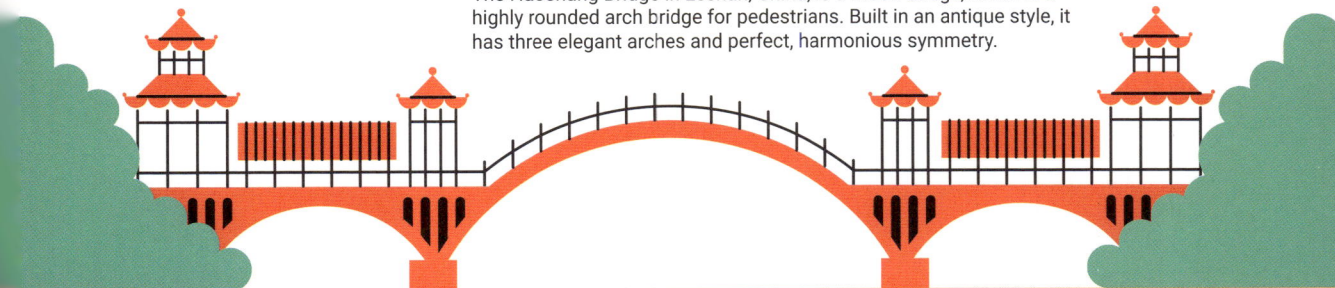

Crazy bridges

Whether out of necessity or insanely creative design, some bridges are breathtaking or just plain crazy!

Lucky Knot Bridge

This bright red truss bridge spans the Dragon King Harbour River in Changsha, China. Design teams in Amsterdam and Beijing worked together to create the rolling pedestrian bridge that symbolises luck and prosperity.

The steepest bridge in the world

Known as the scariest bridge in Japan, the Eshima Ohashi Bridge looks more like a rollercoaster than a road! It is 1.7 km (1.1 miles) long and has a gradient of 5.1% on one side and 6.1% on the other, making it the steepest bridge in the world.

▶ The bridge is tall enough for ships to pass underneath.

Chunhua footbridge

Chunhua means "spring flower" in Chinese and that is exactly what this footbridge looks like. The footbridge is positioned over a busy intersection of large roads in Shenzhen city, allowing people to cross.

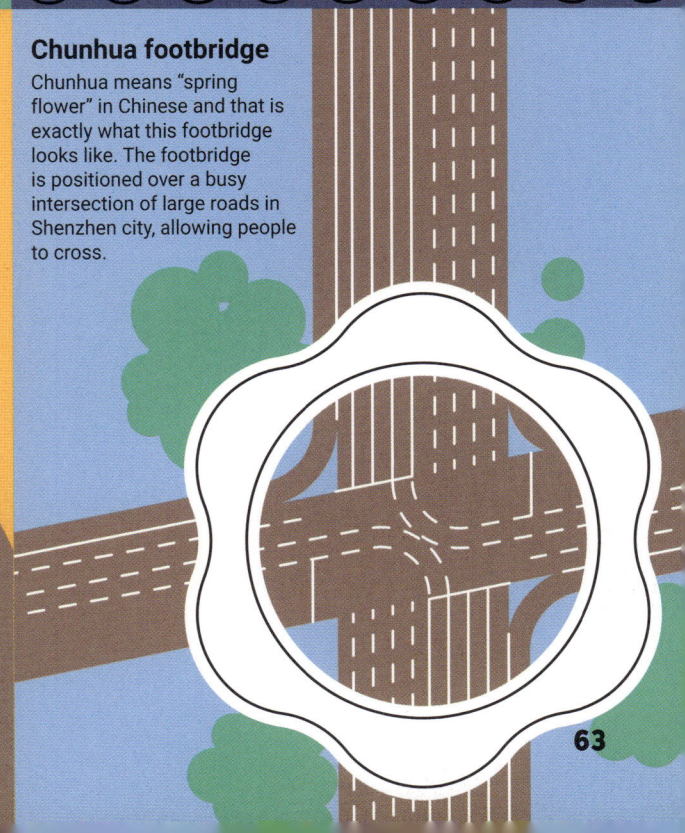

DRILL HOLES AND TUNNELS

Engineers drill holes deep into the Earth to access resources like oil, gas and water. Holes are also drilled for research, for example to find out about climate history by extracting ice cores. We bore tunnels in the Earth's surface to carry passengers, or water or sewage from one place to another.

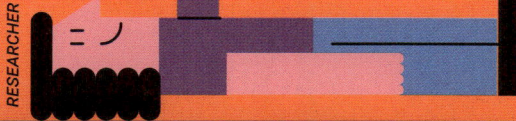

Drilling for oil

Geologists use satellite images and other technology to look for possible oil-bearing sites. When a site has been chosen, they prepare it for the rig. Often, the rig is usually replaced by a permanent platform.

▸ Drill ships are modified to operate in deep water.

Offshore oil rigs

Oil deposits are also found under the seabed and special mobile rigs are used to drill for it. There are several different types. Once oil has been found, the rig is usually replaced by a permanent platform.

▸ Oil spills are disastrous for the natural environment, but properly managed rigs can also bring benefits. Several retired oil rigs have been kept in place and have become the central hubs of unique habitats.

Ice core drill holes

Scientists drill into ice sheets and glaciers and pull out long cylinders of ice. The layers of ice correspond to years and seasons, with the youngest ice at the top. By studying them, researchers can see how climate has changed and predict what might happen in the future.

★ In 2021 researchers in Antarctica extracted ice cores dating back two million years. These are the oldest ice cores ever found.

ICE CORE

RESEARCHER

▸ Drilling barges are used in calm, shallow seas.

▸ Jack ups have legs that can be extended to the seafloor to keep the rig stable.

▸ Semi-submersibles float in the sea on top of submerged pontoons. These are often converted into production rigs.

PONTOON

★ About 30% of oil is extracted offshore and 70% on land.

Onshore oil rigs

Rigs on land need water so the crew has to install a well. First they need to dig a pit to dispose of rock cuttings. Then they begin digging the well itself, often before the rig arrives.

The rig consists of a drill supported by a structure called a derrick. As the drill bores down into the ground, a mixture of mud and water is poured into the hole. Once the drill reaches the oil, the drill and the derrick are set aside and replaced by a pump.

DERRICK

TRAVELLING BLOCK

SWIVEL

STANDPIPE

CROWN BLOCK

KELLY

BLOW OUT PREVENTOR

MUD PIT

MUD PUMP

DRAW WORKS

ENGINES

Barely scratching the surface

Here you can see the structure of the Earth. All of our drilling activities take place in the shallow crust which is just 5-70 km (3-44 miles) thick.

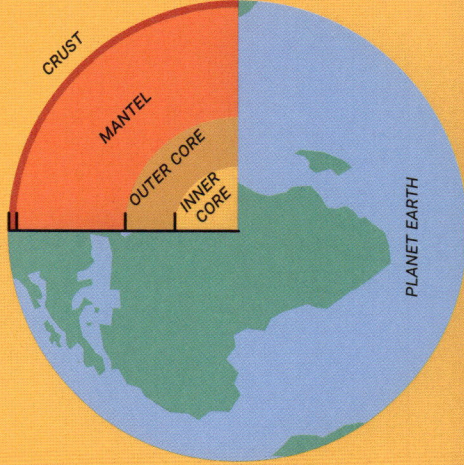

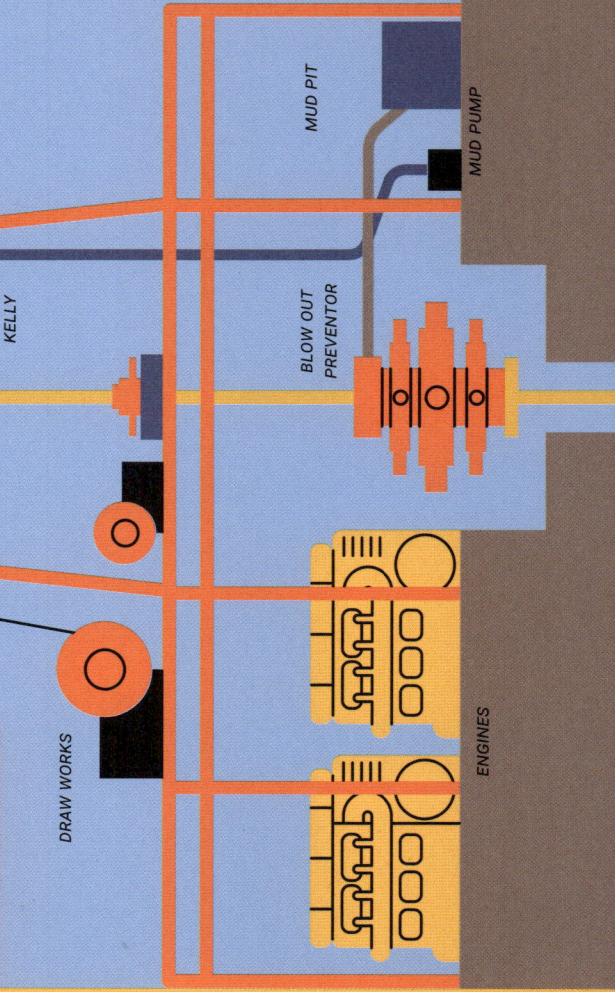

CRUST

MANTEL

OUTER CORE

INNER CORE

PLANET EARTH

Digging into the crust

The Kola Superdeep Borehole is deepest hole humans have dug. The Russian scientists in charge of the project wanted to learn more about our planet's outermost layer, how it was formed and how it evolved

▸ Mount Everest is the tallest mountain and the Mariana Trench in the Pacific Ocean is the deepest place on Earth.

SEA LEVEL

MOUNT EVEREST
8,848.86 METRES (29,031.7 FT)

DEEPEST ACTIVE MINE

MARIANA TRENCH
(ALMOST 11 KM / 7 MI DEEP)

KOLA SUPERDEEP BOREHOLE
(12.3 KM / 7.64 MI DEEP)

Tunnels

People have been building tunnels since Babylonian times over 4,000 years ago. Tunnels can be used for mining, transportation (trains and cars) and as canals for water or sewage.

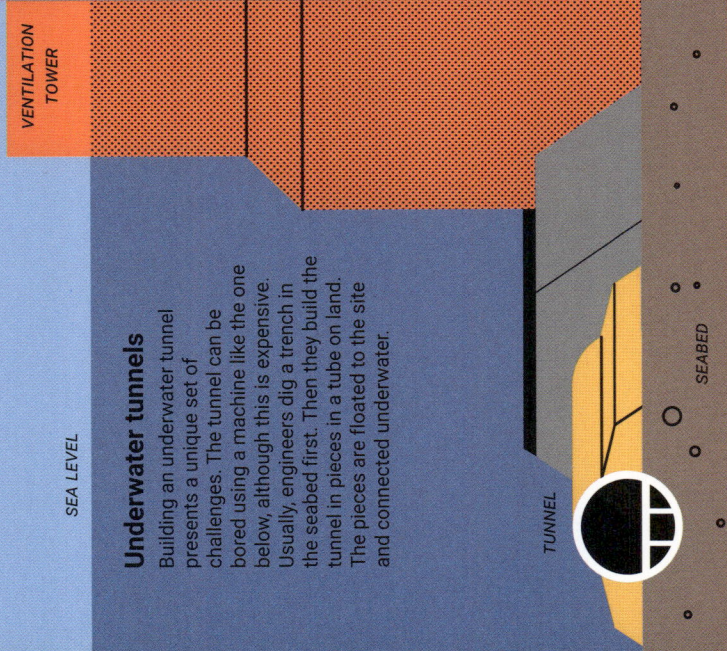

Underwater tunnels

Building an underwater tunnel presents a unique set of challenges. The tunnel can be bored using a machine like the one below, although this is expensive. Usually, engineers dig a trench in the seabed first. Then they build the tunnel in pieces in a tube on land. The pieces are floated to the site and connected underwater.

VENTILATION TOWER

SEA LEVEL

SEABED

TUNNEL

Cut-and-cover tunnel

This is one of the oldest and simplest ways to dig a tunnel. It is most often used for shallow tunnels. It can be quite disruptive as the tunnel is built, when the soil is being excavated and set aside. But once the tunnel is complete, the soil can be returned and beautified with trees, parks and playgrounds.

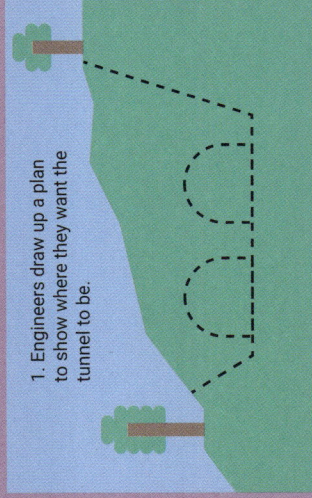

1. Engineers draw up a plan to show where they want the tunnel to be.

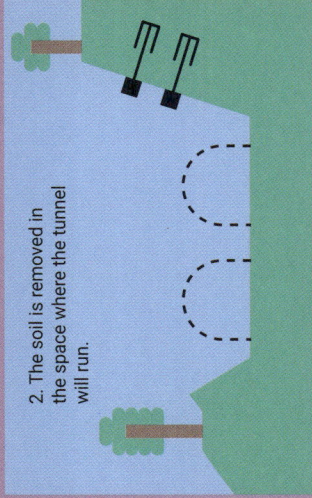

2. The soil is removed in the space where the tunnel will run.

3. The structure of the tunnel is built.

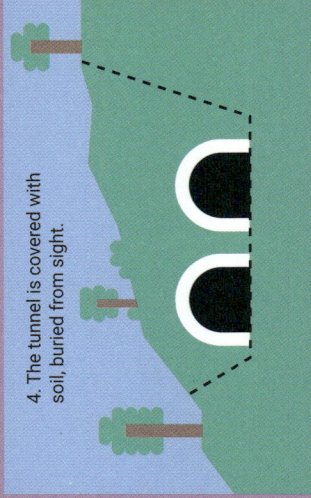

4. The tunnel is covered with soil, buried from sight.

▶ The blow out preventor is a kind of safety valve in the drill that prevents out of control gushes of gas or oil.

DRILL PIPE

CASING

DRILL BIT

ENLARGEMENT OF THE DRILL BIT

▶ The drill bit fits on the bottom of the drill. This is the piece that actually cuts into the ground, so it is very sturdy.

Boring machines

Tunnel boring machines (TBMs) are used to excavate long tunnels through different kinds of soil and rock. They are best suited to building long, round tunnels, for example for underground trains.

How they work

TBMs have a rotating, cutting head at the front which breaks up soil and rock. The waste material is transferred using a screw conveyer to a another conveyor belt system in the shield. It is eliminated from the back of the TBM. Meanwhile, hydraulic cylinders drive the machine constantly forwards.

▶ TBMs are ideal for building subways in cities where above-ground excavation would cause a lot of damage and disturbance to the surroundings.

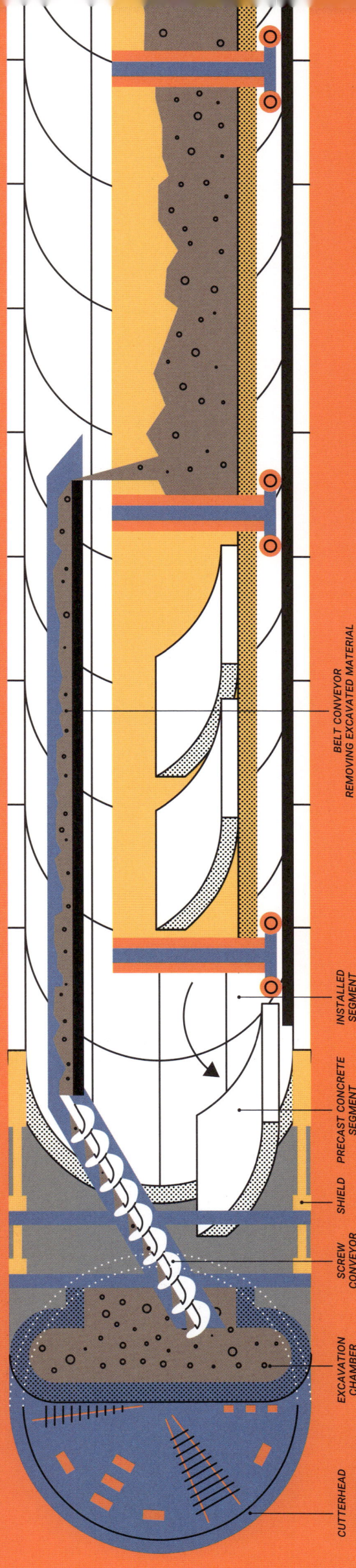

★ Tunnel boring machines are also known as "moles".

Expensive

TBMs are expensive to make and difficult to transport because they are so large and heavy. However, for long tunnels they are more efficient and lead to shorter completion times.

★ At 24.5 km (15.23 miles) long, the Lærdal Tunnel in Norway is the longest road tunnel in the world. At 57 km (35.4 miles), the Gotthard Base Tunnel in Switzerland is the longest tunnel in the world. It is used only by trains.

★ The Channel Tunnel between France and the United Kingdom is the longest undersea tunnel in the world. The submerged part is 37.9 km (23.5 miles) long. It was built using a TBM.

BELT CONVEYOR

REMOVING EXCAVATED MATERIAL

INSTALLED SEGMENT

PRECAST CONCRETE SEGMENT

SHIELD

SCREW CONVEYOR

EXCAVATION CHAMBER

CUTTERHEAD

Biotechnology deals with living things, and includes all the technologies used in the medical world. Medical technology is evolving at incredible speed with a huge range of new treatments and procedures becoming available, including immunotherapy, robotic surgery and personalised medicine.

BIO
& MEDICAL

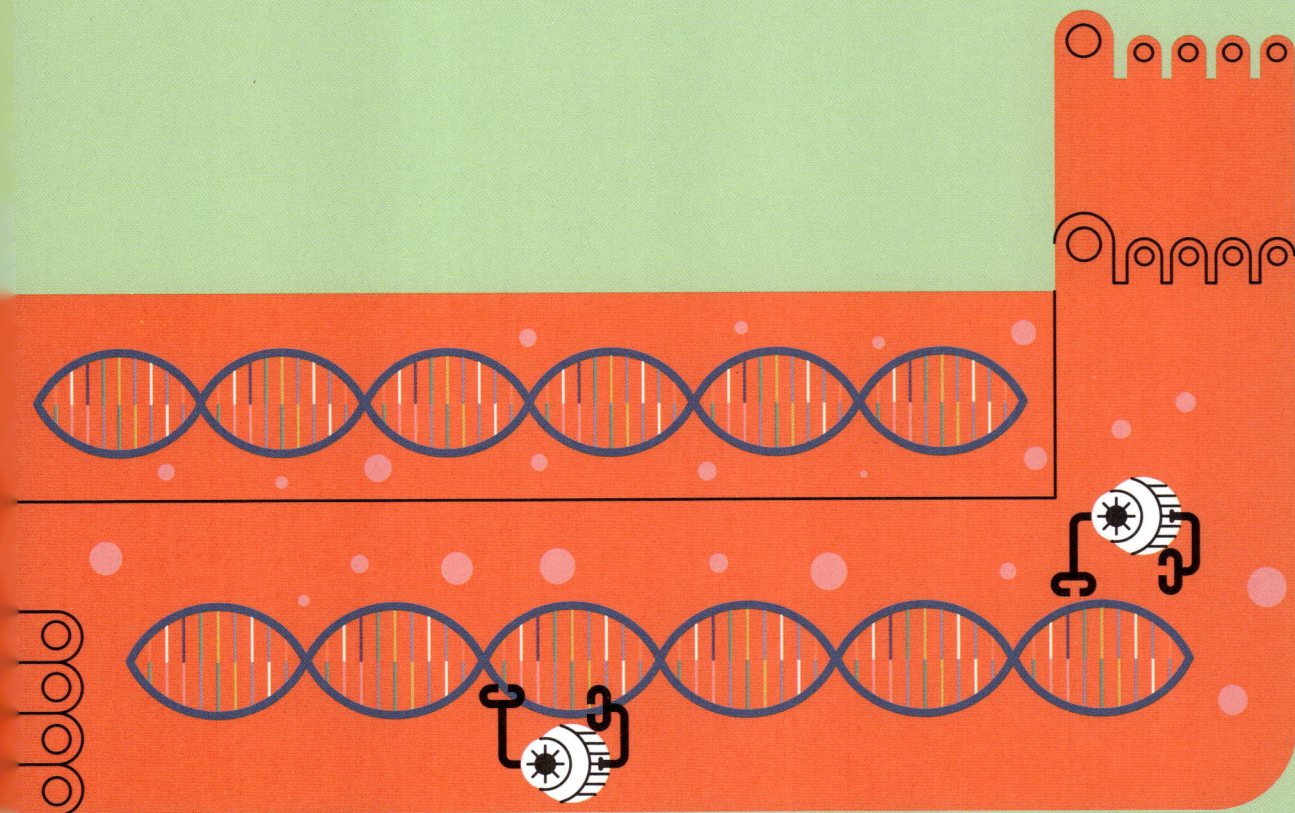

VACCINATION

Vaccines are a safe and effective way to prevent illness and save lives. The WHO (World Health Organisation) estimates that vaccination saves between 3.5 and 5 million lives every year. Like eating healthy food, exercising and getting regular medical check-ups, vaccines are a key way to stay healthy.

Immune systems

Our immune system protects us from diseases caused by pathogens (invaders or germs) such as bacteria and viruses. It learns to recognise invaders and remembers how to kill them if they come back, making us immune to future infection.

▶ An immune cell called a macrophage engulfs bacteria, destroying them.

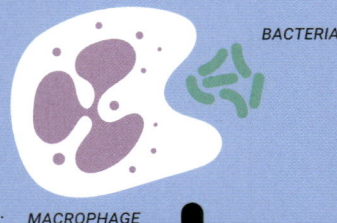

MACROPHAGE

BACTERIA

B cells and T cells

These white blood cells are part of the immune system. B cells produce antibodies that stop invaders before they enter healthy cells. T cells destroy cells that have been infected by them.

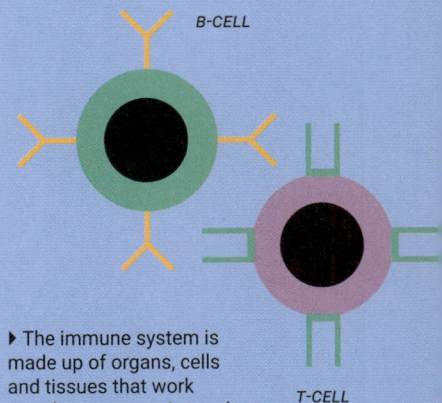

B-CELL

T-CELL

▶ The immune system is made up of organs, cells and tissues that work together to recognise and destroy pathogens.

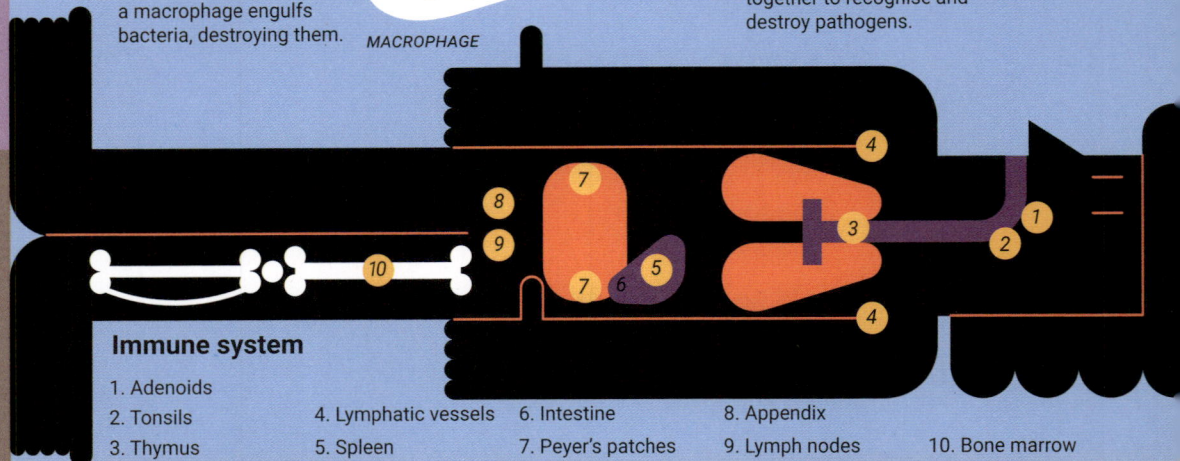

Immune system

1. Adenoids
2. Tonsils
3. Thymus
4. Lymphatic vessels
5. Spleen
6. Intestine
7. Peyer's patches
8. Appendix
9. Lymph nodes
10. Bone marrow

Variolation

Variolation was a forerunner of vaccination. Long before vaccines were used in Europe, people in Africa, India and China discovered that they could prevent a terrible disease called smallpox by exposing healthy patients to a small dose. They scraped scabs or pus off a sick person's skin and spread it on a healthy person to build immunity.

▶ Lady Montagu Wortley learned about variolation while living in Constantinople in the 18th century. She introduced it into the United Kingdom.

LADY MONTAGU WORTLEY

▶ In China, doctors ground scabs from a smallpox sufferer's skin into a powder and blew it up peoples' noses.

UP THE NOSE IT GOES!

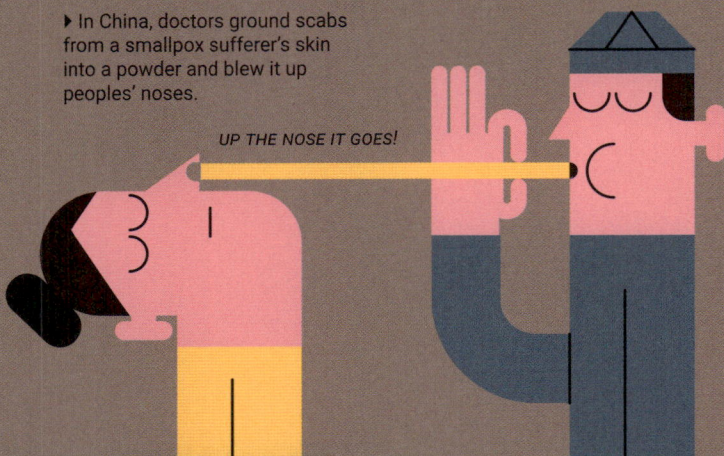

Vaccines and cancer

There are vaccines that prevent some types of cancer. They target two viruses: the hepatitis B virus, which can cause liver cancer, and human papillomavirus (HPV), which causes cervical and some other cancers.

▶ There are also vaccines that treat people who already have cancer. These treatments are called immunotherapy. The vaccines work to boost the patient's immune system to fight their cancer. The technology is new and so far only a few cancers are treated this way but in the future it will revolutionise cancer treatment.

Help save more lives

Every year about 1.5 million children die unnecessarily because they were not vaccinated. Supporting vaccination saves lives!

Don't stop vaccination

Some infectious diseases, like polio, have been almost wiped out by widespread vaccination. If people stop vaccinating in large numbers many deadly diseases will return.

The first vaccine

English scientist Dr Edward Jenner gave the first vaccine against smallpox to 8-year-old James Phipps in 1796. He injected the boy with a dose of a similar but much milder virus called cowpox. After a couple of months he gave James a dose of smallpox to see if he was immune. Luckily he was!

DR JENNER

JAMES PHIPPS

How vaccines work

Vaccines deliver a small, harmless amount of a pathogen. Our immune system immediately steps in to neutralise it. At the same time it forms a memory of the invader. If we come into contact with the same pathogen again in the future, our immune system can recognise and destroy it before we get ill.

▶ The body reacts by stimulating cells in the immune system to create antibodies. The antibodies remember the germ and are ready to defend us against it in the future.

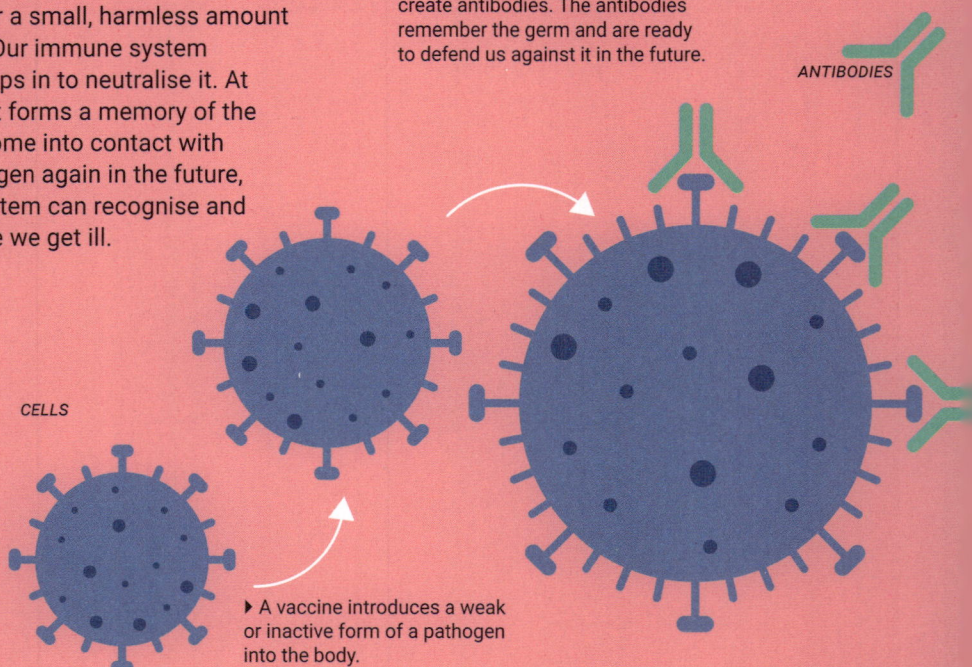

ANTIBODIES

CELLS

▶ A vaccine introduces a weak or inactive form of a pathogen into the body.

Types of vaccines

Vaccines can work in several different ways. Here you can see four different types of vaccine used against COVID-19.

Whole virus
A weakened or inactive form of the entire Covid-19 vaccine is put into the body so your immune system can learn to recognise it.

VACCINE EXAMPLE: SINOVAC

mRNA
Contains instructions that prompt your body to make a protein spike that looks like Covid-19 so your immune system can learn to recognise it.

VACCINE EXAMPLES: MODERNA, PFIZER

Viral vector
An inactive virus delivers instructions for your body to create a part of the Covid-19 virus so your immune system can learn to recognise it.

VACCINE EXAMPLES: ASTRA-ZENECA, JCOVDEN

Protein
Uses pieces of the Covid-19 virus, sometimes from the protein "spike," so your immune system can learn to recognise it.

VACCINE EXAMPLE: NOVAVAX

Childhood vaccinations
Most countries recommend a schedule of vaccines for young children. These protect against common diseases like polio, tetanus, diptheria, measles and whooping cough.

Pet vaccinations
Pets like dogs and cats also receive vaccinations against common diseases, including distemper and rabies. The type of vaccine given varies from country to country, depending on what diseases are common.

▶ When Covid-19 was first identified in December 2019 there were no vaccines and no one had any immunity. Many people died in the first few months. But Covid vaccines were developed very quickly and by October 2021 more than seven billion doses had been given globally.

★ Normally a vaccine will take 10 to 15 years to develop.

Reject vaccine lies
A minority of people oppose vaccination. They are afraid they will make them sick or give them another illness. For example, some believe that the MMR vaccine (against measles, mumps and rubella) causes autism in children. This is false. The MMR vaccine is given at 12–15 months but autism begins even before a child is born. Symptoms don't appear until about 18–24 months (soon after children receive their MMR vaccine) which causes some people to (wrongly) believe that autism is caused by the vaccine.

VACCINE

★ Last century, more than 300 million people died of smallpox. Three out of ten people who caught it died and many more were left blind or disfigured. Thanks to a huge vaccination programme, smallpox has been eliminated. The last case was recorded in 1977.

★ Unlike other drugs which are given to a few people who are sick, vaccines are usually given to very large numbers of people who are well. This is why they have to be tested so extensively.

Herd immunity

To be successful, vaccination rates need to be high across the population. Herd immunity occurs when almost everyone is vaccinated. When almost everyone is immune, then infection rates stay very low.

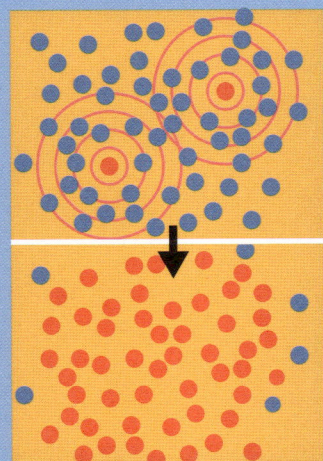

● Not vaccinated but healthy
● Sick and contagious
● Vaccinated and healthy

No one is vaccinated
Contagious disease spreads easily and many people get sick.

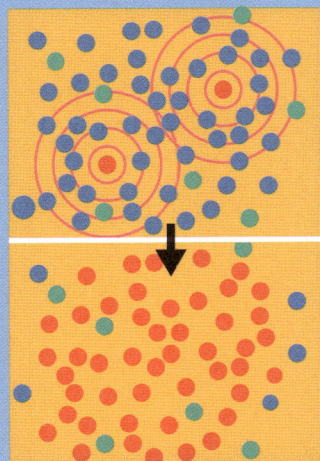

Some people are vaccinated
Contagious disease spreads less easily but quite a few people still get sick.

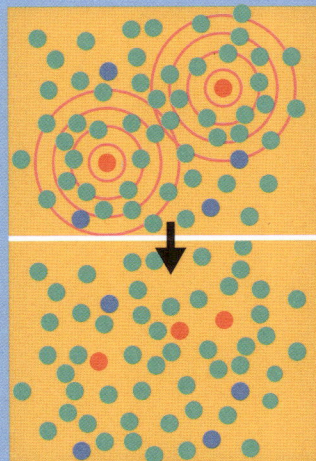

Almost everyone is vaccinated
Contagious disease cannot spread easily and hardly anyone is sick.

How vaccines are developed

It usually takes many years to develop a vaccine. Scientists begin with research to find a vaccine idea that might work. This is tested for safety in laboratories, often using animals. The next stage includes manufacturing small quantities of the vaccine and testing it on a few healthy people. If it is successful, more and more people are tested. These trials can takes years. When everyone is completely sure that the new vaccine is safe and effective, mass production and vaccination can begin.

RESEARCH & DISCOVERY

SAFETY STUDIES

SMALL SCALE DEVELOPMENT

TRIALS ON SMALL NUMBER OF PEOPLE

TRIALS ON THOUSANDS OF PEOPLE

EVALUATION, APPROVAL & MANUFACTURING

ROLL OUT: VACCINE GIVEN TO LARGE NUMBERS OF PEOPLE

SURGERY

Advances in medical technology have the potential to transform health care, ensuring that illnesses are diagnosed and treated earlier in hospitals where highly-trained staff can rely on high-tech tools that allow them to do their jobs efficiently. The most exciting and sophisticated advances are happening in operating theatres, with robotic surgery, 3D printing and stem cell treatments in the forefront.

Origins of surgery

Records show that people have been using surgy to treat injuries, drain and cauterise wounds and sew up cuts for thousands of years. Prehistoric people used splints to heal broken bones.

TREPANATION

▶ The oldest surgical operation we know about is called trepanation. It involved making a hole in the skull to relieve pressure and treat disease in the brain, and dates back at least 8,500 years.

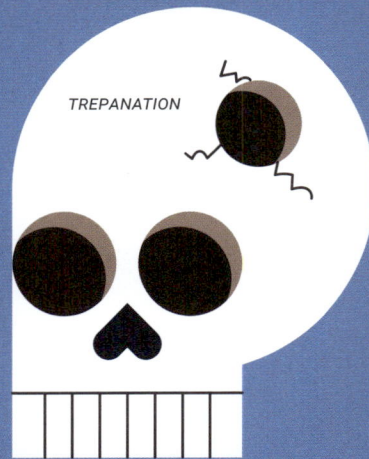

Anaesthesia

Surgery was not very popular until anaesthesia became widespread in the mid 19th century. Before then, either no pain relief was offered or people took large doses of alcohol or opium.

▶ Ether, chloroform and nitrous oxide (laughing gas) were the first types of anaesthetics to be used in surgery. They were all given to patients in the form of gases, to be inhaled.

PATIENT INHALES ANAESTHETIC

★ A Japanese surgeon — Dr Hanaoka Seishū — began carrying out operations using general anaesthesia in 1804, almost 50 years ahead of surgeons in Europe and America.

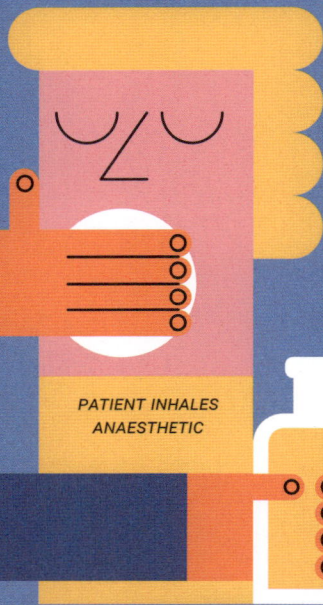

Germ theory

In the mid 19th century the French chemist and microbiologist Louis Pasteur showed that tiny organisms, or "germs" in the air caused disease. They also caused infections in patients during surgery, and up to 40% of them died in the days and weeks following their operations.

▶ An English surgeon called Joseph Lister began using carbolic acid in hospitals as an antiseptic to prevent infection by germs. He applied carbolic acid to dressings, surgical equipment and wounds, and even sprayed it into the air in operating theatres. The death rate from post-operative infections dropped to 15% overnight.

CARBOLIC ACID SPRAYER

★ Robotic surgery is less invasive than many traditional techniques. It also allows surgeons to reach previously inaccessible areas of the body.

The surgeon

Surgeons are seated at a console and have a high-definition, magnified, 3D view of the surgical site. They control the robotic arms in real time using joystick pads in both hands.

Robotic surgery

The use of robotic surgery, also known as robot-assisted surgery, is increasing rapidly in hospitals around the world. It allows doctors to perform many types of complex operations with greater precision and control than is possible with traditional techniques. In robotic surgery, surgeons are still present and in control even though they are usually seated at a console at some distance from the patient. The operations are carried out by high-precision robotic arms, guided by the surgeon from the console.

★ Patients recover more quickly after robotic surgery so they can go home sooner (freeing up hospital beds for other patients).

Simulation surgery

New technologies using VR and AR allow novice surgeons to learn and practice surgical procedures before they operate on real patients. Surgery simulators can combine imaging from MRIs, CT scans and other diagnostic tools to create 3D models that replicate real life situations. Experienced surgeons can also use simulators to plan complex surgeries.

Keyhole surgery

In keyhole surgery, doctors make a tiny cut in the skin just large enough to insert an instrument called a laparoscope. It has a light and a camera on the end and allows doctors to see inside the patient's body. They make one or two other small incisions to insert instruments to carry out the surgery.

▶ Keyhole surgery has many advantages over traditional methods. Patients bleed less, have smaller scars and fewer infections, and can go home sooner.

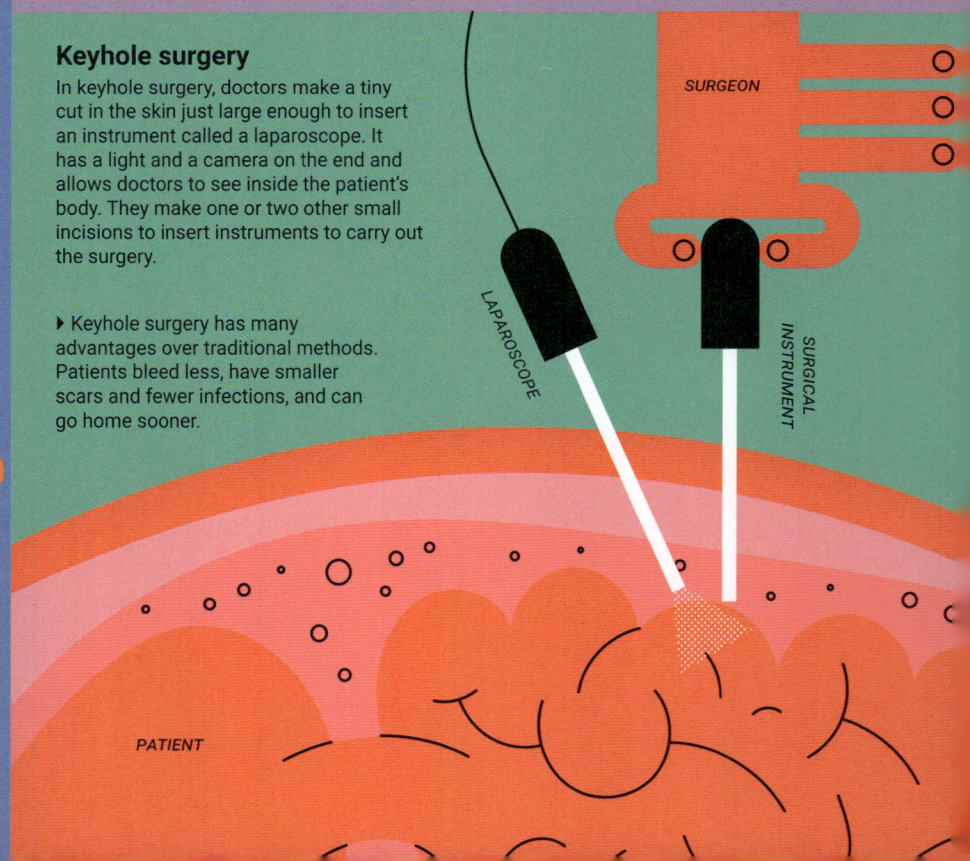

SURGEON

LAPAROSCOPE

SURGICAL INSTRUMENT

PATIENT

SURGICAL ROBOT

5G

▶ Reliable, high-speed communications technology is essential for remote surgery. 5G wireless internet will play a key role in allowing telesurgery to spread around the world.

Remote surgery

Robotic surgery opens up exciting horizons, including the possibility of highly-skilled surgeons operating on patients who are far away. Remote surgery, also known as telesurgery, combines robotics with advanced communications technology. It allows specialist surgeons to treat patients in remote locations or places where doctors with their special skills are not readily available.

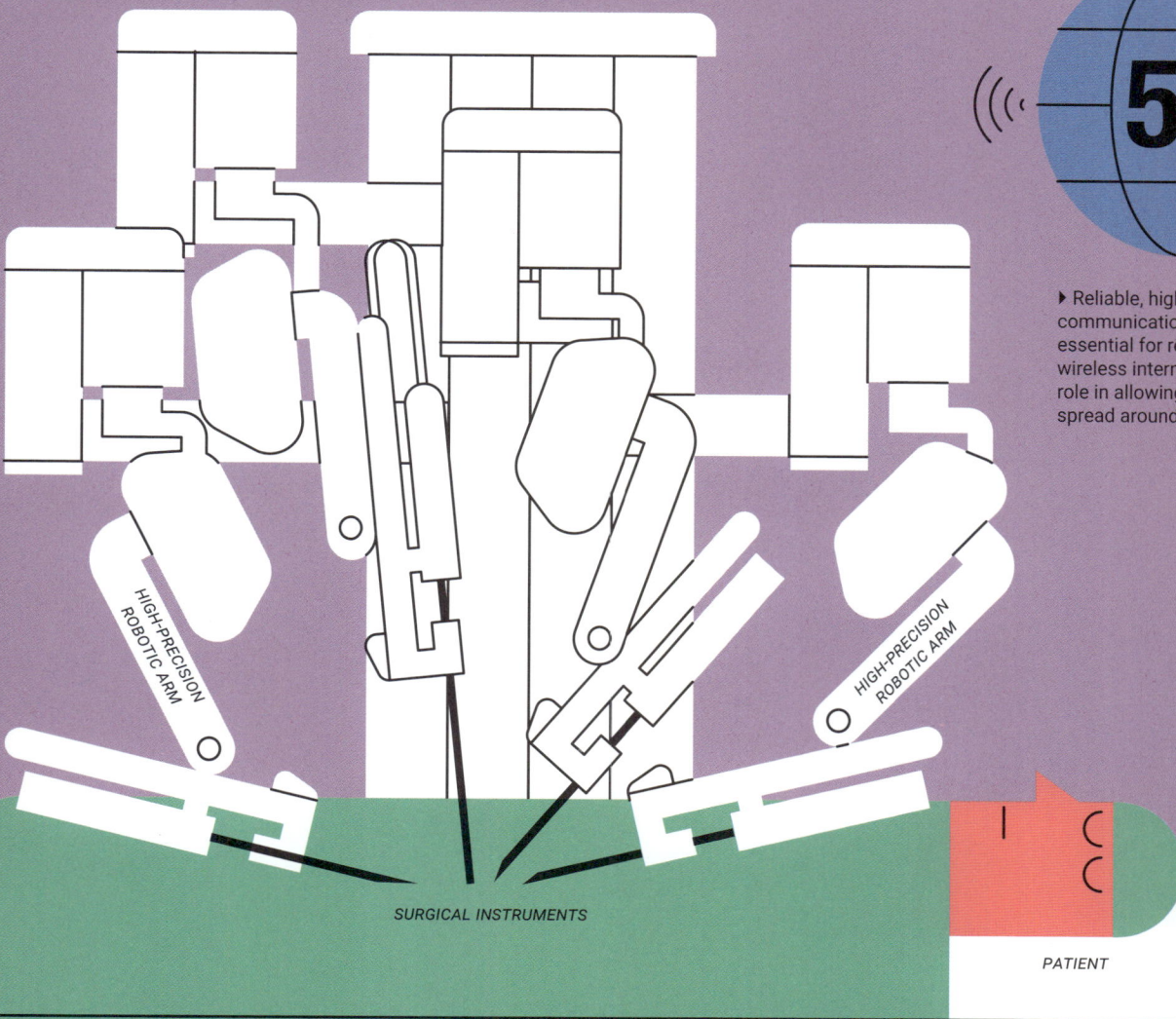

HIGH-PRECISION ROBOTIC ARM

HIGH-PRECISION ROBOTIC ARM

SURGICAL INSTRUMENTS

PATIENT

The robot

The camera in the surgical robot produces a clear 3D image and has the same 360-degree agility as the surgeon's wrists.

Medical technologies

AI
Artificial intelligence is employed in many ways, but it is particularly useful in detecting diseases early and making accurate diagnoses more quickly.

3D PRINTING
Printers are used to create implants for hips, knee and spine surgery. In the future, they may be able to print human organs, including the heart and liver, saving the lives of thousands of people who must now wait for transplants from donors.

CRISPR
This is the most advanced gene-editing technology. By modifying our genes, some of the biggest threats to our health, such as cancer, could potentially be overcome in the future.

HEALTH WEARABLES
Today more and more people use wearable devices synced with their phones to track everything from their steps, blood pressure and oxygen saturation, to sleep patterns and heartbeat. These devices help wearers to know when they have a medical problem so they can get treatment as soon as possible.

VR
Is not just for gaming or accessing the metaverse. It it increasingly used to manage and treat a range of psychological illnesses and conditions, including stress, anxiety, dementia and autism.

Laser surgery

In this type of surgery special beams of light are used instead of surgical instruments. There are many different types of lasers and they are used to treat a range of health issues.

LASER BEAM

▶ Laser surgery is commonly used to treat eye problems, to remove warts, wrinkles, scars or tattoos from the skin, to shrink tumours and for dental work.

Endoscopic surgery

Endoscopic surgery is carried out using an endoscope, which is a long flexible tube with a light and a camera on the end. It is passed into the patient's body through a natural opening, such as the mouth or nose. Images created by the camera are shown on a computer screen. The surgeon can see inside the patient's body and can take samples for biopsies, remove growths or carry out surgery if required.

ENDOSCOPE

COMPUTER SCREEN

PATIENT

GENETIC MEDICINE

As scientists learn more about how our genes work they are able to use this knowledge to treat medical problems. This is called genetic medicine. It is a relatively new type of medicine but it is becoming more and more important.

▶ Many illnesses are caused by variations in the genes we inherit from our family. Doctors can now recognise many of these variant genes. This gives them better options to treat illnesses.

★ The double helix structure of DNA was discovered in the 1950s. It was a very important step forward in genetics.

★ All blue-eyed people are the descendants of one person who live between 6,000 and 10,000 years ago.

The human genome

The human genome is the complete set of DNA, or genetic instructions, needed to build a person. It was first mapped in 2003.

What are genes?

Genes are found on the DNA inside your cells. They carry all the information you inherit from your parents and control the way you look and how your body works and even how you think and behave. Your genes are what make you different from everyone else. Follow the grey arrows below to find out where they are located.

1. Inside cells

Your body is made up of billions of cells. Cells are too tiny to see with the naked eye, but they are the building blocks of every form of life.

▶ Each tiny cell nucleus contains about 1.5 gigabytes of information, which is much more than the largest dictionary.

CELLS

NUCLEUS

2. Inside the nucleus

All human cells have a central part called the nucleus. Inside the nucleus there are 23 pairs of chromosomes.

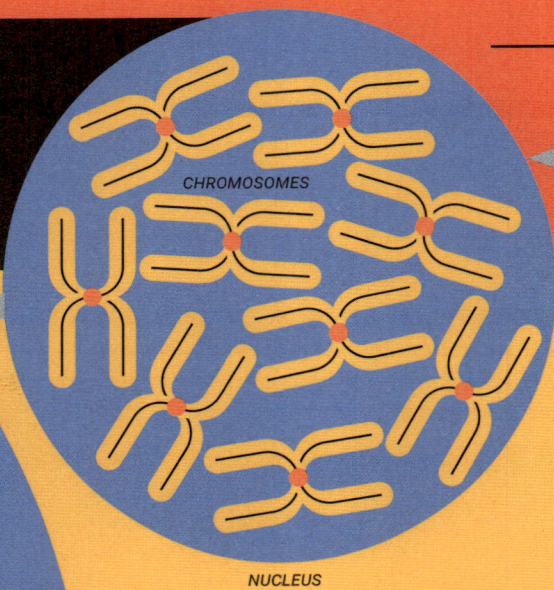

3. Inside chromosomes

Each chromosome contains hundreds to thousands of genes. Chromosomes and genes are made of DNA (deoxyribonucleic acid.)

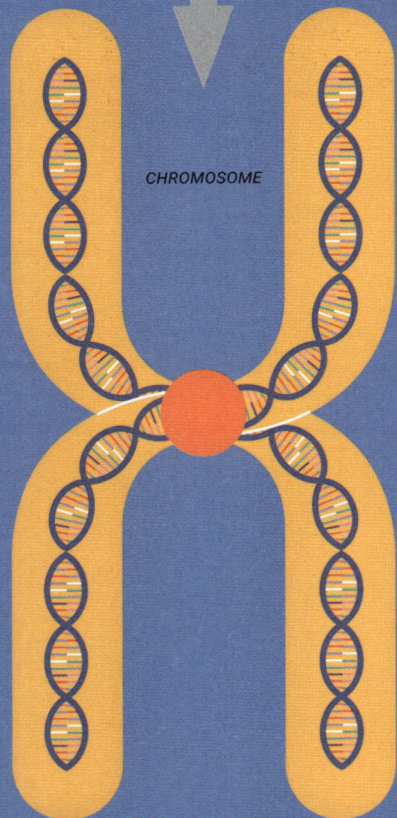

CHROMOSOMES

NUCLEUS

CHROMOSOME

BROWN HAIR IS DOMINANT   BLONDE HAIR IS RECESSIVE

BROWN EYES ARE DOMINANT

BLUE EYES ARE RECESSIVE

Dominant and recessive genes

Some genes are dominant and others are recessive. For example, the genes for brown eyes are dominant over the genes for blue eyes. Children receive a gene for eye colour from each parent. If they get a brown-eyed gene and a blue-eyed gene, they will have brown eyes. They will only have blue eyes if they get a blue-eyed gene from both parents.

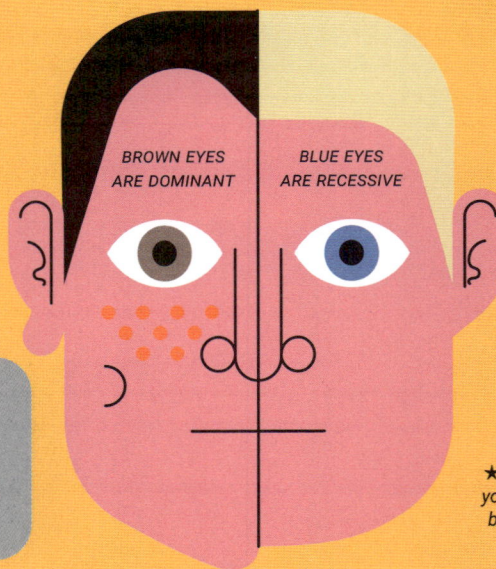

★ If you put all the DNA in all your cells end to end, it would be twice the diameter of the Solar System.

4. Inside DNA

DNA is made up of two chains that coil around each other to form a double helix. DNA holds the instructions for things like eye colour and tallness. Each instruction is carried on a different section of the DNA. These sections are called genes.

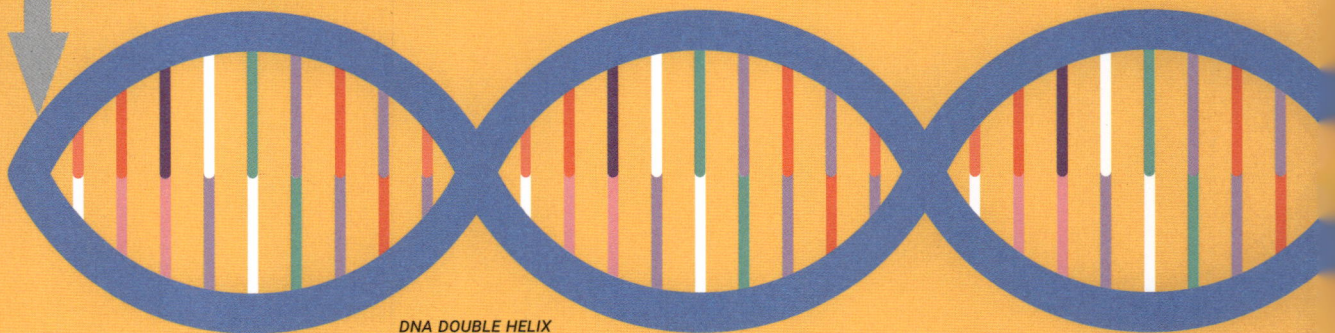

DNA DOUBLE HELIX

Boy or girl?

Of the 23 pairs of chromosomes inside each cell nucleus, 22 are the same in both males and females. The 23rd pair differs. Females have two copies of the X chromosome, while males have one X and one Y chromosome. All babies get an X chromosome from their mothers. They get either an X or a Y chromosome from their fathers.

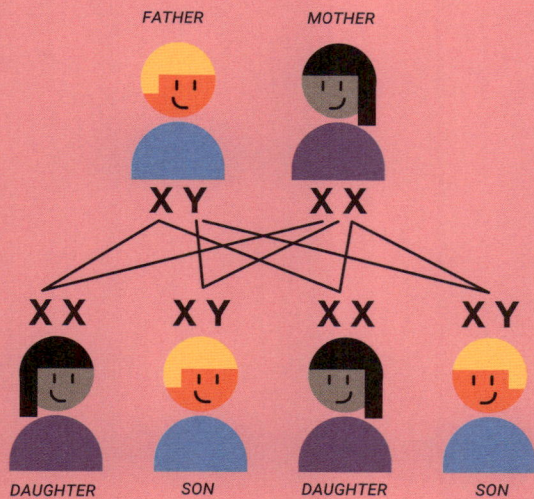

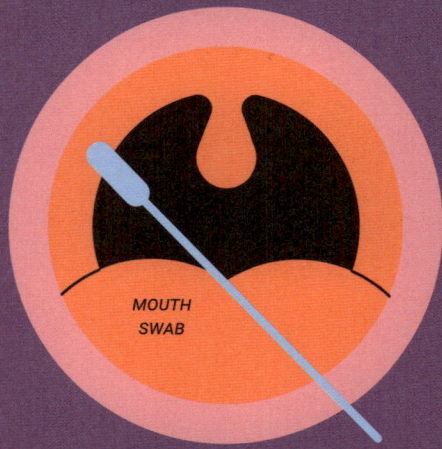

FATHER   MOTHER

X Y   X X

X X   X Y   X X   X Y

DAUGHTER   SON   DAUGHTER   SON

▶ A simple way to gather material for genetic testing involves swabbing the inside of the mouth with a tiny brush.

MOUTH SWAB

Genetic testing

Genetic tests are performed on samples of hair, blood, skin or other tissue. These are sent to a laboratory to be examined. There are many different tests available. In each case, doctors choose the ones that will provide the most useful information.

Personalised care

Our genes affect the way we respond to medicines. A drug that is good for one person can be ineffective, or even harmful, for another person. If doctors map every single patient's genetic makeup, they can use medicines they know will work for them.

★ Personalised medical care is already widely used and has helped many people.

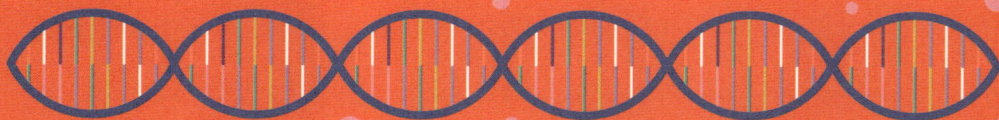

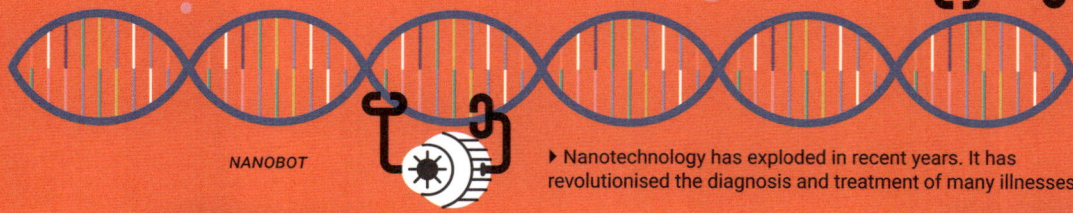

NANOBOT

Nanobots

Nanobots are robots so tiny that they can go inside your body. In medicine they are used to deliver a drug or therapy to a very specific area. Fitted with cameras, they can also show, monitor or even treat disease.

▶ Nanoscience and nanotechnology are the study and use of very small things. A nanometre is one billionth of a metre. A single sheet of paper is about 100,000 nanometres thick.

NANOBOT

▶ Nanotechnology has exploded in recent years. It has revolutionised the diagnosis and treatment of many illnesses.

Gene therapy

Gene therapy is an exciting new branch of medicine and scientists are still studying and doing experiments to see how it works. When they find a gene that is not working properly, they try to replace it with a healthy one. In some cases they have been able to restore sight and cure cancer.

▶ Gene therapy is very expensive. In the future it may become cheaper and more widely used.

Cloning

A clone is an exact genetic copy of another living thing. Scientists make three different types of artificial clones.
1. Clones of genes used for research.
2. Clones of entire animals.
3. Clones of stem cells that can be used to grow healthy tissues to replace diseased cells.

Natural clones

Clones also exist in nature. Some plants and single-celled organisms, like bacteria, produce offspring that are genetically identical to themselves. In humans and other mammals, identical twins are natural clones. They occur when a fertilised egg splits into two (or more) embryos.

★ Cloned dogs and cats don't always have the same temperaments as the pets they were cloned from.

Farm technology in the past

Farming is the oldest industry in the world. Over the centuries there have been many important technological advances.

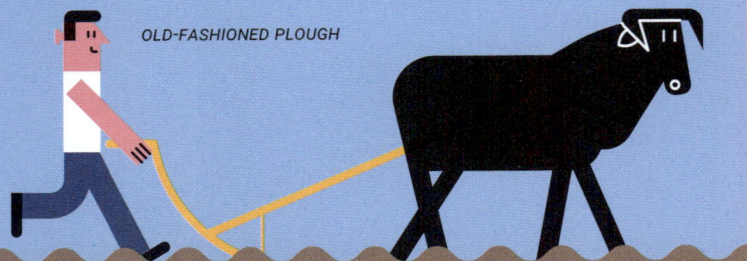

OLD-FASHIONED PLOUGH

The plough

Ploughs are used to open up a furrow in the soil to plant seeds. They were invented in Mesopotamia and China thousands of years ago.

The tractor

Tractors are an essential farm tool. They are used to cultivate land and harvest crops, but also to feed and care for livestock and many other farm jobs.

TRACTOR

Irrigation

Crops need water to grow. There are many ways of irrigating land. Water can be flooded, dripped, sprinkled or sprayed onto the fields.

WHEELED SPRINKLER IRRIGATOR

★ Worldwide, only about 20% of farmland is irrigated, but it produces about 40% of the food we eat.

▶ The Green Revolution also introduced widespread use of fertilisers and pesticides as well as new machinery and better management.

★ The Green Revolution is credited with saving the lives of a billion people.

The Green Revolution

New agricultural technology in the 1950s and 1960s, especially the development of high-yield strains of wheat and rice, dramatically increased food production.

HIGH-TECH FARMS

World population keeps growing, but we have a finite amount of land to produce food for everyone. Efficient, high-tech farming uses **robotics**, **ICT**, **big data analytics** and more, to make better use of our resources. More planet-friendly, it uses less energy, **pesticides** and pollutants.

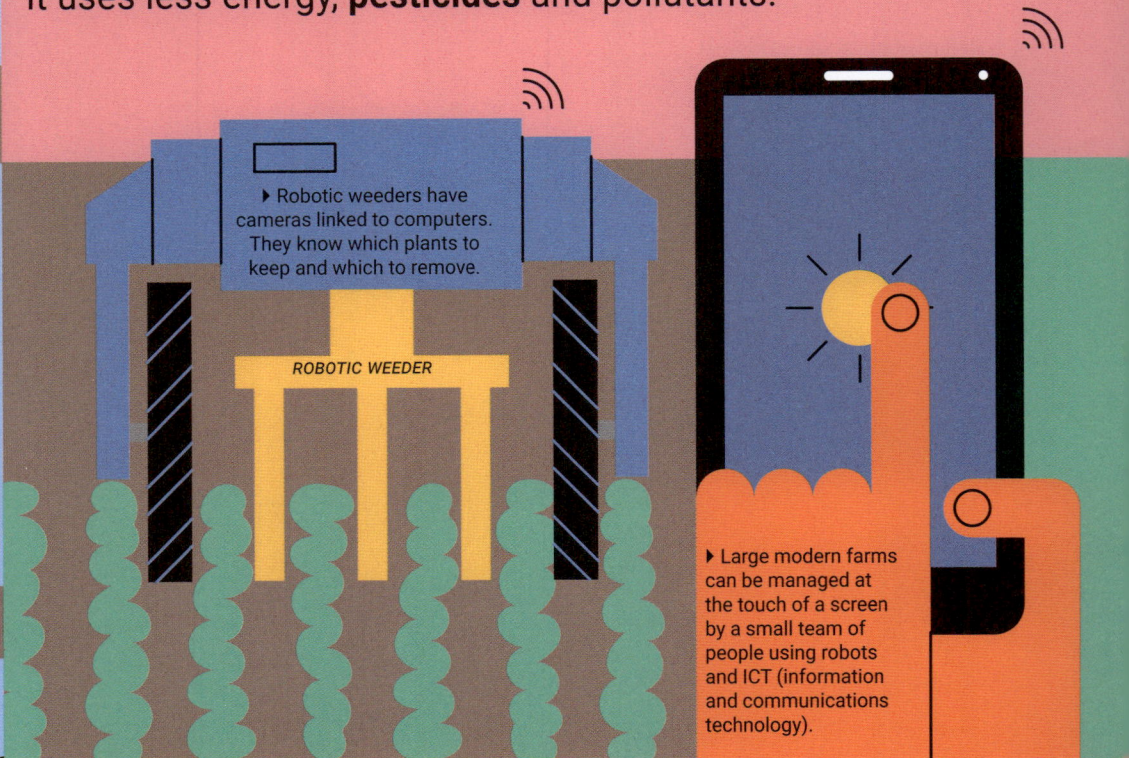

▶ Robotic weeders have cameras linked to computers. They know which plants to keep and which to remove.

ROBOTIC WEEDER

▶ Large modern farms can be managed at the touch of a screen by a small team of people using robots and ICT (information and communications technology).

Hydroponics

Hydroponics is a way of growing plants in water enriched wirh nutrients instead of soil.

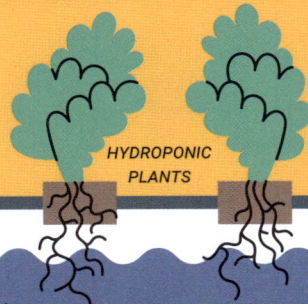

HYDROPONIC PLANTS

▶ Hydroponic food crops can be grown where soil is poor or where there is not enough farmland.

WATER WITH NUTRIENTS

Aeroponics

Aeroponic plants grow in the air. Their roots are misted with water and nutrients.

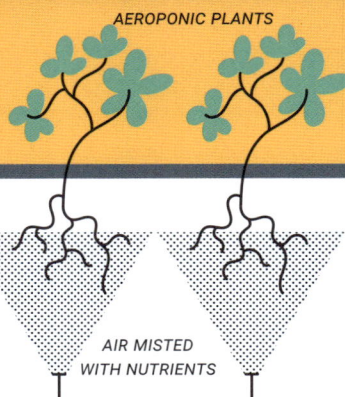

AEROPONIC PLANTS

★ Aeroponic crops use 98% less land and 95% less water than traditional farming.

AIR MISTED WITH NUTRIENTS

Aquaponics

Aquaponics is a mix of hydroponics and fish farming. The fish stay in a tank and their waste has enough nutrients for the plants to grow. Both the plants and the fish can be eaten.

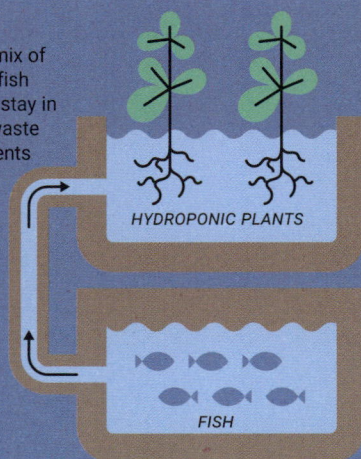

HYDROPONIC PLANTS

FISH

Vertical farming

The world is fast running out of farmland. In vertical farming crops are grown stacked in layers, often using the hydroponic and aeroponic systems shown here (left). In the future, office space that is no longer required because people work from home, may be used for farming.

▶ A skyscraper used half as office space and half for vertical farming.

DRONE

▶ Drones can be programmed to spray crops.

DRIVERLESS TRACTOR

★ When vegetables and fruit are ready to harvest there is no time to lose. Bad weather and labour shortages can hold things up, but robotic pickers can work all night if needed.

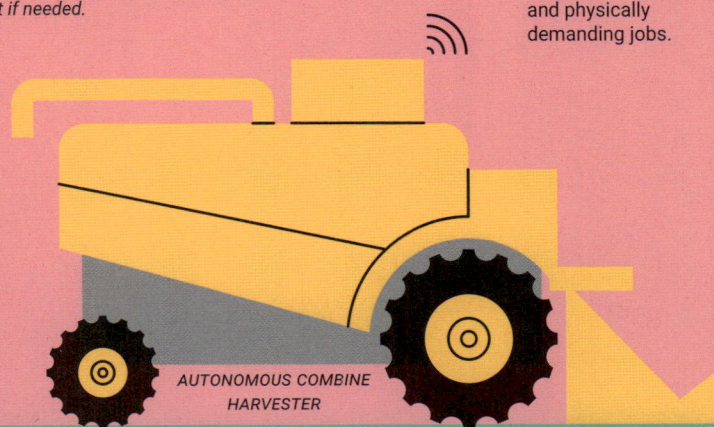

▶ Farm robots do many labour-intensive, repetitive and physically demanding jobs.

AUTONOMOUS COMBINE HARVESTER

Robotics

Farm robots can carry out a huge range of tasks, from feeding livestock and watering, weeding and spraying plants, to sowing and harvesting crops. They save time and reduce labour costs.

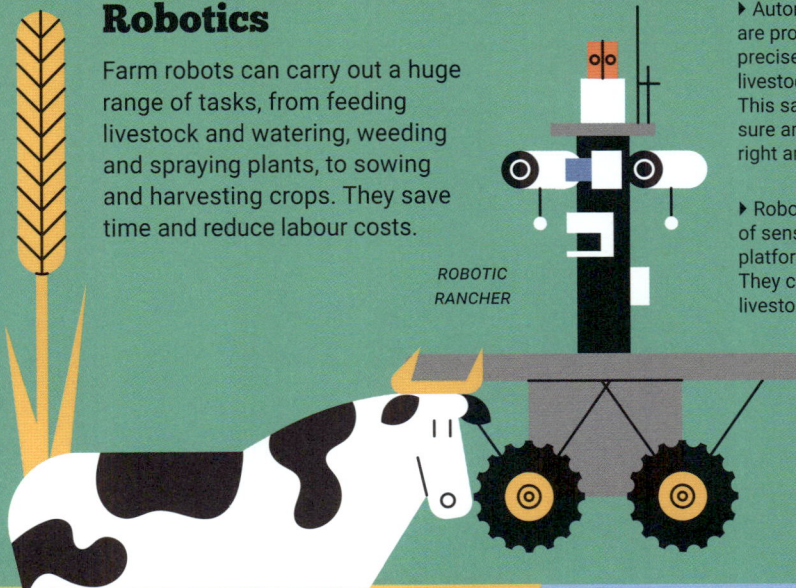

ROBOTIC RANCHER

▶ Automatic stock feeders are programmed to release precise amounts of food to livestock at regular intervals. This saves time and makes sure animals are getting the right amount of food.

▶ Robotic ranchers consist of sensors mounted on a platform with four wheels. They can watch over livestock.

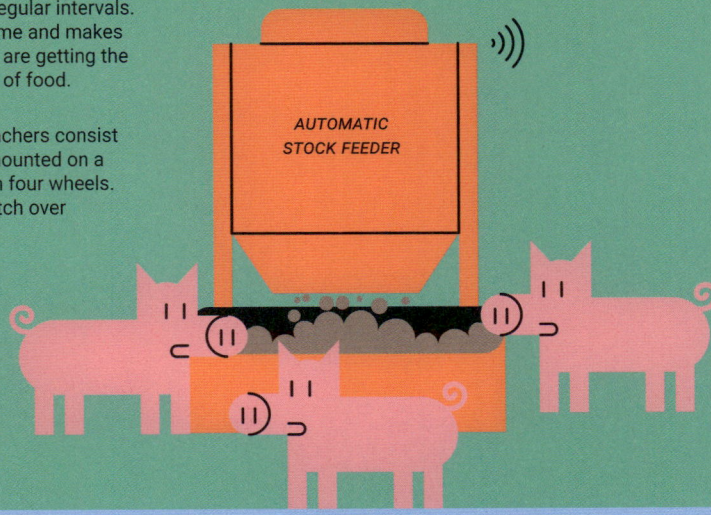

AUTOMATIC STOCK FEEDER

Sustainable farming

Sustainable farming means producing enough food for our needs without compromising the ability of future farmers to do the same. We need to protect farmland for the next generations.

★ Sustainable farming helps protect the environment by reducing soil erosion, conserving water and maintaining soil quality.

Satellite tracking

Satellites map the land they monitor providing detailed information on soil types, climate, moisture levels, land use, crop stages and more. Farmers can use this information to make the best decisions for their land.

▶ Satellites can provide accurate short- and long-term weather reports. They can also monitor climate change.

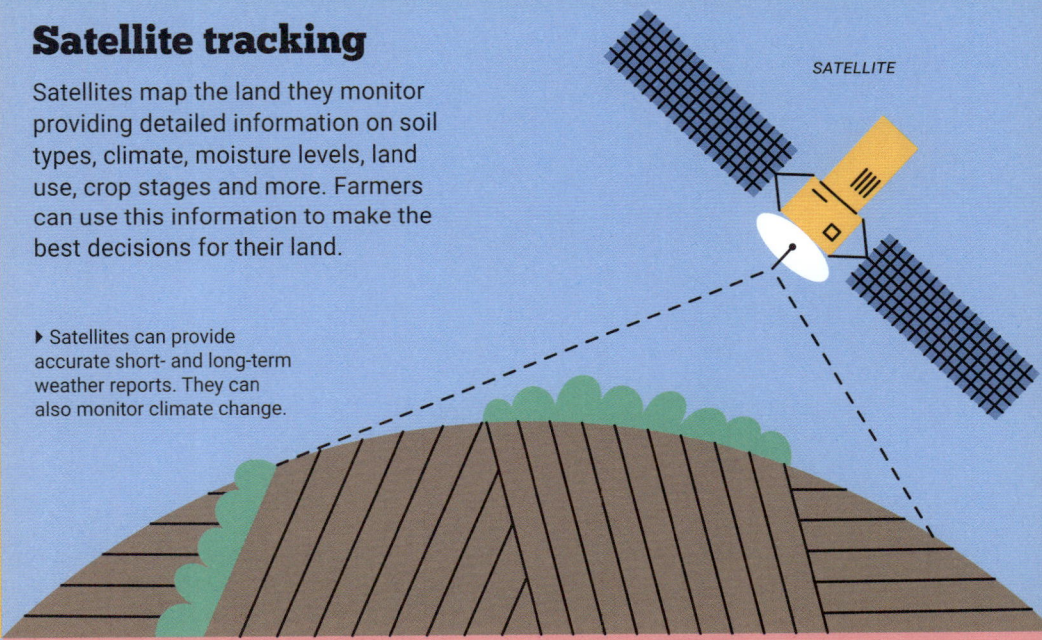

SATELLITE

Soil and water monitoring

Farmers can use sensors to monitor how much moisture is in the soil. They know when irrigation is required and how much is needed for best crop yields.

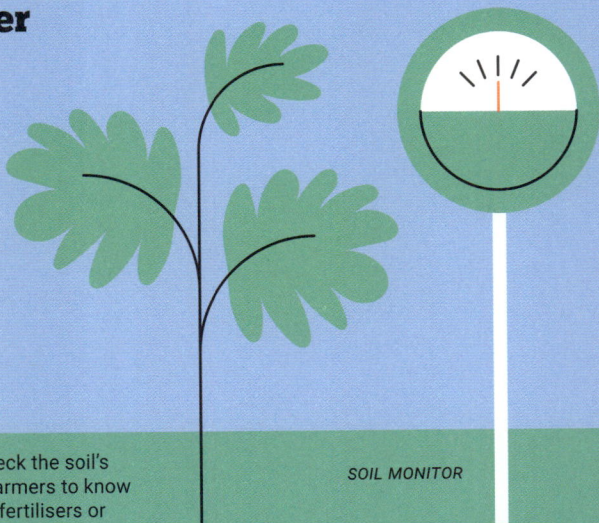

SOIL MONITOR

▶ Soil monitors can also check the soil's nutrient levels. This helps farmers to know whether they need to apply fertilisers or not which saves time and money.

ICT

Farmers require constant access to up-to-date information on a wide range of topics in order to manage their farms efficiently. Innovative use of **ICT (Information and Communication Technology)** gives them just what they need.

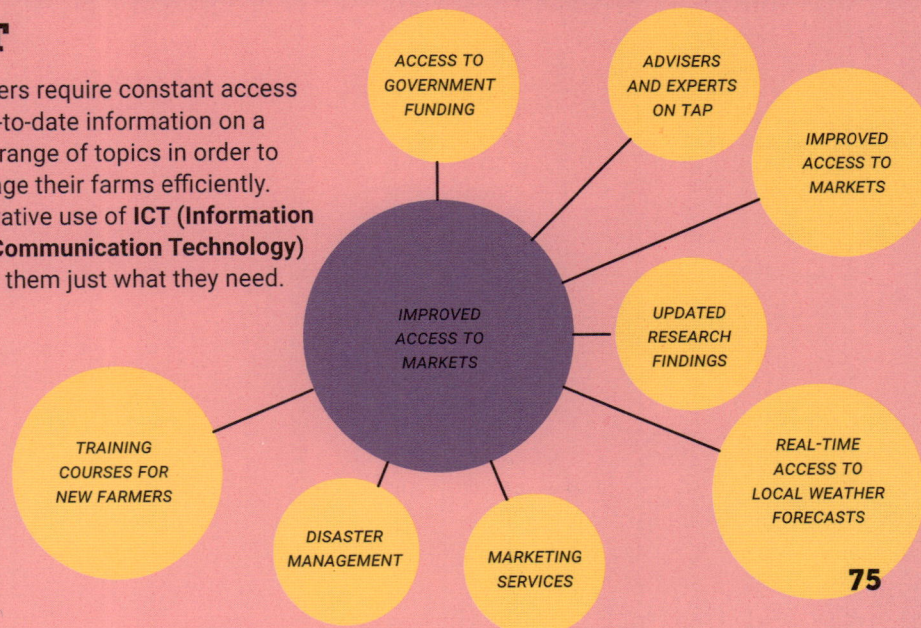

ACCESS TO GOVERNMENT FUNDING

ADVISERS AND EXPERTS ON TAP

IMPROVED ACCESS TO MARKETS

IMPROVED ACCESS TO MARKETS

UPDATED RESEARCH FINDINGS

REAL-TIME ACCESS TO LOCAL WEATHER FORECASTS

TRAINING COURSES FOR NEW FARMERS

DISASTER MANAGEMENT

MARKETING SERVICES

1. Smartphones send and receive text messages via satellite.

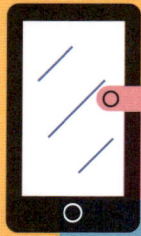

TRUE or FALSE?

2. The first electric car was invented in the 21st century.

TRUE or FALSE?

3. What does "desalination" mean? Choose one of the following:

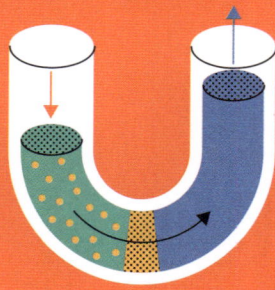

A. Treating water after it has been used in a factory so that it can be safely released back it into the environment.

B. Removing the salt from seawater so that people can drink it.

C. Purifying water in reservoirs before sending it to household taps.

D. Using an aeroplane to shoot chemicals into clouds to produce rain.

4. Three of the following statements about vaccination are true. Which ones are they?

A. Vaccines deliver a small, harmless taste of a pathogen so that our immune systems can learn to recognise it and be ready to act if a real infection occurs.

B. Vaccines are quick to develop, from initial research to roll out.

C. The WHO estimates that vaccination saves between 3.5 and 5 million lives every year.

D. The first successful modern vaccine was developed to fight smallpox.

5. Rank these cars in the order they were first produced

A. Chevrolet Impala

B. Oldsmobile

C. Ford Mustang

D. BMW X3

E. Model T Ford

6. The first high-speed trains, or bullet trains, started operating in Japan in the 1960s.

TRUE or FALSE?

7. Two of the following statements about the Internet are true. Which ones are they?

A. The internet is owned by Bill Gates.

B. Almost all international internet communications are sent via fibre optic cables on the ocean floor.

C. Wi-Fi means "wireless fidelity."

D. The Internet and the World Wide Web are the same thing.

E. The Internet has become the main source of information for millions of people worldwide.

QUIZ

Test your knowledge. See how much you have learned by reading this book. The answers are on page 79.

8. Three of the following statements about the wheel are true. Which ones are they?

A. Gears are wheels with teeth that mesh together and transmit power.

B. Wheelchairs were the first wheeled vehicles.

C. There are more than one billion bicycles in the world, half of them in China.

D. The first wheel was used to make pottery.

E. The spinning wheel was invented in the USA in the 19th century.

9. The James Webb Telescope is the most powerful space telescope ever built. It orbits around the Sun.

TRUE or FALSE?

10. Computer systems are made up of hardware and software. Three of the things listed below are hardware. Which ones are they?

A. Motherboard

B. Apps

C. Keyboard

D. Operating system

E. CPU (Central Processing Unit)

11. What is an avatar?

A. A new friend found in the metaverse.

B. An icon or digitalised version of a person used in video games or in the metaverse.

C. A new cryptocurrency used in the metaverse to buy things.

D. A smelly fish paste sandwich.

12. Fossil fuels, including oil, coal and natural gas, are renewable resources.

TRUE or FALSE?

13. Rank these technologies in the order they were invented

A. Gun powder

B. Stone tools

C. Control of fire

D. Antibiotics

E. Irrigation

14. Generating power using wind turbines, solar panels and hydro-electric stations is less damaging to the environment than using fossil fuels.

TRUE or FALSE?

15. Three of the following features will be used in most high-tech homes

A. Smart kitchen devices to store and prepare food.
B. A smart security system that has cameras to monitor outside areas as well as sensors to detect gas or water leaks.
C. A helicopter pad.
D. Smart toilets that examine waste and tell you when you should visit the doctor.

16. Robots are most commonly used in industry to manufacture goods.

TRUE or FALSE?

17. There are six basic types of bridge.

TRUE or FALSE?

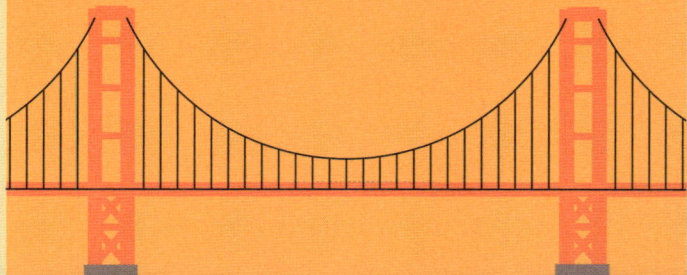

18. Four of the following statements about air travel are true. Which ones are they?

A. In 1935 it took about two weeks to fly from Brisbane in Australia to London.
B. The Concorde is the only supersonic passenger jet that has ever flown.
C. Food tastes different at high altitudes.
D. Supersonic jets fly faster than the speed of sound.
E. Space rockets are also propelled by a type of jet engine.

19. Two of the following statements about smart factories are true. Which ones are they?

A. Drones are always used for deliveries from smart factories.
B. The IoT (Internet of Things) is essential in a smart factory.
C. 3D printing is widely used for mass production in smart factories.
D. Smart factories control the production process electronically from beginning to end.

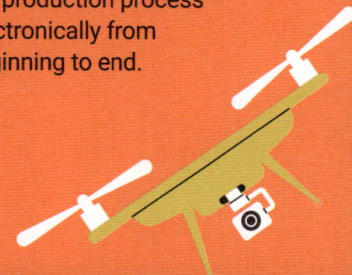

20. Two of the following statements about plastics are true. Which ones are they?

A. Plastic is a synthetic or human-made material that does not occur in nature.
B. Bioplastics are more likely to be biodegradable but they need careful recycling because many also contain toxic additives.
C. Plastics are widely used to build aircraft because they weigh more than metal.
D. Microplastics are good for the environment.

21. Two of the following statements about space travel are true. Which ones are they?

A. We can't visit deep space because we don't have space ships that go fast enough.
B. Wormholes are often used by human spacecraft to cover long distances quickly.
C. Einstein said that nothing can travel faster than light.
D. We have firm scientific proof that aliens have visited our planet in the last few years.

22. Three of the following statements about skyscrapers are true. Which ones are they?

A. Most skyscrapers are topped with a lightning rod with a wire running down to the ground to disperse electricity from lightning strikes.
B. The first skyscrapers were built in Chicago and New York in the 1880s.
C. Modern skyscrapers are not built to withstand earthquakes.
D. Winds are weaker at the top of a skyscraper than at street level.
E. Most skyscrapers have a skeletal frame of vertical columns and horizontal girders.

23. High-tech farming methods use robotics, ICT, Big Data and other technology to produce more food in a planet-friendly way. They use less energy, pesticides and pollutants.

TRUE or FALSE?

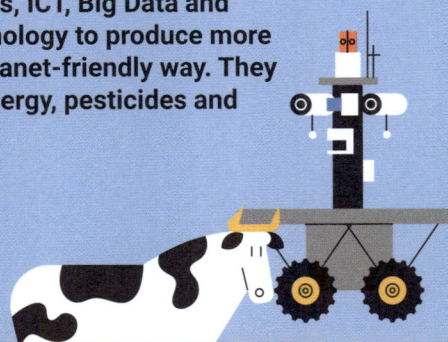

24. Fast fashion products are good for the environment.

TRUE or FALSE?

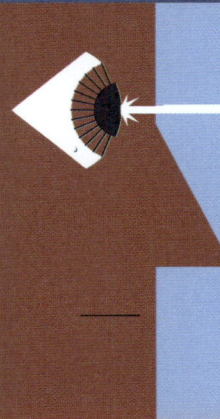

25. Laser surgery uses special beams of light to operate instead of surgical instruments.

TRUE or FALSE?

26. Esports are an explosive growth area in computer games.

TRUE or FALSE?

27. A clone is an exact copy of another living thing.

TRUE or FALSE?

28. TBMs (Tunnel Boring Machines) are best suited to boring short, square-shaped tunnels.

TRUE or FALSE?

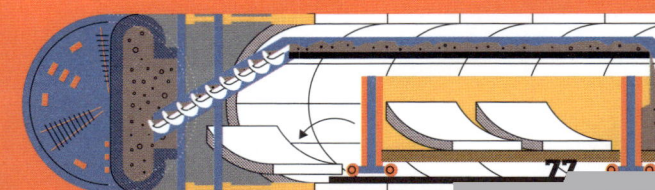

GLOSSARY

Alloy
A metal made by combining two or more metallic elements, such as gold and silver or nickel and bronze.

Aesthetic
Concerned with beauty or the appreciation of beauty.

Anaesthesia
Using substances called anaesthetics to reduce or block pain during surgery and dental procedures. Different combinations of drugs and gases are used to create varying degrees of insensibility, from numbing one part of the body (local anaesthetic) to making someone completely unconscious (general anaesthetic).

Android
A robot or other artificial being that closely resembles a human being. Previously found in science fiction, some of the more recent humanoid robots are very human-like.

Artificial intelligence (AI)
In its broadest sense, AI is intelligence shown by machines as opposed to natural intelligence displayed by humans. It is especially associated with computers and their ability to think and learn. With AI, computers can perform tasks that are typically done by people, such as learning, planning and problem-solving.

Augmented reality (AR)
A version of the real or physical world that has been enhanced by overlaying it with digital images, sounds or information.

Automaton
An early word for robots, or mechnical devices that can operate themselves or follow instructions. Plural is automata.

Big data analytics
When a business has access to ICT, the IoT and other modern technologies, it often receives very large volumes of data that can be overwhelming and difficult to process. Big data analytics is technology that studies this data to uncover hidden patterns, market trends and customer preferences, for example, that help the business to make informed decisions.

Bullet train
A high-speed passenger train. It was used to describe the "Shinkansen" high-speed trains that began operating in Japan in the 1960s. They had a bullet-shaped nose.

Celluloid
A synthetic plastic material developed in the 1860s and 1870s and adopted by the photography and film industries as a support for content.

CHP technology
Combined Heat and Power technology is a very efficient process that captures and utilises the heat that is a by-product of the electricity generation process.

Cryptocurrency
An alternative to physical, real-world money, cryptocurrencies only exist digitally and are not regulated by governments or banks. They are often used as payment systems in digital or virtual environments.

Cryptography
The science of keeping information secret and safe. It is a mix of mathematics, computer science and electrical engineering and is used, for example, for computer passwords and bank (ATM) cards.

Fitbit
A fitness tracker worn on the wrist like a watch, that tracks your day-to-day activity, such as how many steps you take.

FTL travel
To travel faster than the speed of light, which is 299,792,458 metres per second (about 186,282.397 miles per second).

Geothermal energy
Heat which is generated within the Earth. It can be harvested to produce electricity.

Global Positioning System (GPS)
A navigation system owned by the United States government that uses satellites orbiting the Earth and monitoring stations on the ground to provide location information to users.

Grandmaster
In chess, a player of the highest order, especially one who has won an international tournament.

Haptic gloves
Wearable gloves used in virtual environments to allow users to experience realistic touch and interactions through advanced tactile feedback.

Humanoid
A machine that looks like a human being. Robots that are shaped like humans are often described as humanoid.

Information and Communications Technology (ICT)
An umbrella term for a broad set of technological tools and resources used to transmit, store, create and exchange information. The tools and resources include computers, the internet (websites, blogs, emails), broadcasting technologies (radio, television, webcasting, podcasting) and telephony (fixed or mobile, video-conferencing).

Internal combustion engine
An engine that generates power by burning petrol or another fuel with air inside itself. The hot gases produced are used to drive a piston that creates the energy to propel a vehicle.

Internet of Things (IoT)
The IoT is the network of physical objects, or "things," that have sensors, software and other technologies that enable them to connect and exchange data with other devices and systems over the internet.

IP address
A network address for your computer so the internet knows where to send your emails and data. Every computer has a unique address, a bit like a telephone number or street address. IP stands for "Internet Protocol."

Internet Service Provider (ISP)
An ISP is an organisation that gives individuals and businesses access to the internet and other related services.

Kinetic energy
A type of energy that an object acquires due to its motion.

Landline
A telephone that transmits signals through physical media, such as wire or fibre optic cable, rather than through wireless transmission. In recent years, the term is mostly used to mean fixed-line home phones as opposed to mobile phones.

Lidar
A detection system similar to radar which uses pulsed laserlight rather than radio waves to locate, track and identify objects.

Low Earth Orbit (LEO)
Usually referred to satellites, it is an area between about 200 km and 2,000 km (124–1,242 miles) above the Earth. Most satellites orbit the Earth in LEO.

Non-renewable energy resources
Energy sources, such as oil and coal, that are finite and will eventually be all used up.

Nuclear fission
Occurs when the nucleus of an atom splits into two or more smaller parts. The reaction releases an enormous amount of energy, as well as nuclear waste. Fission is used in nuclear power plants to make electricity, and also in nuclear bombs.

Nuclear fusion
Is the process of combining atomic nuclei rather than splitting them (as with fission) to produce energy. This occurs naturally in the centre of stars like the Sun and does not create nuclear waste or greenhouse gases. We don't have the technology yet to use fusion to generate electricity in an efficient way.

OECD countries
The Organisation for Economic Co-operation and Development (OECD) is a group of 37 democratic, free-market economies that work together